D1279171

TESTIFY BOOKS
NEW YORK

Where'd You Get Those?

New York City's Sneaker Culture: 1960-1987

Bobbito Garcia

Editor's Note:
There is a significant amount of slang in this
text. Deliberate effort was made to preserve
the authenticity of these expressions.

Where'd You Get Those? Copyright © 2003
by Robert Garcia. All rights reserved.
Printed in Italy. No part of this book may be
used or reproduced in any manner whatsoev-
er without written permission except in the
case of brief quotations embodied in critical
articles and reviews. For information address:

Testify Books
305 West Broadway #233
New York, New York 10013.

Distributed by powerHouse
Cultural Entertainment, Inc.

First Edition

Designed by Brent Rollins
at ego trip, New York City
Title page illustration and diagrams
on pgs.186-87 by Todd James
Design Assistance by Jen Tadaki

10 9 8 7 6 5 4 3 2 1

Spot-bilt

PATRICK ®

i like PUMA ®

NIKE ®

NIKE and
the SWOOSH name
and stripe are
trademarks of BRS INC.

4174 DYNASTY   HIGH W/RB SIZE

Bata

Bata

MENS BULLET B.B. HI-CUT

81092   10½

CONVERSE ®

KangaROOS ™

 BIH-4421   BLACK   12

Wilson ®

by

Bata ®

COACH WOODEN

BASKETBALL SHOES

STOCK NO. _____   LEATHER OX.   WH/GOLD

53105   SIZE

$ 9.99

SALE PRICE

$ 9.99

Table of Contents

08　Can it Be That It Was All So Simple Then?:
　　The Evolution of the New York Sneaker Connoisseur

20　The Pound

24　WYGT?: Getting Around

26　The '60s: Ragtime

32　'70-'74

54　'75-'78

84　'79-'83

134　'84-'87

174　The End of an Era

176　Fresh Dipped

190　Arts & Crafts

198　Holy Wars

200　The Toothbrush

204　On Ice

208　A Hunting We Will Go

214　"What Size Are Those?"

218　Skippies and Rejects

226　Thou Shalt Not

230　Future Underground Classics

238　NYC Ball Legends

256　Top Ten Lists

258　Chronological Customizations

260　Company Roster

262　Acknowledgments

263　Photo Credits

264　About the Author

Can It Be That It Was All So Simple Then?:
The Evolution of the New York Sneaker Connoisseur

Peep me at age five rocking the Bobby Brady bowl cut. Pardon my skippies!

I am a *reformed* sneaker fiend. I hold this to be to true and actual, yet I'm not quite sure. I still scour the earth looking for that dusty odor to fill my nose on impact when I walk into a sporting goods store (but I keep getting disappointed). I still impulsively shop for new sneakers every three weeks, but when I look at the shelves I'm rarely moved. I still can't help looking down at people's feet when I meet them, hoping someone will blast me with the extra shit, but it rarely happens anymore.

I haven't grown any less fond of footwear. I still wake up every three weeks from some dream where I'm in a down low sneaker store that no one knows about that doesn't exist buying some discontinued model that doesn't exist anymore either. I wake up in bliss. I don't want to sound like some old fart kicking, "Son, they don't make 'em like they used to!" But any sneaker conglomerate will tell you they *don't* make them like they used to. This is fact. Don't be fooled, even reissued models are made differently now, with mass produced, inferior leather compared to their originally issued counterparts. 98% of all post '87, newly designed models are simply cobblestones on a nebulous path.

Most of you have come to this book walking it. This book may disappoint you. For it was not written to celebrate those who have participated in the almost 300% increase in sneaker sales in the last two decades. It was not written for those who pride themselves on owning every Air Jordan that their grandma's Scrabble game partners own too. It was not written to big up sneaker collectors who have over 40 kicks, but have no affinity for any of them. It was not written for the sneaker buyer with no eye for the invisible, no comprehension of why what they are wearing is hot, who wear sneakers that don't tell you anything about their identity. Sneakers have become popular culture, but this book is not about the masses. It is about before.

Before Nike controlled nearly half of the global sneaker market, before sneaker company logos became inescapably visible on pro football and pro basketball uniforms. (And, most horrifically, golf caps). Before the ten million dollar national television ad campaigns. Before the multi-million dollar sneaker endorsements for ballplayers, before the NBA became the merchandising vehicle that it is today. Before chain stores became the main outlet for consumers to buy sneakers. Before sneaker salespersons looked at you like you were Burt Reynolds if you asked for advice on what shoe functioned the best. Before independently owned sneaker shops got shut out of accounts and exclusive releases in favor of big business. Before Ebay, and websites devoted to sneakers.

Before Nike Air Force 1s became popular to non-basketball players, before they became accessible to stores outside New York and Baltimore, before they had embroidered logos that had nothing to do with basketball.

Before yuppies started wearing sneakers with their suits to walk to and from work, before the general public who didn't play basketball found it acceptable and reasonable to wear leather high top sneakers when their only physical exertion consisted of throwing out the trash at night.

The modern sneaker was born in the 19th century. One of its earliest nicknames was a croquet sandal, which may give you a clue about the economic class of people who wore them (croquet sets ain't cheap, fool!). Towards the end of that century, Dr. Naismith invented basketball and in the beginning of the 20th century a few rubber companies popped up to provide sneakers for the new wave of basketball and tennis players in the U.S. In the '50s American youth culture began to bloom. Casual dress became desired and its acceptability was unprecedented. Sneakers were no longer just gym class shoes, but the preferred choice of kids everywhere.

"Wear your sneakers wherever you go, even a smooch in the drive-in show . . . Do anything you want to do, as long as I'm wearing my tennis shoes!"
— Edison Youngblood "Tennis Shoes" Hanover Records, 1959

Thus the sneaker fetish was born.

Converse dominated the basketball market through the '50s and '60s with just one model, namely the canvas Chuck Taylor signature All-Star, which was only available in black or white. P. F. Flyers and Keds were the alternatives for non-ballplayers. There wasn't much reason for consumers to differentiate one from another, or any reason to collect. The Chuck Taylor's design was proven and didn't change from year to year; there was no value to put a pair on ice when it would be available just the same in '55 or '65.

Things would drastically change in the early '70s. On the design side Adidas introduced leather basketball sneakers. And on the streets of New York, Keds put a dead end to Converse's sole dominance, forever. With the introduction of the Pro-Keds basketball line, Converse suddenly had unprecedented competition for the title of number one sneaker on the basketball playgrounds.

There was even more competition before long. Puma popularized suede basketball sneakers in '72. In '77 Pony gained presence in New York, and by '79 Nike made noise too. Converse and Adidas never dropped out the race by any means—they each kept introducing hot new high tops and low tops. The '70s presented choices to the sneaker consumer. Choice of brand, choice of model, and towards the end of the decade even choices of colors available at retail.

Retail outlets were limited however. You could shop for sneakers at a local Army and Navy Surplus Store, a sporting goods store which would sell everything from football helmets to fish tackle, or a shoe store. At any of these three outlets there would be one wall, not even, for sneakers. Distribution was limited, and the models that you'd see the pros or college players wear in *Sports Illustrated* were usually totally unavailable in any store you searched. Today it is unthinkable for a sneaker company to have a pro player wear something that is not available at retail, but in the '70s, that was the norm.

Sporting good chain stores like Herman's were to be avoided at all costs. They only carried overpriced basics. Department stores like Korvettes

were non cypher as well. They mostly carried skippies—brands that were the wack. But it was shoe store chains like Fayva and Thom McCann's that were the ultimate banished spots. They would carry their own brands, like Fayva Olympians, which were cheaply constructed bites of popular brands. Sneaker chain stores like Athlete's Foot (which got its start in '73) and FootLocker didn't have locations, to my knowledge, in New York until the end of the '70s.

With the variables of increased selection but limited resources to obtain them, the hunger inside the animal grew and the sneaker fiend was born. Like the worst heroin addicts in the city (and in the '70s, New York had many of them), cats walked around *fiending* for a sneaker fix. It may have been for a new pair when our parents felt we didn't need them yet. It may have been for a new color, like the Super Pro-Keds in candy apple green, which no one on the block had yet. It may have been for a new pair of Wilson Batas, which no one on the block had even heard of.

The palpable desire of the fiend was nuanced, layered. If you played ball, you wanted to have the best sneakers possible so it could improve your game. Also, playing ball everyday on the concrete was an effective way to wear your sneakers out in just weeks. And worn out sneakers were a justification for a new purchase.

The best ballplayers in the city wore the rarest sneakers, cuz a scout or coach often hit them off with a color that wasn't available at retail. The mentality was to not only feel good on your feet, but to give the perception that you were nice with yours on the court. Stores usually carried white, black, navy blue, and maybe red models, so team colors like green, orange, purple, burgundy, gold, and light blue became highly sought after commodities. Color, conceivably, was more important than the brand. There simply wasn't that much difference in technology between companies, so brand loyalty on the basis of comfort was unheard of. Being a serious ballplayer and having clean sneakers was unheard of too. If you

Bottom left: In 1982, when I was fifteen, I played my second season in the Holcombe Rucker Tournament. I didn't do much scoring, but I was great at clapping for my teammates when they did.

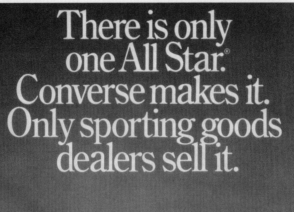

There is only one All Star.® Converse makes it. Only sporting goods dealers sell it.

The Converse All Star is basketball's shoe. Last year 8 out of 10 players in every major college and junior college basketball tournament wore All Stars. They've been worn by every U.S. Olympic Basketball Team since 1936, and have been selected again by the U.S. Olympic Committee for the 1976 Olympics. Converse All Stars are available in 10 team colors, 5 action styles in suede, leather and canvas.

an **Eltra** company

★ **CONVERSE**®

PETE MARAVICH WEARS PRO-KEDS BASKETBALL SHOES.

Pro-Keds: The shoes the pros wear, on the court and off.

were on the court with clean sneakers, it was a possible indication that you didn't play too often, or played soft.

By the mid '70s, the streets changed that perception. Gangs were dominant in the N.Y. of the '60s and early '70s, and the look was rugged. But the mid '70s saw the burgeoning evolution of hip hop culture, and the look changed from being rugged to being fly. Cats were rocking knit polyester mock necks with pleated and stitched AJs (dress pants), and the attending sneaker style became clean. "Fresh out the box" was the preferred look. Stepsies was a game everyone would play when you got new sneakers. The object was for as many people as possible to step on your new pair. But with the advent of hip hop, stepsies was no longer funny. It was grounds for a fistfight. Sneaker prices were increasing too, and spending $25 for Pumas was different than dishing out $12 for Pro-Keds. The sneakers had to stay looking clean for longer to get more bang for the buck.

By the end of the '70s the fiend had two goals—look fresh on the court, look vicious off the court. And there were rewards for being the shit, with hot sneakers that no one else had. Any true sneaker fiend's most cherished memories are of the days that he heard the words, "Yo, money, where'd you get those?" Ah, just writing them makes me smile. The rush of someone noticing your most treasured possessions was immeasurable.

If the sneaker fetish of the '50s and '60s planted the seeds for the sneaker fiend of the '70s, then most certainly the fiend watered the plant that was the sneaker connoisseur of the '80s. Gone were the days of knowing a sneaker like the Chuck Taylors would be available forever. When the Adidas Americana came and went in a roach's eyeblink in '76-'77, it left an indelible mark. The message was clear: models were being introduced more frequently than ever before, and if you didn't get them when they came out you might never see them again. At the beginning of the '80s the value of vintage sneakers became an important factor for the evolving (and tiny) contingent of sneaker connoisseurs. It completed the trinity. You either wanted a pair before they were released, a pair that was available but in a color that no one else had, or a pair that was discontinued.

The way to finesse vintage sneakers was either to put them on ice, which meant you kept them in the box without wearing them for a couple of years 'til they were ripe, or to go hunting. Hunting for sneakers was a ritual shared with only select friends. It was almost like a secret society. You'd see mad kids on the train all wearing the same shit, and then you'd see one kid who had some *magnetic* joints on. You'd become transfixed. He knew you were hawking him, but it was a form of respect. He had to have put as much effort into finding his sneakers and maintaining them as you had, and if you didn't have your flyest joints on to compete you just took an L for the day.

Keeping shit on ice was sometimes difficult if funds were low, and the quest for vintage joints was at times a fruitless endeavor. The next step for the sneaker connoisseur to assert his mastery of taste and underscore his quest to not look like anyone else was to become a sneaker designer himself. If the amount of fiends who would travel on a hunt was a select few, then the numbers of connoisseurs who had the patience to spend the five hours necessary to properly paint their sneakers was even a tinier group. Personal customization was getting a jumpstart in hip hop circles too, with colored fat laces in intricate patterns.

From 1970-1987, the goal in New York was to assert your individuality within a collective frame. The collectives were playground ballplayers, graffiti writers, b-boys and b-girls, DJs, MCs, and beatboxers. The spirit was competitive and progressive, and biting was frowned upon. Whether it was coming up with a new boogie move on the court or a new freeze on the linoleum, ballplayers and hip hop heads alike were pushing the creative envelope at all times. This forward mentality affected what sneakers people wore, how they wore them, and where.

The game changed after '87. Nike rode the jogging boom wave to become the #1 selling outfit worldwide in the early '80s. They missed the boat on the boom in women's aerobics that Reebok capitalized on though. Consequently,

Reebok became #1 in '85. It wouldn't last long. In response, Nike launched a $5 million campaign around Michael Jordan's signature Air Jordan shoe. In '87, Nike launched a $20 million campaign for the Air line. Television advertising for sneakers barely existed prior to the mid '80s. Early sneaker consumers learned about sneakers through print ads, word of mouth, and, most importantly, by discerning for themselves which sneakers looked hot and which didn't. Television advertising proved effective for sales however, as did the endorsement of the greatest ballplayer ever. Between the Just Do It ad and the Jordan/Spike Lee (a.k.a. Mars Blackmon) ad, Nike regained its lead as #1 and hasn't let go of it since. No other sneaker company has even gotten close. By the '90s sneakers would constitute the largest majority of the footwear market, and only 20% of the people buying those sneakers were actually using them for the sport the sneakers were designed for. After '87, overall sneaker sales doubled from the numbers of the early '80s.

Whereas the sneaker fiend was a societal anomaly in the '70s, by the late '80s sneaker fanatics were common. It became normal to buy sneakers not when you needed to replace your old ones, but whenever you pleased. You weren't chastised for having more than five or ten pairs at a time anymore. The revenues generated from all this led to more development for technology. A technology race ensued amongst sneaker companies, but what a lot of designers forgot was that the clean and sleek silhouette of a sneaker's design is what made it desirable. Sneakers produced after '87 were, with few exceptions, over-designed and straight-up ugly. The terrible tragedy of all this was that marketing had become so influential, and the sneakers and athletes had become so iconoclastic, that people were going out and buying all of the new styles in record numbers anyway. Amazing! The first Air Jordan, in any true connoisseur's view, looked garbage. The only person who looked jazzy in them was Jordan himself, yet everyone had them and swore they were the shit. Air Jordans represented the antithesis of

what sneaker culture in New York was all about. It was the first sneaker in New York history that gained popularity on the street that it didn't deserve. It was the beginning of a homogenous style for youth and brand loyalty, two phenomenas that could never have existed in the independent, freestyling era of sneaker culture from '70-'87.

Post-'87 is when the gap between fiend and connoisseur widened to enormous proportions. In '80, Adidas Americanas were sought after because they were unavailable, but if you couldn't find them there were other good choices from the current releases. But after '87, fly kicks that had limited distribution were so hard to find amongst the current releases that a connoisseur had no option but to seek vintage sneakers. It wasn't a choice. It was survival. Original issues of classic joints that had been discontinued became scarce, but luckily when you did find a pair a sneaker store would usually be happy to sell them for just $10 or $20. It was dead stock to them. Little did they know that the value of originals from '70-'87 would skyrocket by '95. By the early '90s, vintage sneakers in Japan were selling at mark-ups from 100% to 1000% of the sneakers' original price. Japanese buyers swept the U.S. for whatever supply was left in old sporting goods store basement's shelves. This left no supply for the growing demand for originals inspired by the Old School hip hop revival of '94-'96. Eventually sneaker companies caught whiff and started reissuing the classics. The comeback or limited edition category now includes some of the most consistent selling products for a number of brands, at times outselling their new models, and sometimes even representing the #1 selling shoe in all categories for a sneaker company period. It's ironic that a model designed twenty years ago can outsell a new model that has hundreds of thousands of dollars in technology, development, and marketing pumped in to it. Then again, that's why I'm writing this book.

New Yorkers in that liberating, glorious sneaker period of '70-'87 wanted to differentiate themselves from each other. Sneakers were how you defined yourself, how you claimed an identity amidst an overpopulated city full of adversity. There was a worldwide mass culture of sneaker consumption, but only in New York, the global Mecca of playground basketball and hip hop, was there the subculture of sneaker fiends and connoisseurs. This group would wind up influencing the sneaker industry, the music industry, the fashion world, the vintage market, and the global consumer market for years after right through to the present day. This book is their story, and my story and the stories of other connoisseurs who either inspired me or were my contemporaries. We were the first generation, and only one, to enjoy sneaker consumption on our own terms.

"Ma, I Don't Want to Wear Skippies Anymore!"

A not so brief personal history before we get to the juiciness . . . I was born September 25, 1966 in Manhattan. My parents were born in Puerto Rico. We lived on 97th between Columbus and Amsterdam on the Upper West Side. My family was pretty serious about ball. My pops Ramon was invited to try out for the Rio Pedras Cardinales of La Liga Superior de Baloncesto de Puerto Rico. My oldest brother Ray played for the first Gauchos at the McBurney Y, and ran in the Holcombe Rucker Tournament and Goat Tournaments of the mid '70s. My older brother Billy was no stranger to the playground either. Pops was a diehard Knicks fan, so whenever they had an away game on channel nine WOR-TV, rest assured there wasn't any other choice of what to watch.

Surrounded by hoops at home, in '73 I too got the basketball jones.

"A basketball jones is when you love basketball so much, you are like a junkie . . . I even put that basketball underneath my pillow, maybe that's why I can't sleep at night . . ."
— Cheech y Chong "Basketball Jones Featuring Tyrone Shoelaces" Ode/A&M Records, 1973

I became the ballboy for Billy's Varsity team at Holy Name Catholic School. I was in second grade, wearing skippies, feeling glum. I kept asking momduke to buy me some Pro-Keds; every kid who was down around the way wore them. When I turned nine in '75 both my parents agreed I would finally be allowed to play outside without their supervision, so that really upped the ante for getting some Pro-Keds. I didn't want to be playing Blackula or Ringalario while getting plastered for wearing skips. Kids were mean, and they'd sing the national anthem of poor people to you ("Skippies, they make your feet feel fine . . .") until you got something official. So one night moms came home with a box. Word up, I put away my Hot Wheels toy cars and track set and my heart started pumping fast. "I got you a pair of sneakers," she blurted, and passed the box to me. "Ma,

Top: My artistic rendering of an early quiver, circa 1981, featuring Pro-Ked Final Four mesh and Converse Dr. Js.

Bottom: Legendary DeMatha High School coach Morgan Wooten's off-season workout sheet. This was my bible in high school.

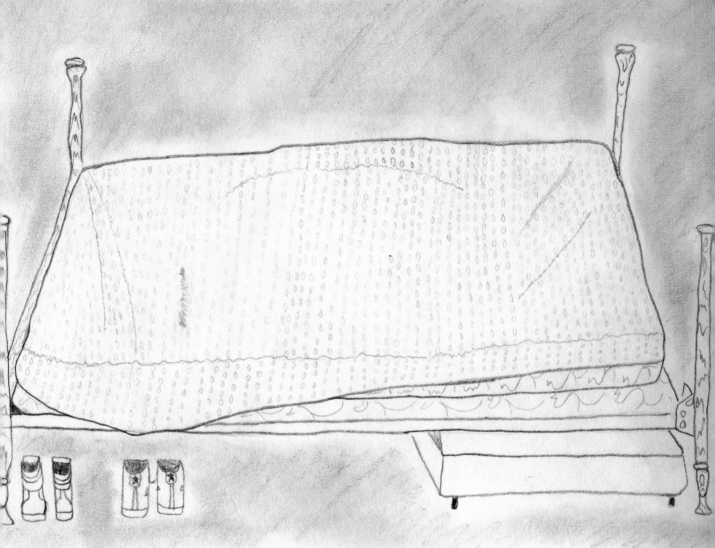

DE MATHA HIGH SCHOOL
Daily Summer Workout

Basketball is a game in which you either get better or you get worse. It has become so highly competitive that in order to perform to the best of your ability at all times, you must work to improve constantly. The summer is the time when a player can work on the individual fundamentals that make him a better player.

1. BALL HANDLING (15 minutes)

 A. Pound ball both hands
 B. Finger tip drills
 C. Pass ball around your mid section
 D. Single leg circle - both legs
 E. Around legs and body both ways
 F. Figure 8 both ways
 G. Figure 8 and drop both ways
 H. Crab run both ways
 I. Side catch
 J. Front catch
 K. Spin ball on finger

these aren't Pro-Keds, these are skippies!" Damn, close but no cigar. I had to go with her to the shoe store myself.

Purchasing sneakers back then was such a beautifully involved process. First the salesman measured my foot with that metal contraption with lines on it that you never see anymore in shoe stores. Then he brought the sneakers from behind the curtain with a short stool in his hand. The stool had a rubber footrest on one side that enabled the salesman to sit in front of me to lace my sneakers while I wore them. I calmly walked around in them to make sure they fit, but of course I really wanted to jump for joy and scream. It was then routine for the salesman to ask if you wanted to wear the sneakers out the store ("Yes."), and if you wanted him to put your old dogged pair in the box ("Nah, you can throw them out.")

I had graduated. I had Super Pro-Keds in blue canvas. I'll never forget what that felt like. It was a coming of age. I literally walked out of the store, got to the sidewalk, and burst into an all-out sprint. I don't even know why. My mom was half a block behind me in stitches.

The moment of glory was short-lived. The next week I saw my boy with Pro-Ked 69'ers that I'd never seen before. I was taken aback. I thought I was cool, but he was cooler. He was a step ahead. By getting my first pair of Super Pro-Keds I was just trying to fit in, but seeing the 69'ers made me realize immediately that I didn't want to just wear popular brands, I wanted to wear the coolest brands and models too. Envy is one the seven deadly sins, and the easiest way to avoid it is to always be ahead of everyone in the sneaker game.

That took funds and license to hunt outside your neighborhood, neither of which I had until '80 when I got my first job. In the interim, I became an apprentice of sorts and followed my brother Ray's path.

When everyone in '74 had on Super Pro-Keds, Ray had on Converse One-Stars. When everyone in '76 had on Clydes in low top, Ray had them in high top. Then in '77 he blasted everyone in the neighborhood and was the first person to rock Wilson Batas and Nikes.

People didn't understand his style, and for Ray they didn't have to. He actually preferred it.

When he was done with his Blazers in '79 he passed them on to me as hand me downs. I was only two sizes from fitting them by then and decided to put them on ice until I fit them. I was glad I did. The fat belly swoosh disappeared in '79, so I had my first vintage sneaker of value stepping into the '80s, but I still wasn't shit. In '79 my boy Vincent freaked everybody when he came out with the rare Jabbars in white on blue suede. Envy, envy, and more envy. At that point they were the most beautiful things I had ever seen on someone's feet.

In '80 I was a freshman at Brooklyn Tech H.S., cutting last period everyday through the winter so that my boy Alix Achille and I could sneak into Columbia U.'s indoor gym. I would only miss playing ball three days in the next eight years. I was more than a gym rat. I was a traveling one and a trespassing one. Wherever there was supposedly an open run or even better an empty gym, I was there.

Second semester freshman year I felt compelled to make my time spent in the classroom as close to being on a court as possible. I memorized everyone's kicks in every single row and seat for all eight periods of the day. I could tell my classmates how many sneakers they had and when they got new pairs better than most of them probably cared to know. There was one kid who always had Clydes in the deffest colors like rust on tan. Puma was the first company to *really* freak stripes beyond the basic team colors. Seeing rust stripes had me flummoxed. I don't think I ever even looked up at his face the whole semester. In my Freehand Drawing class I'd hand in drawings of my bed and the sneakers lined up underneath it. During Chemistry I'd draw all the logos of my favorite brands—the Converse chevron and star, the Pony chevron, the Nike swoosh, the Adidas stripes, the Pro-Ked double stripe with a point, the Puma stripe, the Spalding triple wings, the Bata triangle.

I began to really *study* sneakers. My '80 Nike Blazers, for example, had a sponge tongue, long nylon laces, a light blue terry cloth insole, a suede toe cap, and a cotton thread reinforcement glued to the midsole along each side of the upper. I haven't owned Blazers in 22 years, but I still remember them as if I were sitting on my old couch staring at them. I loved going to sporting goods stores to look at sneakers. I'd take trips with no intention to buy, just browse and see what was out. I'd watch NBA games and not even watch the action, just the sneakers. I hate to admit this, but I'd look forward to players getting injured. It was the only time the camera would zoom in and I could really see their customized sneakers.

In '82 I joined the Upward Fund Youth Basketball Program in Spanish Harlem. I met Mark Pearson, Ted Lake, and John Merz there. We formed a tight bond talking about basketball and sneakers everyday at McDonalds. We'd have two ducats between the four of us, so we'd get four cups of courtesy water and one apple pie to share. Then we'd sit down for hours and kick stories about sneakers we'd never seen before. Between the hunts and the customizing we were all competing amongst each other. We were connoisseurs. If I saw more than five people with the same pair of sneakers I had on I took that as a defeat. It wasn't about being different for the sake of difference. It was about being different with style.

My passion for sneakers continued on through high school and college. Post-graduation, my obsession led to writing the first sneaker articles for *The Source* and *Rap Pages* in the early '90s, and consulting for Nike, Adidas, and Converse. Getting paid to do what I love has been a blessing but honestly I would still be the diehard ballplayer and sneaker connoisseur with or without the professional validation, with or without all the free gear. And as for my quiver, I still have a number of choice vintage collectibles alongside whatever few and far between fly and functional joints I can pick up. I am not a collector. At the rate that I have purchased sneakers over the years it would be really easy to have over 500 hot joints piled up in my room. But as a ballplayer it is impossible to not dog your kicks eventually. Most sneakers aren't worth saving once

they're dogged, and I don't buy sneakers without intending to wear them. I might put a pair on ice, but eventually I want people to see them on my feet, not in some mythical closet.

But if I did have a magical, mythical closet, all the sneakers that you are about to see in this book (with the exception of the Skippies chapter) would be in it. In my estimation these were the most seminal and coveted joints from five periods: the '60s, '70-'74, '75-'78, '79-'83, '84-'87. (If you are true connoisseur you already know how I've grouped them cuz you've skipped the intro and gone straight to the pictures already!) Every flick is of sneakers produced during the time they originally came out. You will not see any reissued models. You will get to hear the New York stories behind them from a connoisseur's view. These are opinions, not fact. The sneakers themselves are fact. The rest is just a bunch of adults reliving their youth as if we were sitting in Mickey D's drinking courtesy water again. ∎

I call these my "step offs," as in
"Step up off me, money!"

The Pound

There are a number of voices that you will hear throughout this book. They come from a myriad of backgrounds and have as many opinions. I interviewed them on the basis that I respected their sensibilities towards kicks.

The Fiend Generation:

Richard "Pee Wee" Kirkland a.k.a. "the Stickman"

"Pee Wee" Kirkland is one of New York's greatest playground legends. He was born in 1945 and grew up in Harlem on 117th between Lenox and Fifth. After leading the nation in scoring at junior college, then a standout year at Norfolk St., he went hardship and was drafted by the Chicago Bulls. He walked away from camp and returned to Harlem, and became an all time Pro Rucker megastar. Unfortunately his career got cut short when he caught a ten-year bid to Federal Prison in '71. While inside, he dropped 135 points for his prison team in an exhibition game against a squad from Lithuania. He left an indelible mark on Harlem with his moves and his style on and off the court. Clyde who? If you talk about playground basketball in New York in the '60s and early '70s, "Pee Wee" was New York's true king of style. Legend has it that he wore fresh out the box sneakers every time he played in a game, and then never wore them again.

Joe "The Destroyer" Hammond

Joe Hammond is widely regarded as the greatest shooter of all New York playground legends—ever. He was born in 1949 and grew up in Harlem. In his most memorable Pro Rucker game, he went up against Charlie Scott (then the leading scorer in the ABA) and Julius Erving and outscored both of them with over 50 points. Joe's rep was so strong at the Rucker that he was invited to try out for the Los Angeles Lakers in '71. He had never even played high school or college ball. Joe wound up walking away from their camp and returned to Harlem. He was infamous for playing games of one on one where the loser would have to give up their sneakers. Of course Joe was never the one walking home in socks.

Joe Skie a.k.a. "Joe Ski," "the White Machine"

You can't play ball in the Lower East Side of Manhattan and not know who Joe Skie is. He is unstoppable, and has been that way consistently through six decades of playground basketball. He was born in 1944 and grew up in the L.E.S. He played at high school powerhouse Power Memorial, St. John's U., and in the Pro Rucker where he earned his nickname for his scoring. Some observers theorize that he's maintained his shape because he's never played a lick of D. Another variable that may better explain his healthy legs and knees is that Joe's grips are always fresh out the box, and always original.

Lincoln Parker a.k.a. "Little Linc," "Zinc Oxide"

Lincoln was born in 1962 and we grew up together on 97th St. He's 5'3" ("5'4" on a good day"), but was a formidable defender who played in City Wide, Whitney M. Young, King Towers and was an all star in the Goat Tournament in '78. He also ran a successful youth program called Poetry In Motion that taught basketball and literary skills. The block we grew up on produced some hip hop legends, most notably Doze of TC5 and Ken Swift of the Rock Steady Crew. Lincoln was older than all of us and he was the first person I knew personally that started rocking the def gear like mock necks and British that were the shit Uptown where hip hop was originating.

The Connoisseur Generation:

Ray Garcia a.k.a. "Little Ray," "Reggie Jackson," "Brother Ray"

If someone had the idea to write this book in late '70s, they would've approached my brother Ray Garcia. He was born in 1958, and I've never met anyone who quite matched his fervor for unique sneakers in the '70s. He was an early practitioner of laborious sneaker customizations so he could have totally different sneakers than anyone else. His mantra: *"I didn't want to see one other person with the same sneakers as me. Not one. I didn't want to set a trend because I didn't even want anyone to have the same sneakers as me afterwards either."*

Theodore Lake a.k.a. "Teddy Nitro," "The Nitro Man," "Ted Ice," "Teddy Sweet," "Ted Grizzly"

When I first met Ted at the Upward Fund in '82, we were both on the sideline sizing up what everyone was wearing in the gym, not paying attention to the game at all. We immediately bonded. Ted was born in 1967

and grew up in Spanish Harlem. Ted was a lefty who scored at will. He dropped 49 points in a Rucker game, and once scored the final sixteen points for Upward Fund in under two minutes to push a game into overtime (thus the nickname "Nitro"). He played high school at Rice and Taft, then Utah Tech, Mattatuck C.C., and finally Elizabeth Seton J.C. Ted was such a sneaker junkie, he once came up a couple of bucks short on a purchase and paid the difference with his last train tokens. He then walked five miles home. It didn't matter, as long as he had a fresh box in his hand he was straight.

John Merz, a.k.a. "Johnny Snakeback Fever," "Spinal Bifida," "J Smooth," "Johnny Jack Hammer"

I met John at the Upward Fund as well. I was impressed with his fundamentally sound game, plus he had boogie. It was rare to see a white kid with a handle in the '80s playing in Harlem. He was born in 1965 and grew up in Brooklyn. He played in City Wide and PAL, then St. Anns H.S. and SUNY Stony Brook. He didn't pay as much attention to scoring as he did to looking good in his sneakers. To John, style was paramount. If you had some bullshits on your feet and thought you were the shit, John would disabuse you of that notion with the quickness. It started for him at age six when he discovered the old Sneaker Factory on Sterling Pl. Today he admits, "I used to shake and pee in my pants when I'd pass there! My parents went on a trip once and left me $76 for the month, and I spent my money the first day entirely at the Sneaker Factory instead of on food!"

Mark Pearson a.k.a. "Sake," "Mark Money," "Biz"

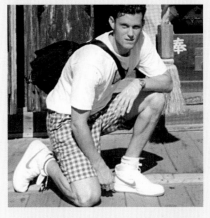

Mark Pearson was born in '65 and grew up in Flatbush, Brooklyn. In the mid '80s you couldn't ride the F or any of the "ding dong" lines without seeing a Sake throw up (or the work of his partners Trike and SET 3). The first time I saw him play was at 86th St. in Central Park in '82. Not only was he dominating the run, but he had on very milky nubuck New Balance 480s, which I had never seen anyone with. Then he walked off the court with his Riverside Church Hawks gym bag (he played there with Walter Berry), and that sealed it. I didn't know him, but I had mad envy. Months later we met at the Upward Fund. I didn't remember his face but I recognized him by his sneakers. He became legendary by choosing to attend Columbia University for no other reason than the basis that the team was wearing customized Nike Franchises when he applied.

"Jazzy Art" a.k.a. "SET 3"

Jazzy was Mark's bombing partner in the train yards and his homestrown on the courts. He was born in 1964 and grew up in Flatbush, Brooklyn. The first time I met him he had on a pair of Wichita St. game shorts with the letters MTXE (Mental Toughness, Extra Effort) on the side. I don't know to this day how he got his hands on them, but that was Art's M. O. He had the right clothing flavor and looked like a ballplayer. Unfortunately his game peaked at Ditmas Junior High. Some people in the crew had props for the quality of their collection. For Art, it was all about the quantity of your quiver. In high school he would line up his joints on *all four* sides of his bed and watch his boys scream in amazement.

Turk Gumusdere a.k.a. "Trike 1"

Born in 1961 in Istanbul, Turkey, Turk moved to Brooklyn when he was eleven. With a mean jumper and 38" hops, he played on a Riverside Church crew that went 64-0, featuring eight future NBA players including Chris Mullin and "Pearl" Washington. Turk got his start in hip hop when he began writing Trike 1 in '74. His whole passion was bringing unique gear style and flavor to the basketball court. His sneaker obsession was so all-encompassing that he didn't don an actual pair of shoes until the day of his father's funeral.

Ahmad Hooper a.k.a. "Mad" (pronounced "Mod,") "Hoop"

Ahmad was born in 1968 and grew up between Brooklyn and the Boogie Down. He played at Lower Merion H.S. (Kobe Bryant's

alma mater—"He went to *my* school!"), Walton H.S., and Hunter College. He also played at Nelson Park where he regularly went up against playground legend "Master" Rob and future NBA player John Morton. His Bronx upbringing also afforded him the joy of witnessing early hip hop park jams with Afrika Bambaataa and Grandmaster Flash. In '87 he counted 77 pairs of dogs in his quiver, with (proudly), "no repeats!" His expertise has come in handy over the last fifteen years as he has worked in various sneaker stores. He's currently at Moe's Sneakers-Coliseum Mall in Jamaica, Queens. If you go there, he's the boisterous one behind the counter with joints on that aren't out yet.

Pete Nash a.k.a. "Pete Nice," "The Prime Minister"

The first time I met Pete in '87 he had on Air Force 1s in white on green. Automatic ups. He was born in 1967 and grew up in Queens and Brooklyn. He played for Bishop Ford H.S. and was All Brooklyn-Queens for Catholic high schools plus Honorable Mention All City. He once dropped 31 points against Holy Cross (featuring All-American Derrick Chievous) in the city semi finals. In '87 he and MC Serch formed the rap group 3rd Bass. They signed to Def Jam Records and released two gold LPs. In '77 he saw Tony "Red" Bruin at Mater Christi H.S. with customized Nike Blazers in yellow on green with his name on the back. That drove Pete nuts and from that point he became a bona fide sneaker junkie who always stayed ahead of the curve.

Blake Lethem a.k.a. "Keo," "Lord Scotch," "Kid Bennetton," "Link 2," "Dose," "Merge," "THE 123"

Blake was born in '67 and grew up in downtown Brooklyn. A respected graffiti writer, he was down with the T.O.P. crew. His hip hop credibility is unassailable. He was blessed to rhyme with (or against) some of the best MCs in his generation, like Biz Mark, Big Daddy Kane, and Kool Keith. Since households funds were low and jokes

at school for reject sneakers were high, Blake honed his boosting skills to feed his sneaker jones ("I'd drool on the store windows on Fulton St.").

Michael Berrin a.k.a. "MC Serch"

Serch was born in 1967 and grew up in Far Rockaway, Queens. After 3rd Bass ended, he started Serchlite Music, signed Nas, and put out Nas' first two LPs on Columbia. His recording artist days may be long gone, but he still performs for people who gaze below his ankles. Serch boasts one of the best current collections worldwide. Unlike other collectors who have classics from the '80s that are recent purchases, Serch amazingly has untouched, boxed classics that have been on ice in his closet for over fifteen years. That's will power! He claims that, at times, the act of putting on a new pair of grips was more satisfying than sex!

Dante Ross a.k.a. "System"

Dante was born in 1965 in San Francisco, then grew up in L.E.S. and BK. He worked at Rush Artist Management and toured with Eric B. and Rakim and the Beastie Boys. As an A&R for Tommy Boy and Elektra, he signed acts such as De La Soul, Brand Nubian, Pete Rock & CL Smooth, and KMD. As a producer with the Stimulated Dummies he's done music for Everlast and Santana. As a young skateboarder he dogged a lot of sneakers, so he got into owning multiple pairs early. He would steal and then sell anything he could (toothpaste, Bustelo coffee, fireworks, etc.) to support his sneaker habit. He even wore sneakers when accepting his Grammy Award-completing the outfit with a suit!

Mike Drake

Mike was born in 1967 and grew up in the Dunbar Projects of Harlem, USA. He made NY Post All Division at Brooklyn Tech H.S., went on to play D2 at American International College, and then played pro in Puerto Rico. By the age of twelve his shoe size was thirteen, so finding fly joints was a task. But he rose to the occasion, and by age seventeen had amassed over 70 pairs of rare oversized sneakers. Mike loved sneakers so much as a teenager that when he was forced to wear shoes (rarely) he actually took the insoles from his kicks and put them in his shoes. He always wanted a remnant of sneakers on his feet.

Jorge Pabon a.k.a. "Fabel," "Paser," "Per," "Pas"

Fabel was born in 1965 and raised in Spanish Harlem. He is best known for popping as a member of the Electric Company and Magnificent Force (with Mr. Wiggles) in the early '80s, and as an enduring member of the Zulu Nation and Rock Steady Crew. A master of sneaker and gear customizations, he is one of the originators of the super duper fat lace style of the early '80s. For him just buying a fly pair of joints wasn't enough. The true test was how someone could flip them. An archivist of hip hop gear, his head to toe outfits were on display at the first hip hop exhibit at the Brooklyn Museum. He's presently at work on a documentary on hip hop fashion from '75-'85.

Jorge Alvarez a.k.a. "Kurious," "the Magician"

Kurious was born in 1970 and grew up in the same building as I did. He released a rap LP on Hoppoh/Columbia in '93, and played summer league ball for Central Baptist. He became a sneaker addict simply to avoid being an outcast on the competitive block we grew up on. There were guys like Kirk Rodriguez who would switch fly sneakers three times in one day! Kurious' missions took him as far as Virginia to cop rare joints (like the

treasured pair of all green Adidas Forums). He was generous about telling heads where he got his sneakers, but only because he knew that by the time they'd find the spot (usually out of state), the stock would be sold out.

Schott Lee Jacobs a.k.a. "Schott Free"

Schott Free was born in 1969 and raised on Staten Island. As an A&R he signed seminal hip hop acts such as Wu-Tang, Mobb Deep, and Big Pun to Loud Records. He played CYO for Sacred Heart, then at Staten Island Academy. He once scored 36 points with twelve boards and eleven assists in a game, and represented his borough in the Golden Hoops all-star game. He learned the finer points of sneaker consumption early. This included the realization that if you loved a pair that not a lot of people had, buy them immediately. Even one day of hesitation could cost you your size. Schott claims that ever since he's had his own dough—and hasn't had to depend on momdukes for kicks— he gets somebody saying something about his kicks every other day!

Michael Greene a.k.a. "Emz"

Emz was born in 1972 and raised in the Bronx. He wrote EM ONE, then EMZ, and has been a popular radio and club DJ for over a decade on both coasts. He's worked for Loud Records and Interscope, and has done beats for Tupac. His quest to be unique steered him to rock crazy combos as a youth (like one aqua Chuck Taylor and one yellow), but his current collection of rare '80s kicks clears him of any prior violations. It is one of the top two collections I have ever seen. His favorite response to unworn classics he wears on occasion? Awed silence.

Steve Brock

Steve was born in 1964 and raised in the Bronx and New Rochelle. As a batboy for the Yankees during the '80 and '81 seasons he signed a record fifteen sneaker contracts. On the road with the team, his $100 per diem went $1 for a burger, $99 to kicks. He also became the sneaker buyer for Royale's with locations in New Rochelle and the Albee Square Mall in Brooklyn, with patrons like legendary collector Biz Markie. By his senior year at New Rochelle H.S., he was such a rabid collector that he was able to wear a different pair of sneakers every day for the entire school year (that's 152 pairs). He'd wear his weakest joints in January, after Christmas, when everyone was rocking their new sneakers. In his words, "It was like New Year's Eve to someone who partied all the time. I'd let them have two weeks and then piss them off again with some ultrasonic shit." That's some legendary shit!

Prof. Will Strickland

A self-proclaimed "sneaker whore," Will was born in 1970 in Detroit, and eventually wound up in New York. In high school he made 2nd Team All State in Texas, then played at Rice U. and pro in Brazil. He has worked at Epic and Bad Boy Records, and also taught a course on hip hop culture at the University of Massachusetts. He enjoyed scouring the discount racks as a youth to secure slept-on models. His penchant for finding hot ball kicks made his Texas classmates say, "You must not be from here with those shoes on." (They were more into track and football.) He dealt with the flack and has kept his eye keen ever since.

The Sneaker Survivalist: Udi Avshalomov

Udi was born in 1970 in Isreal, and raised in East New York. At age fourteen, he was the youngest buyer at any sneaker store that mattered in the '80s, when he and his family opened the legendary Broadway Sneakers. Years later he opened his own current operation, Training Camp, and it has maintained the same rep for having that next shit you can't find anywhere else. His tenacity for consistency made a big impression on me when I first opened my own store, Bobbito's Footwork, in '96. He has consulted Nike, Puma, Timberland, and has designed shoes for Phat Farm and Wu-Tang, but don't think he's just business. He's a connoisseur as well, and owns 400 never-worn pairs that he's stashed since '87. ■

Where'd You Get Those?:
Getting Around

The following lists for each period feature the brand, model name, street nicknames, materials and colors for each shoe. An asterisk next to a color denotes that is was hard to find or customized for college and pro athletes. Please note that certain shoes' production years may not coincide with the time period it was available in New York. All sneakers are listed in order according to their relevance in New York. Basketball sneakers, then other categories (like running or tennis), are listed in Basic Classics according to their popularity in hip hop circles and basketball courts combined. The more I saw a particular model the earlier it appears on the list, but that doesn't mean it was necessarily a flyer sneaker than something less popular. Not everyone that wore shit in New York was original. That's why it's called Basic Classics. The Rarest Gems are listed according to how unavailable they were in New York, and how seldom seen they were otherwise. The most subjective category is Slept On Butters. I listed sneakers according to how severely they were overlooked relative to how dope they were.

"Hey man, where'd you get that smooth-ass kufi?" "Shoo-bee-doo, my brother! Make a left on 8th right past the chicken spot.": Butch Purcell and Earl "Black Jesus" Monroe chatting it up at the Pro Rucker in 1972.

The '60s—Ragtime

Basic Classics—Basketball

■ **Converse All Star Chuck Taylor a.k.a. "The Rags," "Ragtops," canvas high top and low top in black, white**

Converse jumped off in 1908, founded by Marquis M. Converse. Their canvas basketball sneaker was named the All Star in 1917, and then in 1923 the shoe became the signature Chuck Taylor. Chuck was a basketball ambassador who gave clinics throughout the U.S., South America, and Europe. The Chuck Taylor has sold over 750 million pairs in its history, making it the #1 selling sneaker of all time. It was the quintessential basketball and hanging out sneaker for New York in the '60s. It's design and N.Y. availability has remained a constant from the '60s to present.

Greg "Elevator Man #2" Brown, Harlem ballplayer (born '54): My first pair of Converse was a Christmas present, and it was like holding a camera! No other toys mattered.

Coco 144, pioneer graffiti artist (born '56): We'd say, "Don't get the sneakers that slip and slide, get the sneakers with the star on the side. Pick up your Converse."

"Pee Wee" Kirkland: We used to call them "the Rags" because they were canvas like a ragtop. Converse was subliminally considered #1. It was the psychological effect of the star on the ankle and the name All Star. Everyone was trying to be a star. People who played the game well mostly wore Converse. People who didn't play too well mostly wore Keds. You couldn't find me in a pair of Keds for any reason. Converse was the one.

Joe Ski: Back in the day everybody on the court wore white high top Chuck Taylors.

Joe Cruz, South Bronx ballplayer (born '46): We wore the white low cut to hang. It was hard to find the black low cut, and when Converse came out with colors in the '70s it freaked people out!

"Pee Wee" Kirkland: When I'd go to big affairs I'd dress up, but I'd have on Converse. That wasn't common back

then. I'd have on some silk pants, silk shirts, and an Alpaca sweater (which was the shit).

You could only style a pair off the court but for so long because playing ball eventually dogged them. You got ridiculed when your foot was coming out the front. Dragging your foot going for a dunk would wear them out real fast. They'd joke, "When's it going to happen?" like really meaning, "When you gonna get a new pair of sneakers?"

Joe Ski: They had to last you the whole summer. You didn't get a new pair every month.

Joe Cruz: My moms used to buy the $6 irregulars (with the irregular stamp at the heel) at Paragon's. I think Converse put those out to help us out in the projects!

Joe Ski: We shopped for them at Peck and Chase on Orchard St. If they were $11 you'd tell the guy, "My mother's poor and we don't have no money," and he'd give them to you for $8. He'd remember your sad "I ain't got no money" face. They'd hold sneakers for us too. You'd give a deposit of $4. If you didn't come back within two weeks you'd lose your money. In the two weeks between you'd squeeze the rest from your parents, clean the house, take out the garbage, anything.

"Pee Wee" Kirkland: We used to go downtown to Paragon's to get 'em for $9 or $10. They sold them in Harlem, but not for the same price. This one kid around the way was up on Paragon's, then he told someone else. You know how the ghetto is. If the drum beats and you out there, you hear.

Joe Ski: We'd go to Moe's on 13th and A. He'd sell you Chucks a size nine and a half on one foot and size nine on the other. He'd given the other one away! But you'd take it cuz they'd be $3 less. Guys would wear a size nine, and buy a ten and a half cuz there'd be no nines left. They couldn't wait. The sneakers would only come in every six months.

Joe Cruz: In the mid '60s Converse came out with Chuck Taylors with weights in blue on the lip of the toe

A game of 21 up at Dyckman. One cat with 69'ers, one with Chucks, and one bozo with shoes and church socks.

We go right on winning players, coaches, games, titles. Our 48-year record as the leading basketball shoe maker testifies to the unbeatable construction of Converse "All Stars".

Converse
Chuck Taylor
ALL STAR
BASKETBALL SHOES
HIGH CUT OR OXFORD

CONVERSE RUBBER COMPANY
MALDEN 48, MASSACHUSETTS

You can measure the **difference!**

CONVERSE
'Chuck' Taylor
ALL STAR
OXFORD OR HIGH CUT
BASKETBALL SHOES

Break-away Speed
Pinpoint Pivots
Hairline Stops

Lightweight
Marvelous Comfort
Fatigue-free Fit

CONVERSE RUBBER COMPANY MALDEN 48, MASSACHUSETTS

—because they want only the Best

more **coaches** specify...

more **players** wear...

CONVERSE
ALL STARS

CONVERSE
ALL STAR
BASKETBALL SHOES

CONVERSE RUBBER COMPANY MALDEN 48, MASSACHUSETTS

P.F. FLYERS
Pf
POSTURE FOUNDATION

YOU'LL find yourself in a new world of *fun* with "P-F"! The X-Ray picture shows you just why. For here is an exclusive built-in feature that revolutionizes canvas shoe comfort. Look at all the new models... many in color, in styles to please the whole family! See them today. Remember to insist on "P-F" Canvas Shoes!

Everything you do is more fun with "P-F"

Oxfords, in all white or blue—in styles to suit the needs of children to grown ups.

The scientific foot protection that guards against flat feet, puts extra pep, spring and endurance in your legs.

1. This rigid wedge gives the bones of the foot proper orthopedic support, keeps them in their natural, normal position. **2.** The sponge rubber cushion assures comfort for the sensitive area of the foot.

"P-F" *means Posture Foundation*

One of several sport oxfords in white or colors, for the well dressed man.

Popular athletic shoes in sand, black, brown, blue for "little" men and "big" men.

Attractive moccasin type oxfords in blue, brown, beige, white— for growing children.

"P-F" *Canvas Shoes made only by* **B.F. Goodrich and HOOD RUBBER**

Here are some ads that your grandmother saw back in the day while she was changing your maduke's diapers.

because wearing ankle weights were so popular. That's one of the ways "The Goat" got his hops.

■ P.F. Flyer, canvas high top and low top in black, white

B. F. Goodrich was making sneakers in the early part of the century right along with Converse. In the early '60s they sold a large quantity of the P.F. (Posture Foundation) Flyer. The P.F. Flyer's popularity in New York was essentially with pre-teens and didn't last past the mid '60s. The shoe disappeared at the turn of the decade.

Coach Sid Jones, United Brooklyn Pro-Am Team (born '51): Every pre-teen wanted to be the fastest kid on the block. We came up racing and doing relays against other blocks. This is way before we got into basketball. From '60 until '63, P.F. Flyers were *the* shoes we wanted cuz we actually thought the shoes made us run faster. We responded to the name Flyer. I thought, "Man, I can fly."

Dee Adams, former Milbank coach (born '58): They had this commercial with these little white kids running fast and jumping, and the tag line was, "Run Faster, Jump Higher."

Fab Five Freddy: In the commercial they zoomed in on the kid's sneakers so you could see what they called the "magic wedge." We'd wear sneakers down to nothing, so I ripped my P.F. Flyers open trying to get the magic wedge (which I never found). My moms wasn't too happy!

Brother Ray: I don't remember anything about the P.F. Flyer other than repulsion, utter horror and fear of having to wear them! They were cheapo cheapos.

Greg "Elevator Man #2" Brown: If you were a serious ballplayer maybe you could pull off some skippies like the

Decks by Keds, but no way could you wear P.F.s on the court. No way!

Coco 144: As a kid our choices were between Converse, P.F. Flyers, Decks, or cornballs. If your moms was really cheap she bought you cornballs at John's Bargain Stores where most of the patrons were welfare recipients. Cornballs were no-namers below even skippies! P.F. Flyers were fresh until the late '60s when Pro-Keds came out, and then the Flyers became wack.

Rare Gems—Other

■ Onitsuka Tiger Marup Nylon Sp, nylon/suede low top running shoe in white on blue, blue on white

Kihachiro Onitsuka founded Onitsuka Tiger in '49 in Kobe, Japan. He started by making canvas basketball shoes out of his crib. In '77 the company was renamed Tiger Asics. Asics is an acronym for the Latin phrase, "Anima Sana In Corpore San," which translates to "a sound mind in a sound body." The '67 Marup was one of the first pairs of running shoes that really blew up beyond the runners' market. It sold over 400,000 pairs. Completely slept on in the streets of New York, these sneakers were waaaay before their time.

■ Onitsuka Tiger Mexico 66, leather/suede low top running shoe in blue on white

The '66 Mexico was t. e first Tiger shoe to feature their signature renowned stripes. Flavor Flav on the hype tip.

■ **Onitsuka Tiger Corsair, leather low top running shoe in red on white with blue accent**

The '69 Corsair was part of Tiger's '72 Olympic line and was one of the starting blocks for jogging shoes. Its design inspired Nike's Cortez running shoe.

Slept On Butters— Basketball

■ **Spalding Deluxe SS a.k.a. "Red Bottoms," canvas high top and low top in white and black**

Baseball Hall of Fame pitcher Albert Goodwill Spalding founded his sporting goods company in 1876 in New England. Spalding designed the first official basketball, then started making basketball sneakers in the early 1900s right after Converse. In the '60s they introduced the Deluxe SS. It lasted in N.Y. from '60-'67 and was the only other sneaker besides Chucks to gain respect under the rim.

Coach Sid Jones: Converse and Spalding were the sneakers you had to wear to be accepted on the court. Spalding had an orange sole and I thought they looked better than Converse.

Greg "Elevator Man #2" Brown: They were rare, and were the first sneaker I remember anyone saying, "Where'd you get those?" when they'd see them. If you had them on you were bad!

Joe "The Destroyer" Hammond: The rubber toe on the Spalding protected my foot well, but then I moved on to Converse. ■

Detail from Spalding catalog circa1962.

- *Spalding's famous cushioned "Sport Arch" for healthful comfort*
- *Colorful two-tone trim*
- *Contour-cut ankle lines*

"SS"

67-111 (SS-W)

67-112 (SS-B)

67-11 (SSW-LC)

'70-'74 The Emergence of Leather, Suede and the Pro Rucker

Before '70 was the Dark Ages of sneaker culture compared to what came after. Leather and suede sneakers (in colors beside black and white) very slowly made their first entrance into New York stores, and people didn't know how to react! The major showcase for these new sneakers in the street was none other than the Pro Rucker Basketball Tournament, played up on 155th St. and Eighth in Harlem. The league peaked in popularity in the early '70s, as kids hung off fences and trees just to watch their favorite playground legends. The kicks that these legends wore were being noticed and sought after. Some of the sneakers couldn't be found, heralding the beginning of limited supply and hungry demand.

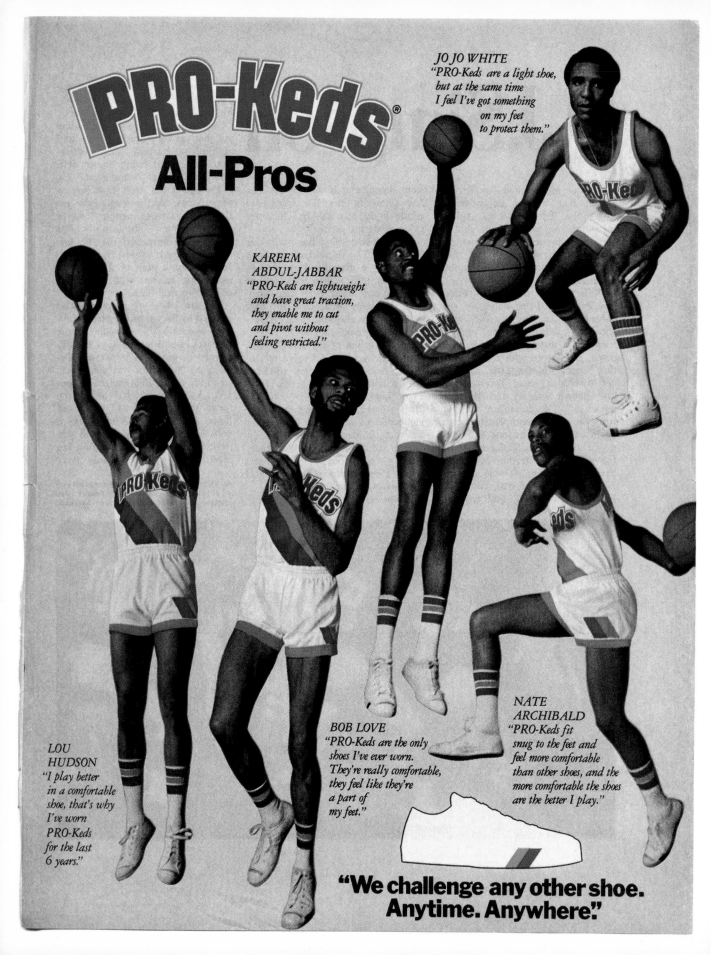

Previous spread: Dr J plays before a packed house at the 1972 Pro Rucker.

Left: It's hard to believe by today's standards, but NBA players were steadily rocking low top canvas in the early '70s, as this 1971 Pro-Keds ad illustrates.

Following spread: "I hope this game starts soon, my butt hurts!": Kids line the fence in anticipation of seeing Bob Love of the Chicago Bulls (second from the left) and Dr. J (far left) about to catch rek on 55th.

Basic Classics—Basketball

■ **Pro-Ked Super a.k.a. "69'ers," canvas high top and low top in white, black, blue, red, *green**

The U.S. Rubber company jumped off in 1892 when nine companies merged, and in 1916 they released Keds canvas sneakers. Keds sold a bananas amount of sneakers throughout the country for decades, mostly to kids and females. Around the mid '60s Pro-Ked 69'ers started popping up on ballcourts in N.Y., and by the early '70s they became the first classic sneaker (other than Chucks) for New Yorkers on and off the court. Their availability, though, would waffle back and forth until '86 when Pro-Keds closed shop (until their eventual recent re-launch).

Lincoln: Even back then there was the notion of being accepted if you had certain products. Pro-Keds were one of those products. All the cats in school that played basketball and baseball had Pro-Keds.

Joe Ski: I tried Pro-Keds when they first came out. Not everybody was wearing them, so you'd look crazy coming on the court with them.

Brother Bill: I wasn't an aficionado of Pro-Keds. I saw girls wearing them. Girls would never wear Chuck Taylors, which were for ballplayers. The whole world was divided between ballplayers and nons. 90% of the world wasn't even aware of our state of mind.

Dee Adams: The 69'ers were more of a street shoe than a ballplayer's shoe. All the young hustlers in Harlem were rocking them, and then I saw the kids pick up on them after that.

Snake, pioneer graffiti artist: In '71 the low top black ones were popular with two shoe strings on each shoe in different colors overlapping each other.

■ **Pro-Ked Royal a.k.a. "Super Pro-Keds," canvas high top in white, blue, red, black, *green; canvas low top in white, black, red, blue, *green, *gold**

By '70 Uniroyal owned Keds and became the first company to specifically market ballplayers to the influential New York scene with player endorsements of popular New York natives Kareem Abdul Jabbar and Nate "Tiny" Archibald. They were obviously targeting New York in the hopes of putting a dent in the Converse-dominated market. It worked.

Joe Cruz: The low cut Super Pro-Ked in navy blue or white took the sneaker world to another level of fashion.

KRS-ONE, legendary MC: The Super Pro-Ked is the greatest sneaker ever introduced to mankind! I loved them. It's bugged how flat they were compared to today's technology.

Seth Rosenfeld, film director: Once the Supers came out in '72 the older 69'ers (which I always thought were fresher) became really hard to find.

Gerry Erasme, former Syracuse U. point guard: I remember like it was yesterday. I got Pro-Keds in '72. They were just starting to gain recognition but not many people had them. I liked the way the thicker sole looked.

Put yourself in their shoes. Pro-Keds.

There is only one All Star. Only Converse makes it. Only sporting goods dealers sell it.

The Converse All Star is basketball's shoe. This year 8 out of 10 players in every major college and junior college tournament wore Converse All Stars. Converse All Stars have been worn by every U.S. Olympic Team since 1936, and All Stars have been selected again by the U.S. Olympic Committee for the 1976 Olympics. They are available in 10 team colors, 5 action styles in suede, leather and canvas.

★ converse

an Eltra company

Put yourself in Nate Archibald's shoes.

Nate spends a lot of time on his feet. So it's no wonder his feet spend a lot of time in our shoes.

Sure, the Royal Plus is tough. But with our cushioned arch support, padded tongue and collar, it's not tough on your feet.

And to a pro like Nate, comfort counts. Because to win, you've got to stay on your toes.

UNIROYAL

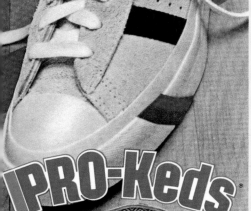

IPRO-Keds®

IPRO-Keds®
SPRING 1976

Previous spread, left: In the early '70s, Pro Keds went underground with this Harlem Globetrotters subway ad campaign.

Previous spread, middle: This 1975 Converse ad reveals a pride in sporting goods stores' distribution that doesn't exist anymore in today's mass market sneaker world.

Previous spread, right: New York City native Tom "Gator" Pauling displaying how his Chuck Taylors added height to his J.

Left: "Tiny" repping it for the PJs at Patterson Projects in the Bronx, circa 1971.

■ Converse All Star Chuck Taylor a.k.a. "Chucks," "Cons," canvas high top and low top in black, white

"Chuckies" were still hot on the b-ball court, but in this period they lost a little bit of their footing as far as producing the off-court butters.

Jazzy Art: Everybody wore skippies until your moms decided that she was going to spend the dough on Chuck Taylors! When I was in sixth grade, my mom dropped twelve bucks for a pair. They lasted a week! They were *not* built to last. Around my block there were gangs that wore dungaree jackets with their name on the back, like the Savage Skulls, the Young Saigons, and the Young Vietnams. They were all rocking Chucks.

■ Pro-Ked Royal Plus a.k.a. "Tinys," "Royals," and "Suede Super Pro-Keds," suede high top and low top in white on blue, white on red, *black on white, *black on gold, * white on green *white on carolina, *black on red, *white on purple, *white on maroon, *brown on tan, *gold on navy

The very first Royal Plus in '70-'71 had three stripes on the uppers similar to Adidas. I don't know if Adidas beefed or not, but the next year Pro-Keds settled in very nicely with two stripes. They were made until '78. Nate "Tiny" Archibald blew these up while playing for the Kansas City Kings. In '72-'73 he became the first player in NBA history to finish number one in scoring (with a 34 points per game average) and assists (with 11.4 per game) in the same season. He made the Bronx very proud.

Lincoln: The suede Super Pro-Keds were the next level, and came out after the canvas Super Pro-Keds. There were posters of "Tiny" on the side of buses, and I stole one and put it in my room. If you had those joints you were bad. They would turn your feet blue because the dye from the suede would get all over your socks. Truthfully, the reason I got them wasn't even to play ball. They just looked smooth with jeans.

Sake: The Royal Plus was the bomb!

Frosty Freeze, Rock Steady Crew b-boy: I bought a pair in '81 when they were real hard to find. They were the last pair in the store. The red suede really stood out.

■ Converse One-Star, leather high top in black on white, leather low top in black on white, white on black; suede low top in black on natural, black on gold, *white on green, *black on orange, *white on red, *white on blue, *white on purple, suede high top in *white on red

The '74-'75 One-Star marked a significant trend—available for a year then gone forever—that years later would become standard in the sneaker industry. It was one of those moments that sent a clear message to connoisseurs: Get your shit now or forever hold your peace (or piece).

We've put our basketball shoes on the line in every Olympic year since 1936. Converse All Stars.® They color the action.

Berlin 1936,
London 1948,
Helsinki 1952,
Melbourne 1956,
Rome 1960,
Tokyo 1964,
Mexico City 1968,
Munich 1972.

★ **converse**

an Eltra company

Selected again for use by
the U.S. team for
the 1976 Olympic Games
in Montreal.

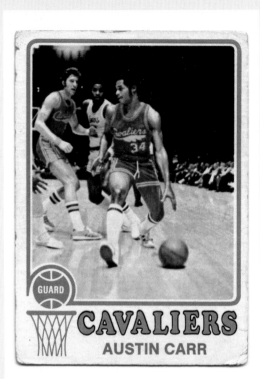

CAVALIERS

AUSTIN CARR

GUARD

116030 Supergrip
A special model for High School and College players. White form fitting leather uppers. SOFTPROTECT heel padding for comfort and secure fit. Adjustable arch support. Long wearing sole of vulcanized gum rubber provides good traction.

116020 "Greenstar"
A newly developed basketball shoe with a rich looking dark-green velour leather upper, white stripes. SOFTPROTECT foam padding surrounds ankles and heel for extra support and comfort. Vulcanized gum rubber sole. Ideally suited for teams needing dark shoes.

116040 "Promodel"
A basketball shoe for players who prefer high tops. Combines all features of the "Superstar" along with foam padded uppers that completely surround the ankles.

115041 "Official"
A very light and comfortable shoe for basketball Officials and Coaches. All black leather uppers, black gum rubber sole. Arch support. SOFTPROTECT heel padding. Special wedge underneath heel relieves strain of standing on feet many hours each day.

116060 Shooting Star
The only basketball shoe with ventilated nylon uppers. Nylon material that breathes, allows perspiration to evaporate. SOFTPROTECT ankle and padding for secure fit. Vulcanized gum rubber sole. A great shoe for a moderate budget.

116310 "TOURNAMENT" red

116300 "TOURNAMENT" blue

116320 "TOURNAMENT" gold

"TOURNAMENT"
Here is a shoe that really attracts the crowd's eye. A dazzling variety of team colors add the finishing touch to any uniform. Top quality velour leather specially cut and tanned to hold up under the constant stress of basketball.
Vulcanized gum rubber sole reinforced for longer wear at ball-of-foot and heel. Excellent traction. Special padding for protection of heel and Achilles tendon, designed to keep the shoe snugly on foot during games.

Previous spread, left: All-time New York legend Bernard King at the University of Tennessee, wearing Converse One-Stars and showing off his quick release form.

Previous spread, right: Converse brags about their basketball dominance throughout the decades in this 1975 ad.

Top left: Note that the Cleveland Cavalier to the left of Austin Carr is wearing the rare red on gold Tournaments.

Joe Ski: The One-Star came out with blue or red uppers, but the only people you'd see wear those colors were hippies.

Brother Ray: They were the first sneakers I loved just because of the way they looked. They weren't out for very long, and then you couldn't find them anywhere. Back then sneakers were never reissued after they were taken out of production. I liked my One-Stars so much that when they got busted I just sewed them. I didn't think I'd be able to find them ever again.

Rare Gems—Basketball

■ Adidas Greenstar, velour low top in *white on green

The Dassler Brothers Sport Shoe Factory kicked off in 1924 in Germany when Rudolf Dassler joined his brother Adi, who had started making sport shoes in his moms' washroom in the early '20s. In '48 they had beef with each other and parted ways. Adi then founded Adidas. People may despise the Celtics for winning so much, but no true sneaker connoisseur can ever front on the Celtics' grips. They have perennially had the illest customized black or deep forest green joints while the rest of the NBA has primarily always stuck with white. In '68 some of the players switched from Chucks to the Adidas Blackstar, the granddaddy of suede Adidas basketball shoes. The Celtics wore the Blackstar for two years until Adidas came out with the '70-'72 Greenstar. Sneaker companies were just beginning to break out of the dark ages and provide color beyond the black and white minimal selection. The world became a better place because of it.

■ Adidas Supergrip, leather low top in black on white

The '70-'71 Supergrip were similar to the Superstars except they had a leather toe box instead of a rubber one. You couldn't find a soul with them in New York.

■ Adidas Shooting Star, nylon/leather in black on white

The '70-'71 Shooting Star was the first nylon mesh basketball shoe. Adidas called it, "airnet uppers." This sneaker was way ahead of its time. Nylon mesh didn't catch on in New York until ten years later.

■ Adidas Tournament, suede high top and low cut in *white on navy blue, *white on blue, *white on green, *white on red, *white on gold, *red on gold, *blue on gold; leather in black on white

The '72-'74 Tournaments were the same as the Greenstar just made in different flavors for other NBA squads. These were strictly pro and college material. I have never seen an actual pair in any store or on anyone's feet in New York, aside from the photo of Dr. J at the Pro Rucker with a pair he copped from his playing days at U Mass. The red on gold and blue on gold weren't even in the Adidas catalog and must've been specially customized.

Timo Pape, Adidas Germany: Adidas was founded on the premise of specifically designing shoes for athletes to improve their performance. Adi's belief was that if the athletes will wear it, then the consumers will wear it. I'm not surprised that customized colors of the Tournament weren't available in stores.

Top left: Brooklyn's own Greg "Jocko" Jackson flying high while playing for Guilford College in leather Adidas.

Bottom left: Queens native Ernie Grunfeld taking it to the butter while playing for U. of Tennessee in leather Converse All Stars.

■ Adidas Pro Model, leather high top in black on white, *red on white, *blue on white, *white on white, *gold on white

Both Adidas' popularity and availability were extremely limited in New York. The Pro Model set it off for Adidas with ballplayers in New York based purely on function. The first Pro Model came out in '65 and was the first modern era leather basketball shoe ever made. The rubber shell toe cap, which was inspired by the shape of a seashell, came in '69. In '68 the San Diego Rockets of the ABA became the first squad to rock Adidas, and in the same year the NCAA title game had players from both U. of Houston and UCLA wearing Adidas. In the following years, a young Harlem ballplayer with no college or pro experience wore them, and as Joe Hammond's legend grew so did the spread of Adidas in N.Y.

Greg "Elevator Man #2" Brown: At first people thought the funny looking toe was the ugliest, plus they were $15 compared to $7 for Converse. My father thought I was crazy to pay that much. But it was about status. Joe Hammond had them! He was the first person to wear them in N.Y., and he was like the Elvis of basketball.

Joe Ski: The first time I ever saw leather basketball shoes I was at the Pro Rucker. Joe Hammond came out wearing Adidas. Everyone was asking him, "Where'd you get those?" and he brushed it off saying, "My boy sent them to me." He had new sneakers every three games. He knew a lot of people and was making big money. He had it that way. When leather sneakers came out people weren't really wearing them on the street until '75. But this was the first time I actually saw them on the court. I figured they must've come from another country! Hammond dropped 55 points that game and he kept telling people, *"Don't step on my feet!"* I'll never forget that! It was hilarious. If someone stepped on his sneakers he'd stop in the middle of the game and rub it off. I went from wearing Chuck Taylors to Adidas Pro Models. They became my #1.

Coach Sid Jones: The first time I ever saw leather sneakers it was in the early '70s. They were called the Collegians and had two stripes. Adidas came out right after them and took over. Leather was something new, and we didn't know if we should stick with canvas Cons or be different.

■ Adidas Superstar, leather low top in black on white, *red on white, *blue on white, *white on white, *gold on white

The Superstar, introduced in '69, was the low top version of the Pro Model, and the first leather low tops ever. Similar to the Pro Models, they first appeared in N.Y. strictly on top level ballplayers' feet. And even they had a hard time finding them in stores.

Greg "Elevator Man #2" Brown: The only store that sold them was Carlsen Imports. You had to show a school ID and be a ballplayer, and then this old Jewish man would sell them to you.

Joe "The Destroyer" Hammond: Shell toe Adidas were one of my favorite sneakers ever. I got my first pair in '70 when Adidas started coming out. You could hear them skidding on the floor a lot, and we liked that noise. I always wore low tops, and would just tape my ankles.

■ Converse All Star, leather high top in blue/red on white, low top in blue/red on white, white on black; suede low top in *black on natural, *black on gold, *white on green, *white on orange, *white on red, *white on blue, *white on purple

The leather '70-'73 All Star was Converse's competition to the Adidas Pro Model and Superstar, and it was the second leather basketball shoe ever seen in New York.

■ **Puma Clyde, suede low top in white on blue, *orange on natural, *orange on blue, *blue on orange, *black on gold, *white on red, *red/green on black; high top in black on natural**

Rudolf Dassler founded Puma in 1948 in Germany. The '72 Clyde was the first signature suede shoe for a pro ballplayer, endorsed by Knick guard Walt "Clyde" Frazier. Everyone that I interviewed pointed to the Clyde as the first suede sneaker they ever saw on the streets of New York. It was instant impact. With initial limited availability, the Clyde was unequivocally the most sought after shoe of this period, and would later become one of the staple shoes for hip hop enthusiasts until '85. Legend has it that Clyde once wore blue on orange on one foot and orange on blue on the other. I cannot confirm this. Clyde was known for getting freaky deaky though. In the '70 NBA Championship Series he wore blue laces on one foot and orange on the other with white Chuck Taylors.

Dee Adams: I bought Clydes in '72 at Lee's on 125th off St. Nick. I wore them to ball and brothers laughed at me. They called them skips. They eventually caught on because ballplayers started sporting them at the Rucker. Everyone in Harlem played ball, so we were all influenced to start wearing leather and suede because we saw all the top ballplayers doing it.

Brother Ray: Walt Frazier wore Pumas, and I immediately wanted them. I bought them at Carlsen Imports. Back then when you bought sneakers you *had* to look at the tread. The Puma bottoms had squares with diamonds, which was totally different than the tread of other brands.

John Snakeback Fever: Clydes were like wearing a piece of plywood and suede strapped to your foot. There was no arch in there, no nothing. You had to wear eleven pairs of socks to make them comfortable.

Lincoln: The first fly sneakers I got were Clydes in white on blue in '73. They also came in black on gold, but you could only get those at Paragon. I saved $20 from my allowance but still didn't have enough. They were 25 bucks. I

wanted these joints so bad, and my homeboy worked at a store right next to Paragon. He stole $10 out the register to hook a brother up with some Pumas, and I brought him back his change!

Greg "Elevator Man #2" Brown: When Puma came out with the Red, Black, and Greens in '73 they couldn't keep them in stores in Harlem. I wore a pair in a game at Boston U., and my coach said, "Uh, uh! You're getting too militant."

■ **Bata Bullet, canvas high top and low top in black on white**

Bata jumped off in 1894 in Czechoslovakia, founded by Tomas Bata. The '72 Bullet appeared in New York faster than a speeding you know what. It was one of the earliest canvas models of any brand to have their logo placed on the uppers outside the ankle.

Leroy 'La Luscious Lee' Shaw, playground legend: When I played High School our coach bought Bata Bullets for the squad and sold them to us for $8 each. They were alright!

Rare Gems—Other

■ **Adidas Italia, leather running shoe in green on white**

The '70-'72 Italia was a simply gorgeous European shoe, but it never made it across the Atlantic to the hood. Too bad, the money green stripes would've had the prepubescent hip hop generation buying lime 10¢ icees by the pound. ■

Top left: Legendary NBA match-up and legendary rare sneaker match-up: Jerry West wearing gold Superstars and Walt Frazier taking him out in orange Clydes with orange laces.

Right: "Hey kid, stop making me look bad in my own photo shoot!": Walt tries to rip little man in a Colgate toothpaste print ad.

Bottom left: Red Clydes make an early appearance at the Pro Rucker in 1972.

While older, upper-echelon players began to wear leather, younger ball players stayed with canvas, as this photo of an early '70s Gauchos squad at the McBurney Westside Y depicts.

The New York Rucker All-Stars in 1973, featuring the likes of Dr. J, "Tiny" Archibald, Billy Paultz, Freddie Crawford, Greg "Bubba" Gary, Hawthorne Wingo, Ron Behagen, Bill Pless and Vincent White.

'75-'78

The Emergence of Choice and the Connoisseur

From '75-'78, sneaker brands started releasing more models in addition to their older mainstays. Pony, Nike, and Adidas had limited distribution, but when found they provided alternatives to Converse, Pro-Keds and Puma. It was the emergence of choice, and the emergence of the sneaker connoisseur went hand in hand with this development.

Bottom right: The blue Pro-Keds tab on the back was the sign of officialness.

Basic Classics—Basketball

■ **Pro-Ked a.k.a. "69'ers," "Uptowns," canvas high top and low top in white, black, blue, red, green, purple, maroon, gray, brown**

'69'ers were so popular in Harlem and the Bronx that they became the original "Uptowns." (Nike Air Force 1s would gain the same nickname 20 years later.) They were the unofficial canvas hip hop sneaker for everyone who didn't have the funds to step up to suede Pumas. The Godfather of hip hop, Afrika Bambaataa, wore these proudly for years when he DJ'ed park jams in the '70s.

Scotch: *The* sneaker was the Pro-Ked 69'er low. There was nothing else out that mattered. If you didn't have 69'ers, then you had rejects on. And they'd dance around you and sing, "Rejects! They cost a $1.99! Rejects! They make your feet feel fine! Rejects, they wipe yo' mama's be-hind!" I heard that all day until I finally copped some.

Dante: I wanted brown "Uptowners" *bad*. I begged my mom but she could only find the standard blue joints that everybody had.

■ **Puma Clyde, suede low top in white on blue, black on gold, white on red, *gold on black, *blue on gold; suede high top in white on white**

During this period, the Clyde was rarely seen on Puma's intended market of ballplayers. It became the first non-canvas basketball shoe to gain staying power as fashionable New York street wear.

Jack Steinweis, former Puma worldwide President: We'd sell a lot of Clydes in the winter. It snowed a lot, and all the merchants would put salt on their sidewalks. The salt would eat away at the soles, and two weeks later kids had to buy new Clydes. We'd see a snowstorm and get happy.

Fab Five Freddy: Games like stepsies and all that changed when Clydes came out. It changed the concept of being fly.

Seth Rosenfeld: Clydes were the perfect sneakers to sport with anything. We'd cut the bottom of our Lee jeans to leave fringes and Pumas would look fresh with them. We'd also rock AJs, which were called Gabardines in Brooklyn, and were also known as Overlaps. They were gabardine and polyester pants, a variation of the double knit pants of the generation before us. They were dress pants, but we wore them with Clydes cuz they looked so hot.

Dante: My first Pumas ripped and started talking out the side after two months! I never liked them after that.

■ **Pro-Ked Royal a.k.a. "Super Pro-Ked," "Supers," canvas high top and low top in white, blue, red, black, *green, *maroon, *purple, *carolina, *gold, *orange**

The Super Pro-Keds were the first pair of name brand sneakers owned by a lot of heads in my age bracket. As we got older our fashion taste buds became more sophisticated, and the Super Pro-Keds were eclipsed by the end of the '70s by the influx of leather models. But they had a strong run, and were popular with homeboys and homegirls alike.

Gerry Erasme: In '76-'77, I was the only person on the squad at Power wearing Super Pro-Keds still. Kids were wearing Nikes, Shell toes, and Clydes, but I couldn't let go of my Supers.

New York City legend Butch Lee (#15), on the verge of cracking his defender during a game at Marquette University circa 1975.

- Top quality, single unit outsole construction for top traction and wear characteristics
- Soft and strong leather upper padded tongue and ankle collar for maximum comfort and support
- Heel wedge helps reduce leg strain and an extended lip counter provides support and comfort for the toughest competition
- Lightness and durability help make our Professional All Star the best technically designed basketball shoe on the market today
- All colors available in sizes 15, 16, 17
- Case wgts.: 25 lbs. (12 prs. per case)

19763 White Ox/Blue Trim
19102 White Ox/Red Trim
19106 White Ox/Green Trim
19108 White Ox/Lt. Blue Trim
19293 White Ox/Gold Trim
*19295 White Ox/Maroon Trim
*19297 White Ox/Orange Trim
*19299 White Ox/Purple Trim
19764 White Hi/Blue Trim
19103 White Hi/Red Trim
19107 White Hi/Green Trim
19109 White Hi/Lt. Blue Trim
19294 White Hi/Gold Trim
*19296 White Hi/Maroon
*19298 White Hi/Orange
*19300 White Hi/Purple Trim

*Maroon, orange, and purple team orders only, see your Converse representative for details.

All Star Professional Basketball Shoes

“When I get through promotin', every kid in New York is going to want a pair of these new Converse All-Stars.”

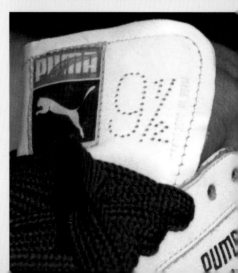

Lower left: When Dr. J got his first Converse endorsement check, he was smiling real big.

Prime Minister Pete Nice: We had a tournament in '77, and I wanted to break in my brand new Super Pro-Keds. I folded them and put them under my mattress overnight. Of course the next day I got eight blisters anyway, but we won.

Fabel: As a kid we played "Hot, Peas, and Butter, Come & Get Your Supper." That had me running and jumping over shit in abandoned buildings. My Super Pro-Keds were definitely getting ragged. The first thing to go was the little blue Pro-Keds tab in the back. I tried to glue it back with Elmer's Glue because I wanted heads to know they weren't fake. The second thing to go was the two stripes on the side. The rubber would peel up on the sneaker and get little fringes. I would wear my Pro-Keds busted sometimes because they weren't vickable. Who was going to take beat up old sneakers?

■ **Converse All Star Pro Model a.k.a. "Dr. Js," leather high top and low top, blue on white, red on white, *green on white, *light blue on white, *gold on white, *maroon on white, *orange on white, *purple on white, *white on black, *gold/royal blue on white**

In '76 the ABA merged with the NBA, which increased Julius "Dr. J" Erving's visibility immensely. He went from being a Pro Rucker/ABA legend to being an American household name and a bona fide sports hero. Converse signed him to an endorsement deal (for only $25,000 initially), and it was the wisest move they ever made. If you searched hard enough you could find the team colors in certain stores, and the shoes' comfort was an instant success on the court. Dr. J put Converse back on the bus map.

Pete Nice: The first time that I went nuts over sneakers was when my father had Dr. J give a clinic at Bishop Ford in '76. He had on custom Dr. Js with his name burned on the high top. I had to get a pair of those.

Dante: In '77 my whole basketball team—me and eight motley kids—went to a basketball clinic at Fordham U. Dr. J and Larry "Dr. K" Kenon gave each of us leather All Stars. We were crazy welfare kids so we were open!

Serch: I worked a newspaper route when I was nine and saved up for a month to buy $35 Dr. Js. My mom was real angry because that was a lot of paper. The leather cracked on me crazy, so my man Tito told me to put baby oil on them. They were so flavorful.

■ **Puma Basket, leather high top and low top in black on white, white on white, *royal blue on white**

Never quite as popular as their suede counterpart, The '71-'85 Basket was basically the leather version of the Clyde. They were perfect for heads who dug the Puma stripe but didn't want to spend the time cleaning their suede with a toothbrush.

Frosty Freeze: They felt like I was walking on solid ground! They weren't very comfortable to dance in.

Bobby Jones plays in PUMAS

PUMA®

Dist. by: **BECONTA** INC.

Stars and stripes

Promodel

Abdul Jabbar

Abdul-Jabbar white

Shooting Star

Star players like Kareem Abdul Jabbar, Billy Knight and Doug Collins choose adidas quality three stripe footwear. They know that adidas provides the ideal footing for feats. So if you're out to score, join today's winners in adidas.

adidas® 🔺®

The all-sports people

Opposite: A classic rare grips battle between Jim Boylan of Marquette U. and Phil Ford of UNC during the 1977 NCAA Championship. Boylan sports light blue Puma Baskets while Ford wears Carolina blue Dr. Js.

■ Adidas Jabbar, leather/suede high top and low top in royal blue on white, white on white

NYC native Kareem Abdul-Jabbar won the NBA chip in '71 and '79, and was a product of legendary Power Memorial High School. Much love to Kareem, but none of that really mattered to the success of these joints in New York. They could've been Mayor Ed Koch's signature shoe and they still would've been hot. Adidas' distribution was finally improving in New York by '78 and the Jabbars caused an immediate stir. Whereas the Superstars' first audience was strictly ballplayers, the '78-'84 Jabbars were immediately popular with hip hop heads and ballplayers alike. In fact, contrary to popular belief, it was the Jabbars, not the Superstars, that started Adidas' legacy as a brand of choice for hip hop's style council.

Jazzy Art: The first leather sneakers I got were Jabbars. I wouldn't even wear them outside! They were so fly.

Rare Gems—Basketball

■ Custom D.T.'s, leather high top in *red/blue on white

David "D.T." Thompson was one of the greatest leapers in NASA history when he played in the ABA and NBA with the Denver Nuggets. He was the only person I know who ever wore '77 Custom D.T.'s. Talk about personalized!

■ Onitsuka Tiger Fable, suede high top in *white on green

In reaction to Adidas' Superstar, Tiger released the '74-'75 Fable (which stood for fastbreak). The green suede upper with the natural toe box was sick, and was the first dual-color suede I ever saw. They left me utterly flummoxed.

Johnny Snakeback Fever: I was transfixed when I saw these on Dave Cowens. Carlsen Imports carried them, or maybe I imagined that they did because I wanted them so badly.

■ Converse All Star Pro Model a.k.a. "Walter Davis," leather with suede toe box in *purple on white

Walter had a sweet arch on his jumper, but that couldn't compete with how taster's choice his Pro Models were in '78. I don't know how he ended up with a suede toe box when not even Dr. J had one, but Davis had the only pair, and they were never released commercially. Sweet Georgia Brown.

■ Adidas Superstar "Half Shells," leather with suede/rubber toecap in *red on white, *blue on white, *white on red, *white on green

The Half Shells were made from '74-'78 and were strictly pro and college material (Darn!). The only pair I ever saw in New York were the "Quinn Buckners" in white on forest green that Mark Pearson bought at Gerry Cosby.

Sake: When I found the Holy Grail—the green suede Half Shell Adidas—at Cosby's, the quest was over. I definitely got sucked left and right every time I sported them. It was ridiculous! I made sure I wore them up at Rucker and Riverside.

Top left: Dave Cowens of the Celtics shocking the crowd with ill Tiger Fables.

Right: David Thompson had so much hops he almost jumped out the frame of this photo!

Bottom left: Walter Davis of the Phoenix Suns proves that ballet moves are possible when you're wearing Converse Dr. Js.

This page, top: "Hey Rick, turn around and check out my fly kicks after I finish laying you up!": New York native Mike Riordan of the Washington Bullets wearing red suede Half Shells.

This page, bottom: The mega-coveted green suede Half Shells were worn by Celtic players and staff members alike. That guy on their bench probably had no clue as to how rare they were.

adidas

■ **Adidas Superstar II, cangoran leather low top in *royal blue on white**
■ **Adidas Pro Model II, cangoran leather high top with gum bottom in *red on white**

Cangoran was a synthetic substitute created to give poor kangaroos a break. Their leather was often used in the '70s for sneaker manufacturing until it became illegal to bring it into the U.S. I have never seen the '78 Superstar II or Pro Model II anywhere, at any point. They may have been only available in Europe. Lucky bastards!

■ **Nike All Court, canvas low top in black on white, light blue on white, white on black**

Even though canvas was phasing out slowly, if you found the '75-'78 All Courts during those years you were alright with me.

■ **Adidas Americana, leather and leather/nylon mesh high top and low top in *blue/red on white**

The '71-'80 Americana was worn by many ABA ballplayers starting in '71, and was the official sneaker of the ABA in '75. Accordingly the stripes matched the red, white, and blue of the ABA rock. The Americana had many different looks, from the '71 version with nylon mesh uppers and an all leather toe box, to the '74 half suede/half shell toe box,

to the '79 nylon mesh/suede toe cap version. Easily the most sought after sneaker of the decade.

Jazzy Art: You could not find Americanas. You knew they existed and might have seen a pro wear them once or twice. Those were the extra shit.

Scotch: It was the ultimate to wear Americanas with a white tube sock with red/blue stripes.

Joe Ski: The multi-colored stripe fascinated me. I'd run into the store and just try them on and fantasize.

Gerry Erasme: I had three pairs of the soft, buttery nylon mesh Americanas. I loved those! I don't remember anyone else having them.

Johnny Snakeback Fever: Bill Hanzlik played for the Sonics from '80-'82 and wore a pair of Half Shell Americanas with two green stripes and a gold stripe in the middle instead of the blue/red combo. I watched his shoes instead of the game. They just blew my mind.

■ **Puma Super Basket, leather/suede high top and low top in white on white, blue on white**

The '78 Super Basket were really just that, super basketball shoes. If anyone finds them out there call me up and I'll trade you a copy of this book for them!

Serch: I had special Super Baskets with German words printed on the box. The toe was all suede. When I saw them I almost came on myself.

YOU ARE NOW THE PROUD OWNER OF FAMOUS
COACH JOHN WOODEN BASKETBALL SHOES
Designed and manufactured by Bata Shoe Company, Inc., USA

STYLES:
SUPPLE LEATHER - Genuine Full-Grain
SUPER TWILL - with Skin-Fit Lining

FEATURES:
1. Toe Designed for Spring Action
2. Non-abrasive Side Seam
3. Shock Absorbing Swept Back Heel
   Design (prevents bruising)
4. Comfort Padded Counter
5. Full Ankle Hugging Scoop Cut
6. High, Special Molded Padded Tongue

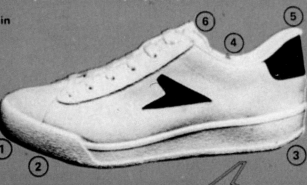

CARE FOR SHOES:
- Always wipe soles with a clean dry cloth before and after each wearing.
- After wear, open shoes wide so they may dry thoroughly.
- The Leather Uppers (also leather toe cap on Super Twill Style) should be cleaned with a soft brush
  dampened with a very mild soap solution and water. After cleaning, allow to air dry completely.

NEW...COACH JOHN WOODEN BASKETBALL SHOES!

A Revolutionary Concept in Sports Footwear!
Polyurethane Sole for extraordinary LIGHTNESS
for better coordination and speed!
Move Faster! Jump Higher! Stop Quicker!

Reduces Fatigue. Improves Endurance.

Polyurethane Soles for TOUGHNESS.
Longer Lasting - Indoor and Outdoor.

EXPERT CRAFTSMANSHIP!
FINEST MATERIALS!

Endorsed by history's
greatest basketball coach

Coach John Wooden

BATA SHOE COMPANY, INC.
P.O. Box 85, Belcamp, MD 21017

PONY. The most complete line in basketball—designed to give you that extra step.

6550

6524

1548

6561

6523

6551

6522

"MVP"—Same features for comfort, lightness and durability as in the "Pro" shoe. High quality resin coated suede uppers in excitingly new colors.
6531 Green Suede/White
6547 Off-White Suede/Red
6541 Camel Suede/Dark Brown
6548 Royal Blue Suede/Yellow
Men's Sizes 6½-12, 13, 14 & 15

6541

6548

6531

6547

6542

6544

6559

Choice of Bob McAdoo, John Havlicek, Paul Silas and many other NBA-Superstars.

The Breathables, the first and only basketball shoes to use a polyester mesh that cools feet down like a breath of fresh air. Protects the athlete's feet and reduces degree of perspiration.

"Pro"—"Official NBPA approved shoe." Super light weight shoe with supple leather uppers, side stitched band for reinforcement and snug fit. Built-in wedge plus comfortable suede insole and full arch support. High abrasion sole for excellent traction and wearability. Off-white suede trim can be dyed in team colors.

6550 Lo Top White Smooth Leather/Off-White
6551 Lo Top White Smooth Leather/Black
6561 Hi Top White Smooth Leather/Off-White
All styles in Men's Sizes 6½-15
1548 MVP Royal Blue/Yellow Hi Top Suede Basketball Shoe
Men's Sizes 6½-12, 13, 14, 15

6522 Breathable Lo Top White Mesh/Off-White
6524 Breathable Hi Top White Mesh/Off-White
Men's Sizes 6½-12, 13, 14 & 15
6523 Breathable Blue/White Lo Top Mesh
Men's Sizes 6½-12, 13.

6559 Top Star—White smooth leather basketball shoe. Padded collar and terrycloth insole with excellent arch support. High abrasion rubber sole and toe bumper. Good traction and durability. Unique shoe developed for the top players with same sole design as "Pro" model and priced very competitively.
Sizes 3-12 & 13
6555 Top Star—White Leather Hi Top (Not shown)
Sizes 3-12, 13, 14, 15.

6544 Top Star Navy Suede/ White Hi Top Basketball Shoe
Sizes 3-12, 13, 14, 15.
6542 Top Star Navy Suede/ White Lo Top Basketball Shoe (Both in Men's Sizes 6½-12, 13, 14, 15)
6545 Top Star Red Suede/White Hi Top (Not shown)
Sizes 3-12, 13, 14, 15.

Previous spread: I never thought I'd see these sneakers again, but miraculously they popped up just before this book went to press. Aren't we all lucky?

Left: Pony catalog page, circa 1977.

■ Wilson Bata John Wooden, nubuck high top and low top in red on white, *blue on white, *gold on white

Ashland jumped off in 1913 in Chicago as a sporting goods company, and three years later was renamed Wilson after its president Thomas Wilson. Wilson was the largest distributor of Converse sneakers for 35 years until '77. Wilson then formed a new short-term relationship with Bata. John Wooden was the most successful college coach at that point, having won ten NCAA Championships in the twelve years between '64 and '75. His signature shoe was worn by a number of pros during the '77-'78 NBA season, but Wilson by Bata didn't put up satisfactory numbers so the line was deaded by '78. It was one of the most collectible sneakers for connoisseurs ever.

Brother Ray: The Batas were indestructible. They were the first sneakers I saw with a polyurethane bottom. I loved them. I had them in natural nubuck which was between leather and suede. I couldn't find them again after they first came out.

Jazzy Art: I was playing in a game at Van Der Veer Projects in Brooklyn in '82. Van Der Veer was nuts and really wild. I got little respect, being the only non-African American there. I had on Batas that I bought five years after they'd first came out. The tongue had three perforations, to fold nicely around your foot. I'm surprised they didn't keep making them. I painted the red logo gold and that shit was *hot*. The minute I got in the game people in the crowd screamed, "Yo, that kid's wearing rejects!" I felt mad low. People were laughing. They didn't understand. One kid on the other team came over at halftime and said, "Those are Batas, right? Those are cool." That one kid giving me props meant so much more than all the knuckleheads laughing. Being up on Batas was like a secret society so I felt redeemed; still mad, but redeemed.

■ Pony Top Star, leather high top and low top in black on white; suede high top in *white on red, white on navy blue

Pony kicked off in 1972 in the US as a sports lifestyle company, founded by Roberto Mueller. In '77, fifty NBA players switched to Pony. The '77 Top Star was their economically priced model and it drew mixed reaction from those inside the paint.

Joe Ski: When Pony came out not too many people were wearing them.

Brother Ray: My Ponys were the first sneakers I had that people really reacted to. The stripe was different, and they were good sneakers.

Joe "The Destroyer" Hammond: I wore Pony one time and threw them out after the game. The suede lost its shape real fast.

Butch Purcell, legendary Pro Rucker coach: Harry James was a ref at the Pro Rucker, and he worked for Pony too. He'd open up his trunk and give out free sneakers to players. That was the first time I ever saw street promotion like that.

■ Pony Pro Model, leather/suede low top in *white on white, *black on white; leather/suede high top in *white on white

The '77-'82 Pro Model was the most durable of any Pony basketball shoe ever released.

■ Pony Pro Model Breathables, polyester mesh/leather/suede high top in *white on white; low top in *white on white, *white on navy blue

Ah man, why didn't I know about the Breathables when they came out in '77! I missed the boat on these, regrettably so.

Sake: My first pair of real kicks were nylon mesh Ponys in '77. Ponys were the flyest shit in the store.

■ **Pony MVP, suede high top in *yellow on royal blue; suede low top in *yellow on royal blue, *white on green, *dark brown on camel; leather low top in *red on white**

The greatest nugget on the '77 MVP was the official gold "National Basketball Players Association" approved stamp on the side. That may have been the best piece of detailing ever on a sneaker. Pony was the first company I saw to commercially release two tone uppers in fruit flavors like gold on blue. Pony was also early in finessing dark brown on camel as well, which was genius. That color was so rare I've never seen anyone with them on, or even ever heard anyone mention them.

Ted Nitro: If you were to throw on the original pair of Ponys in yellow on blue that had the gold NBA stamp on them right now, you'd be bugging a lot of old timers out. Guys would probably pay for them right off your feet. A real sneaker connoisseur would say, "That kid got some shit with him."

■ **Pro-Ked Royal Plus Dura kool, polyester mesh high top in black on white, royal on white, red on white, green on white**

The '76 Dura kool was dura-rare, but do you get the picture yet? Mesh is unstoppable. Take note.

■ **Pro-Ked Royal Master, leather high top and low top in black on white, navy on white, royal on white, red on white; suede high top and low top in natural on natural, white on navy, white on royal, white on red, white on green, white on black**

The '77 Royal Master was the last Pro-Ked basketball shoe to have the two equally wide stripes on the uppers.

■ **Nike Blazer, leather high top with fat belly swoosh in black on white, *red on white, *green on white, *blue on white; suede high top with fat belly swoosh in white on blue, *white on green, *white on red, *white on gold**

Phil Knight and his former U. of Oregon track coach Bill Bowerman founded Nike in '72 in Beaverton, Or. Phil had been importing Onitsuka Tiger running shoes through his company Blue Ribbon Sports since the '60s. There were talks of a merger, but in '72 Blue Ribbon branched off and formed its own brand. The ball squads at U. of Oregon, U. of Washington, and the NBA's Portland Trailblazers were some of the first ballplayers to wear the '72-'78 Blazers. It was Nike's first high top basketball shoe. I only saw each of the green suede and red suede pairs once, both times in Spanish Harlem. A friend of mine claims he once saw them in gold

Bottom right: Maurice Cheeks was killing it in these customized Nike Blazers. This pair was purchased at an auction in Philadelphia over twenty years ago.

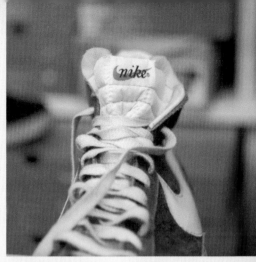

Tony "Red" Bruin showing off his hops and stupid rare green suede Blazers at the 1978 Wheelchair Classic.

suede. These are all like UFO sightings, because no one believes that I saw them in red and I don't believe that my friend saw them in gold. Maybe we were fiending to have them so bad we hallucinated them and as time passed it became reality. But I know this for fact—I have dreamed that I have seen gold suede Blazers at least once a year for the last decade.

Gerry Erasme: The first time I saw Nike Blazers was at the Goat Park in '76. I had never seen anything like it. Stephan Dweck's brother was the first kid to have 'em on the block. He could play, and was definitely feeling himself. I asked, "What are those?" And he said, "Nikes, money, you don't have these?" I was like, "What the hell is a Nike?" Like what is this stripe, what is that supposed to be? I remember a group of us sitting around and just staring at his shoes. *Digesting* them. I didn't know if I liked them, but they grew on me quickly. Nike started doing college team deals and Syracuse wore them. That opened my eyes up and after that I was done!

Lincoln Parker: One night in '77 at PS 163, they were playing a tournament game and don't you know that the only white kid in the whole gym comes in wearing the original Nike Blazers in red on white. The kid had game! He was baking 'em, but his team lost. He was the first cat I had ever seen with them. I didn't know much about them or where to get them, but I knew that I wanted a pair.

Brother Bill: I loved Blazers. They were all I wanted to buy.

Sake: Blazers in white on blue suede would definitely be top five of all time. They could be found on Delancey St. Maybe you'd see the green suede Blazers once in a while. I don't know how the fuck people found them. I would've cut off my hand to get them. The red ones were also on that level.

Johnny Snakeback Fever: The greatest sneaker I ever saw was the Nike Blazer in blue suede. I loved those. There was a four-month span that I knew I could get them. I missed out.

Tony "Red" Bruin, high school legend: Sonny Vaccaro was doing promo for Nike and he gave me Blazers for the '78 Wheelchair Classic all-star game. They had yellow stripes on green suede with my name customized in the back. Everyone in the gym was staring at them and talking about them! They took on a life on of their own!

Pete Nice: Tony Bruin wore the same green suede Blazers in the City Championship. It was nuts! He was my idol. He was the top player in the country. He was devastating with a 40" vertical. He almost beat Dr. J in a dunk contest when he was a sophomore. He wore an ace bandage on his thigh, so I wore one too. For no reason! My thigh was fine. My father thought I was nuts. Seeing "Red" with those Blazers made me a sneaker junkie, and afterwards any Nike sneaker that came out I'd get.

■ **Nike Bruin,** leather low top with fat belly swoosh in white on white, red on white, black on white, *white on green; suede low top in *white on blue, *white on red, *white on orange, *white on green, *black on natural

The '72-'82 Bruin was Nike's first low top basketball shoe, but its impact wouldn't be felt in New York until after '80, when hip hop heads started rocking them.

Joe Skie: Nike struck New York around '77. I bought a pair of Bruins at Paragon's. I walked up to West 4ᵗʰ St and people were asking me, "What are those?" I was the firs person in all of the Lower East Side with Nike. They were so hard to find.

Right: "Slick" Watts was slick indeed, with his shaved dome-piece and customized yellow on green Pro Models to dip up with his uni.

Far right: You know the kids on either side were eyeing the man in the middle, because he got his hands on Superstars while they were still wearing canvas.

■ **Adidas Pro Model**, leather high top in black on white, red on white, blue on white, white on white, *gold on green, *purple on white, *royal blue/gold on white
■ **Adidas Superstar**, leather low top in black on white, red on white, blue on white, white on white, *gold on green, *gold on white

By the mid '70s three-quarters of all NBA players were wearing either Pro Models or Superstars. The ones that NBA players wore had many different looks from full shell toe box to half suede/half shell toe box to all leather toe box. For the regular kid on the street, though, the full shell was the only style available, or I should say, unavailable. These were very hard to find through the early and mid '70s.

Lincoln Parker: The first cat I ever saw in Adidas was Ray Garcia. He had the Pro Model. After seeing him with them I went out and bought them. Broadway Shoe Center wasn't carrying them yet, so I had to go to Paragon. I was biting, but I wasn't going to ask him where he got his joints. I was just going to say, "Fuck it, I'm wearing them, too. Cat just gotta deal with it!" I balled in them shits all summer long and they were lovely.

Brother Ray: The Pro Models from the '70s were the best sneaker ever made, period.

Slept On Butters—Other

■ **Tiger Asics California**, nylon mesh/suede/leather low top running shoe in forest green on white/light blue, royal on yellow, orange on yellow

Tiger named the '78 California after the state where jogging started because they wanted to have integrity in the Japanese market. The only heads who would think of combining green and light blue at that point were graf writers, so while the designers at Asics may not have been throwing up pieces after work, they forever get props for having a forward eye for color combos.

■ **Kaepa**, leather low cut tennis shoe

Kaepa jumped off in '75, founded by tennis player Tom Adams. The concept of the double vamp upper happened by accident. Tom Adams broke a lace during a match and tied the broken piece as a separate lace on the same shoe, creating two sets of laces. He dug the idea and then customized his uppers by cutting them in half with scissors. He put his idea into production, and these tennis shoes saw light from '75-'81.

■ **Brooks Vantage 430**, suede/nylon mesh low cut running shoe in white on blue

John B. Goldenberg established Brooks in 1914 in Connecticut and manufactured ice skates and cleats. In the '70s Brooks became known primarily for its running shoes, but I actually liked the brand because third baseman Craig Nettles of the New York Yankees endorsed them. I liked Brooks cleats so much I'd wear them to walk home on the concrete after my Little League baseball games. I remember seeing the '77-'82 Vantage 430 in a runner's magazine and wishing I had the ducats and heart to sport them.

■ **Puma Easy Rider**, nylon/suede low cut running shoe in dusty blue on white

I picked up a pair of the '77-'86 Easy Rider in the mid '80s at Carlsen Import just before they closed. I had no idea they were from the '70s at the time. Their design was straight fly. ■

"Hey, Frank, I heard they have hot dogs at the finish line!": If only their shape-ups were as fly as their sneakers. The cover of Tiger's catalog, 1975.

Left: An early New York appearance of the Addidas Americana, on the feet of Artis Gillmore at a Rucker national invitational game at City College in 1973.

Right: Note the Nike Blazers (far left) on the feet of a foward-thinking Gauchos player, circa 1978.

'75-'78 was just the lay up line compared to the game that ensued from '79 to '83. Sneaker design became technical and New York distribution got serious, and we consumed all of it like never before. Hip hop culture matured and b-boys, graf writers, and DJs became just as much of an influence on what people wore as the playground basketball stars were. This was the period when connoisseurs really galvanized a bona fide and recognizable sneaker movement, which still resonates today.

'79- '83

The Emergence of Technical Basketball Sneakers and Hip Hop Comes of Age

© Martha Cooper

Basic Classics—Basketball

■ **Puma Clyde, suede low top in white on blue, white on red, white on turquoise, silver on black, *white on green, *white on light blue, *white on purple, *navy on natural, *royal blue on natural, *burgundy on natural, *green on natural, *black on gold, *royal blue on rust, *baby blue on navy blue, *navy blue on sky blue, *rust orange on tan, *cream on burgundy, *black on red; suede high top in white on white, white on blue**

The quintessential Clyde of this period was manufactured in Yugoslavia. The mold that they were built on was almost a triple E width (normal molds are a D width). Space is a valuable commodity in NYC. Wearing Clydes was like stating, "I don't own shit, but I'm gonna own this sidewalk when I'm walking on it." On trains, cats would stand in front of the doors in a b-boy stance with their heels touching but their toes pointing as far opposite as possible. Then the hard rocks would take up two seats with their legs open. People would be scared to ask them to close their legs so that they could sit. The sneaker which best exemplified this bravado was the Clyde.

Sake: Like a bird has plumage, Blake called Pumas "Umage." He took off the p and made that shit plural.

Serch: I called Pumas "Germans".

Crazy Legs, Rock Steady Crew: One of the biggest misconceptions about back in the day is that Adidas and Pumas were popular to dance in. Pumas were too wide and flip floppy . . .

Doze Green TC5: I had a big old salamander foot! Pumas let my feet breath.

Crazy Legs: Doze's Pumas would fly off his feet all the time! He was so clumsy, one time he broke Ken Swift's mom's coffee table like that.

Mike Drake: My first day at Brooklyn Tech I wore Pumas in silver on black that I bought for $25 at the Dunbar Bar on 150th St. They were selling hot sneakers at the bar!

Fabel: When they started coming out with the flavorful colors, I really liked the cream on burgundy ones. Then they came with the exotic shit like turquoise. They were hot to death.

Seth Rosenfeld: I was unstoppable in the baby blue on rust ones, I've never seen anyone else with them.

Emz: The rust on tan ones were the illest color ever and very, very hard to find when I was a kid, but I found them in the back of Jew Man in '92. I was bugging out and went crazy!

Scotch: The rust on tans were the official Puerto Rock ones on my block. If you had those, you kept two toothbrushes in your back pocket. Cats came out with plastic bags over each one! Seriously! Shower caps over Kangols too!

Schott Free: The Clydes in sky blue on dark blue were the first pair I really begged my mom for, and I hated her for a week for not getting them for me. I was like, "Yo, I'll never ask you for anything again."

Frosty Freeze: I bought the navy blue on sky blue ones at Jew Man. They *really* stood out, girls loved them and wanted them too, but I couldn't tell them where I had gotten them.

Ahmad: The first time I saw mint green Clydes it knocked me down. Oh my God!

Andre Kyles a.k.a. DJ Omega Supreme (formerly of Organized Konfusion): At Latin Quarters people were stepping on my spearmint Pumas in white on mint green. That got me upset. I almost knocked this kid out who got too close.

Come Chantrell, renowned Paris collector: The Clydes were beyond sneakers. They were the perfect shoe. In the '80s they bridged the gap between shoes and sneakers via their color schemes.

Previous spread: Rock steady, baby! Ken Swift and other Rock Steady Crew members showing multiple styles while wearing Adidas, Pumas, Pro-Keds, and Nikes.

Top left: Frosty Freeze wows the crowd (including Keith Haring in the front row) while wearing baby blue on navy Clydes. Bust how he dipped up his top.

ASKE

Walt Frazier

906815U
Black/Red

PUMA® Inspired by Walt Frazier, and dedicated to the Master of Cool, the PUMA is an updated version of our original "Clyde." A perfect choice for basketball or casual wear. Durable, top quality suede is teamed with a diamond outsole for super traction and long wear. **Sizes: 3-15**

90681K	**90681J**	**906815S**
Green/Natural	Navy/White	Black/Black
90681RW	**90681US**	**90681U**
Burgundy/Natural	Red/Black	Red/White
906815F	**906815**	**90681TT**
Black/Royal	Black/Silver	Grey/Silver (not shown)

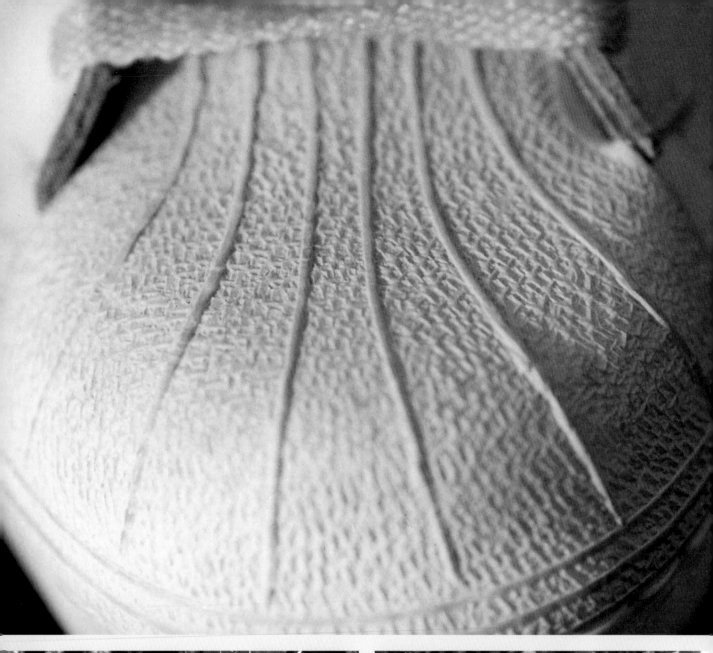

Bottom left: Apple red 69'ers in the midst of a backspin.

Bottom right: Shell Toes working the crispy footwork atop the linoleum at Rock Steady park, circa 1981. Check out the spectator on the right wearing white on white Nike Blazers with no shoe strings in 'em.

■ **Adidas Superstar a.k.a. "Shell toes," "Shells," "A.D.s," leather low top in black on white, red on white, blue on white, white on white, * "money" green on white, *white on forest green**

The '69-'87 Shell toes hit their peak in popularity during this period when they were being manufactured in France. You can identify them by the black/copper logo on the tongue. When I got to Brooklyn Tech H.S. in '80 about half the school (which included African American, Asian American, Latin American, and European American students from all 5 boroughs) was wearing them. I instantly thought they were played out and never owned a pair. As common as they were, it was how people wore them, customized them, and accessorized them that elevated them to icon status.

Doze Green TC5: Superstars were bad for bombing and hard to rack because they were too chunky.

Crazy Legs: Adidas looked fly but they hurt your toes when dancing cuz they were too heavy.

Fabel: Those damn things would chafe your toenails down to the bone. The Shell toes had an impact way before Run-D.M.C. made them popular. We liked them because they looked fly and sort of armored. Plus white on white low top Shell toes could match with anything.

Dante: Got to give credit where credit is due, and the first group of people to really wear Shell toes were Chinese cats from Chinatown. They'd wear them all bummy style though, but still, they had them before everyone else.

Andre Kyles: In '82, everybody was rocking Adidas three stripe suits or Sergio Tacchini and Head terrycloth suits. Fila hadn't even come out yet. It was an exotic thing to be coming out of Queens with the Shell toe. Run-D.M.C. were big around the way but were still only a local thing.

Johnny Snakeback Fever: I didn't like Superstars. Even though I loved Run-D.M.C. musically, once they came out wearing Shells they became the wackest shits out.

Scotch: When they came out with green stripes, It made me smile. For a long time they only had blue, black, red, and white. The green was so beautiful we called it "money green," even though it had nothing to do with the color of money. It just sounded tough.

Dante: Green was an ill flavor because it was rare to find. I liked wearing it to annoy people because even though I was a Knick fan, the Celtics were the super whiteboy shit.

■ **Pro-Ked a.k.a. "69'ers," "Uptowns," canvas high top and low top in white, black, blue, red, *carolina, *green, *purple, *burgundy, *gray, *brown**

The 69'ers had their last stand during these years and phased out in popularity and availability by '82.

Crazy Legs: 69'ers in red high top were my shit! Top three sneakers to b-boy in ever.

Fabel: The low top Pro-Keds 69ers in red were bright like "boom!" and you could see them from a block away.

Bobbito: I called that flavor apple red.

Schott Free: Word, the apple reds. This kid around my way named Silk with a curly wig came out one day in a red nylon shirt, red nylon BVDs, his jeans, and a pair of red 69'ers. He wanted to play but it got too hot. He took his jeans off and was just balling in his BVDs and his red 69'ers, and he was dicking cats!

■ **Converse All Star Pro Model a.k.a. "Dr. Js," leather high top and low top, white on white, navy blue on white, red on white, *royal on white, *green on white, *light blue on white, *gold on white, *maroon on white, *orange on white, *purple on white, *black on white**

The '79-'83 Dr. J's design became a lot more sleeker than its earlier versions. Consequently the low tops popped up on some very select hip hop feet. On the ball side, the high tops were top choice on the playground in '80-'81. I knew ballplayers who wouldn't wear anything but Docs on the court although they'd wear other brands off of it. Power Memorial H.S. wore them in purple and would play The Treacherous Three's "Body Rock" during halftime. That shit would have me amped in the stands! You couldn't find purple at any store in the state.

Ahmad: Dr. Js were my first premium joints. I had made the basketball squad so my moms mailed me a pair. I was like, "What is this? Ma, I can't play in these." She said, "Let me tell you something. Your father, Richard Hooper, played in those and he was All City at Boys and Girls High. Those is ball sneakers. I can't get you no $90 kicks. The sneaker don't make the ballplayer." When I showed them to Bobbito he told me, "Those are official." My whole outlook changed.

Johnny Snakeback Fever: God forbid you tied them tight and then you got the javelin foot. All of the sudden your All Stars would look like a giant banana! That was the worst.

Kurious: Oh, my goodness, Dr. Js were definite top ten of all time! I had the green on white in low top. They looked kind of *long* and doofy. I used to ball in them, so I'd choke them and the front would get swollen. It looked like my dick with a woody!

Ted Nitro: When I wore Dr. Js I felt I jumped higher, and I tried to imitate his moves. Deep down I knew I could not do those moves. I'd watch Paul Westphal play on TV, and felt if I wore his Nike Blazers then I'd shoot with both hands as well as he did. If you wore Dr. Js though, you were not gonna jump like Dr. J Let's be real.

Jazzy Art: Mike Newlin played for the Nets in '81 and wore some wild ass Dr. Js. They looked like turf shoes, and might have been because Mike Newlin was a bit of a nut. One time he jumped into the stands to fight with the fans at the Boston Garden.

■ **Adidas Jabbar, leather/velour high top and low top in royal blue on white, white on white, red on white, silver on white**

By '81, the '78-'84 Jabbars were way overshadowed by the popularity of the Shell toes, but they are a much forgotten early hip hop classic. Peoples' memories get skewed when a sneaker doesn't get reissued and put back in front of their faces.

Fabel: The Jabbars were the flyest for that time frame until the Shell toes came out. Awesome.

Scotch: Those were so milky I'd drive across three states and pay whatever for them right now.

Top right: Mike Newlin of the Nets bugging out while wearing turf shoes on the parquet. Note World B. Free on the right, with rare sky blue Blazers.

Middle right: Ken Swift expanded b-boy horizons by donning Converse Dr. Js to break in. Notice the red stripe on his right sneaker and the white stripe on his left.

19294 Gold Trim Hi, 5-15, 16, 17

9293 Gold Trim Ox, 5-15, 16, 17

9296 Maroon Trim Hi, 5-15, 16, 17

295 Maroon Trim Ox, 5-15, 16, 17

9298 Orange Trim Hi, 5-15, 16, 17

adidas
"K. ABDUL JABBAR"
Endorsed by:

Abdul Jabbar High

Abdul Jabbar Low

Top left: Jabbars were so flavor, b-boys were backflipping over them in joy.

Bottom right: Lester Conner of Oregon State wore Blazers in orange. They were so beautiful that they gleamed in reflection off of the floor.

■ **Nike Blazer,** leather high top in white on white, black on white, red on white, blue on white, *green on white, *yellow on white, *light blue on white

The '79-'81 Blazer trimmed down its swoosh from its earlier version and added a stitched cloth foxing. Nice touches, but it could never regain the sense of reverence inspired by the fat belly swoosh Blazer. It did find its way onto a lot of feet and was the first Nike basketball shoe to gain across the board New York acceptance. People were no longer unsure about Nike, especially Nike street promo guru Sonny Vaccaro was hitting off some of New York's top high school players with personalized freebies.

Jazzy Art: Our boy Chris Logan played for Holy Cross. He showed up with Nike Blazers with his name in purple on the back box. Well, of course I was wishing that I wore fucking size fifteen, and could get adopted and change my name to Logan! Those shits were bananas! Back then Nike was hungry.

Steve Brock: When I signed with Nike as a batboy I made a dream list with my all time favorites like the green on white Blazers and Bruins. The Nike rep said he could get me specially made Blazers from colleges. The first pair was customized with Western Michigan U in the back box. I flipped! I went over to Iona and finagled four pairs of burgundy on white Blazers with Iona in the back box. Then I started to really scam, writing letters to colleges telling them I was a good ballplayer interested in their program who also collected sneakers. The dopest pair were the Air Force 1s in olive from Army in '84.

■ **Nike Bruin,** leather low top in white on white, black on white, red on white, blue on white, *purple on white, *orange on white, *burgundy on white, *yellow on white; suede low top in white on navy blue

Similar to the Blazer, the Bruin lost its fat belly swoosh by '79 but in this instance, it helped the shoe. The fat belly was too much on a low top, and the ensuing sleek swoosh won over hip hop heads slowly but surely.

Fab Five Freddy: I wore a pair of Bruins in the photo shoot for the poster for the Wild Style film. Damn, a brother was up on some shit! Nike wasn't even dominant yet. The whole shape of the swoosh was what did it for me.

Doze Green TC5: I wore those when I'd go bombing with Seen and Mare 139. They were easy to rack cuz I could flatten them in half and stuff them in my pea coat pocket.

Steve Brock: I worked at a sneaker store, and I'd take the Nike catalog home to read before I went to sleep. Some people watch TV or listen to music, but I'd be poring over the catalog, dreaming of acquiring every color. The day I did get every color you couldn't tell me shit.

Bottom right: Ralph Sampson wore Pro-Ked Shotmakers during his early '80s campaign at UVA, where he was named College Player of the Year.

■ **Pro-Ked Royal Master a.k.a. "Pro Models,"** leather high top and low top with "add on bottom" in royal on white, red on white, black on white, natural on white, *green on white, *orange on white;

■ **Pro-Ked Royal Flash,** suede high top and low top with "add on bottom" in black on white, white on black, *white on red, *white on blue, *white on green

The '79-'82 Royal Master and '78-'80 Royal Flash were the best combination of basketball performance and style that Pro-Keds ever made. These remind me of everything good about playing ball in Spanish Harlem as a teenager.

Turk: The suede dye they used was like Kool Aid mix that they dipped the shoe in cuz it fucked up all your socks.

Johnny Snakeback Fever: I had a pair of Pro-Keds in white on blue suede with the add on bottom. I wore them with candy stripe blue/white laces, wide and untied with a sock under the tongue, to see "Pearl" Washington play against "Beetle" Washington in '81 at Brooklyn College. I was the only white guy in the stands. People were sweating me after that game. I can't believe someone didn't just throw me down on the ground and take them, and then beat me down for having worn them!

Scotch: When Mark got his Nike suede Blazers I wanted them badly too, but I couldn't afford them. I got the Pro-Keds with the add on bottom in white on blue suede instead. I took a razor and cut off the stripes so that they could look closer to the Blazers. I was five feet tall with a size thirteen foot, so they looked like a big blue boot!

■ **Pro-Ked Shotmaker,** leather high top and low cut in red on white, blue on white, natural on white, black on white, *light blue on white; suede in *white on royal, *white on black, *royal on white, *brown on tan

The '78-'80 Shotmaker was a good entry level leather sneaker for young teens, like myself, to make the transition from canvas, especially if you couldn't afford the Royal Flash. ("You can't afford it, you can't afford it!")

■ **Pony Pro a.k.a. "David Thompsons,"** leather high top and low top in red on white, blue on white, black on white, white on white, *green on white, *orange on white

In '79 David Thompson of the Denver Nuggets signed up with Pony. Pony's NBA endorsements were strong (with players like Bob McAdoo), and the '79-'82 Pony Pro gained presence in New York via the Pro-Am circuit and with their sponsorship of the Holcombe Rucker Tournament in the early '80s. With the name Pony printed on the t-shirts of the best 11-18 year-old ballplayers in Harlem, kids couldn't help but notice.

Kurious: The David Thompsons' leather looked futuristic to me.

Jazzy Art: Darryl Dawkins had a contract with Pony, but one game he wore Converse on one foot and Pony on the other. It was out of control! You'd never see that happening today.

■ **Pony Starter,** leather high top and low top in red on white, blue on white, black on white

If you couldn't afford the Pony Pro Model, then you were rocking with the '79-'82 Starter. Thing was they really were only for starters, not finishers. With poor construction they never picked up steam amongst ballplayers, and were relegated to casual wear, which they were best suited for anyway because of their simple design.

Schott Free: In fourth grade, I showed up with Pro-Keds that were so damaged the coach pulled me to the side and said, "Tell your moms to get you a fresh pair." I looked at the whiteboys on my team and they all were rocking Nike Blazers and Bruins. I was leaning towards Nike, but then I said to myself, "Naw, I'm Black. Let me keep it original." I wanted Converse Dr. Js, but my moms wasn't willing to kick up the extra eight beans. Ponys were less expensive so I took them. If I ever see those come out again I'm going to have to cop seven pairs so I can be like, "What! I'm a grown man now!"

Opposite: New York high school legend Tony "Red" Bruin dips it on the baseline at Syracuse U. while wearing Pony Pro Models.

FOR THE RIGHT MOVES, GET THE RIGHT SHOES.

David Thompson, Denver Nuggetts

The right moves in basketball start with the right shoes. The same goes for any other game you play.

So the first smart move to make is to get the right athletic shoes. Shoes that are right for your foot, right for the surface you play on, right for the way you play the game.

Which is why you ought to bring your feet to The Athlete's Foot. And put your feet into Pony.

At The Athlete's Foot we specialize in shoes for athletes. We train our people to know the features of every make and model we carry—the materials used in soles and uppers, the last, the construction. Because all these things count big when it comes to keeping you in the

action and out of trouble.

That's why you should check out the Pony shoes that help put the "fast" in UCLA's fast break and the "D" in Syracuse's defense.

College stars and pros count on Pony scientifically-advanced action shoes to help them make their moves.

So whether you choose one of the Pony Pro or Starter leather models, Lo or Hi Tops, you'll get the same performance that NBA All Stars from David Thompson to Bob McAdoo rely on.

Whichever Pony you choose, you'll have the right shoes to make all your moves.

So make your next move to The Athlete's Foot.

362 stores nationwide

PONY

Nobody knows the athlete's foot like

The **Athlete's Foot**®

STARTER, Lo and Hi/PRO 80, Hi and Lo

■ **Adidas Top Ten, leather high top and low top in blue on white with red accent, white on white, *silver on white, *red on white a.k.a. "Indianas," *black on white, *green on white, *orange on white, *white on black, *white on forest green, *white on red with silver accent, *white on green with silver accent**

The '79-'83 Top Ten was the first highly advanced technological sneaker that really made a difference in terms of comfort. On the most highly padded tongue ever (at that point), it had a logo that read "Endorsed by the Top Ten Basketball Pros." Who knew who those top ten players were, and who cared? The Top Ten was a revolution. Any sneaker before it had to be broken in for a couple of days before it was ready to play in. The Top Ten was the first sneaker that could be taken fresh out the box and worn comfortably on game day. They were also one of the first sneakers to have an initial list price of $100. I didn't see them in New York stores until '81, and Paragon was one of the first to carry them. My cousin's boyfriend worked there but I still couldn't afford them, even with a discount.

Lincoln Parker: When Rod Strickland was at DePaul, he had special customized Top Tens in blue/red. I saw him up at Kings Towers and those shits were smoking.

Gerry Erasme: I had Top Tens in '80. Wherever I went people just stared and said, "Those look like moon boots!" Nobody had seen anything like it up to that point. They were so comfortable that I'd even wear them in the snow.

Ahmad: The Top Tens were the illest Adidas ever. Isiah Thomas wore them in red on white when he led Indiana to the NCAA title in '81.

Jazzy Art: John Merz went and bought a pair the minute they came out. I traded him a couple of shirts for them. I was pimping them! Everyone asked, "Where the fuck you get them pieces from?" I'd say, "Don't worry about it!"

Steve Brock: If I had to point to one sneaker that changed the direction of where sneakers were going it would be the Top Ten. It was the first shoe that had a $100 list price. If you had on Top Tens, people knew that sneakers were a priority in your life.

Johnny Snakeback Fever: I had just bought a pair of brand spanking new low top Top Tens in red on white in '84. Roosevelt Chapman borrowed them from me at a New York City Pro-Am game. He had just graduated from U. of Dayton and was the man, having been the NCAA Tournament high scorer with 26 a game. He went out and scored 46 in my sneakers! To have Roosevelt Chapman score 46 in my Top Tens was like him sanctifying them.

Scotch: If I was bombing the elevated trains I wanted ankle support and the Top Tens were ridiculous for that.

Top right, middle right: Customizations galore! Mad college squads were blessed with exclusive make-ups of the Top Tens. Here you can see them in orange on white, white on green, and white on black.

Rick Barry, Inventor.

When Rick Barry helped us create the [adi]das Top Ten basketball shoe, he knew [it w]ould have the severest critics of all: [the] U.S. "Top Ten" players.

So Rick pressed for every advantage. He insisted we develop the upper with a [spec]ial Foreflex℠ cut that lets the foot flex [free]ly and in the correct position. And had [us a]dd an Ankle Saver℠ support system [for i]ncreased protection.

He had us remove a semi-circle from [the h]eel-counter to prevent heel irritation. He watched as we perforated the toe [area] to ensure proper ventilation.

And he demanded we build the deep [herring]-bone sole with a turning disc and a [serrat]ed edge for softness, traction and flex. Then Rick tested our adidas Top Ten [on th]e "Top Ten". They all gave it their [stamp] of approval. Now all we need is yours.

The adidas Top Ten is worn by "Top Ten" players Doug Collins, Marques Johnson, Kermit Washington, Adrian Dantley, Bob Lanier, Bobby Jones, Billy Knight, Sidney Wicks, Mitch Kupchak and Kevin Grevey.

adidas ◈
The science of sport

Top Ten High
Uppers: Full grain leather. Sole: Rubber. Herringbone profile. Top basketball shoe with excellent ankle support, foreflex cut and durable rubber sole. U.S. Patent design 262751.

AG 2105	white/navy	AG 2260	white/black
AG 2246	white/neutral	AG 2277	white/green
AG 2253	white/red	AG 2806	white/silver

Top Ten Low
Uppers: Full grain perforated leather. Sole: Rubber. Herringbone profile. Top low-cut basketball shoe. Excellent padding, foreflex cut and durable rubber sole.

AG 2095	white/navy	AG 2291	white/black
AG 2239	white/neutral	AG 2301	white/green
AG 2284	white/red	AG 2796	white/silver

Top: A young b-boy flaps out the tongue of his Chucks before going down on the cardboard.

Promodel
Uppers: Full grain leather. Sole: Rubber. Herringbone profile. Rubber toe cap. Chrome leather insole. Sole bonded and stitched to upper.

AG 1032	white/black		AG 1379	white/green
AG 1324	white/blue		AG 1386	white/neutral
AG 1331	white/red			

■ **Converse All Star Chuck Taylor a.k.a. "Chucks,"** canvas high top and low top in black, white, navy blue, red, *light blue, *gold, *burgundy, *maroon, *purple, *forest green, *orange, *paprika brown

There was a ballplayer from Crown Heights who I had gym class with in '80-'81 at Brooklyn Tech. He was the only crusader still wearing canvas on his feet, but I had to give it up to him. His red Chucks were always fresh out the box, laces always b-boy neat, and he always wore red t-shirts to dip them out. That's when I knew Chucks had staying power, even at a point when functionally they paled in comparison to the cushioning that leather sneakers were providing. They just looked too def to be forgotten. During the first summer that I played in Rucker in '81 at least one out every five ballplayers out of Harlem in the midget and biddie division wore Chucks.

Jazzy Art: Michael Ray Richardson once wore black leather Chuck Taylors when he played for the Knicks in '81. They had his nickname "Sugar" embroidered on the side. It was out of control.

Turk: Colored Chucks were frowned upon in Brooklyn in the '70s, but we came out rocking reds and light blue.

Fabel: I wore my money green Chuck Taylors with a green BVD. They were fly.

Joe Cruz: In the '80s Converse came out with the ice cream colors like pink, which was popular with the hippies.

Crazy Legs: They were one of the top three shoes to b-boy in.

■ **Pony McAdoo,** suede low top and high top in white on blue, *white on red

The '79 McAdoo low top was very reminiscent of the Nike Bruin, but the McAdoo tag crushed all competition! I always gave the nod to Bob McAdoo anyway, because his name was fly and we were both born on September 25th. He also led the NBA in scoring in '74, '75, and '76, and was the league MVP in '75 when he averaged 34.5 points per game. Wallop! The high tops were the flyest fashion pieces Pony ever had in their catalog.

■ **Adidas Pro Model a.k.a. "High top Shells,"** leather high top in black on white, royal blue on white, red on white, natural on white, * "money" green on white, *orange on white

The '65-'87 Pro Models may not have been as popular as their low top twin brother Superstars, but they did have a b-boy presence. On the ballcourts they paled in comparison to the mega-comfortable Top Ten, but by '83 my whole crew thought it was kind of fly to play ball in them as a retro affair, since other heads were moving on. A true connoisseur always thinks two years ahead.

Jazzy Art: The Pro Models were 50 bucks growing up, and that was just the end of the world!

■ **Converse All Star Pro Mesh,** synthetic leather/nylon mesh high top and low top in black on white, red on white, navy blue on white

The '81 Pro Mesh was the budget version of the Dr. Js, like real budget. Not only were they less expensive, but the mesh was cheap and they weren't even real leather! They looked real flavor for the first couple of outings, but lost their groove swiftly. Maybe that's why Converse only put them out for one season. They were popular with us shorties though, and no one can take that away from them.

■ Puma Sky a.k.a. "Ralph Sampsons," leather high top and low top in navy blue on white, natural on white, red on white, *white on navy blue, *white on red, *white on green, *white on turquoise

"Tiny" Archibald wore the '83-'84 Skys in white on green with the Celtics in '83, plus Riverside Church was handing them out to their players. That was about all it took to make me a believer. People were o.d.'ing on Puma Clydes so Skys were a nice way to escape the mundane.

Sake: I called them the "Dolphin Pumas" because they had that weird dolphin nose in the front.

Johnny Snakeback Fever: I was afraid of getting robbed in my Pumas Skys in white on green. Nobody else had them, and they were so loud. They were the sneaker equivalent of that dunk Vince Carter did on that seven footer.

Andre Kyles: I was asked if I would sell my "Ralph Sampsons" in white on green right off my feet. I was like "Nah, but that's a brilliant gesture!"

■ Converse All Star Pro Star a.k.a. "Bernard Kings," leather high top and low top in red on white, navy blue on white, white on white, *black on white, *light blue on white, *purple on white, *gold on white, *white on green

What's the last shoe that Magic Johnson and Michael Jordan wore in the same year? The '83-'84 Pro Star in light blue was the team sneaker of UNC Jordan's junior year, and Magic wore them in purple that same season for the Lakers in the NBA. But the man really behind the Pro Stars was Bernard King, who broke all kinds of scoring records for the Knicks in the playoffs in '84 with a 42.6 points per game average, shooting 60% from the field against the Detroit Pistons. Like Biggie Smalls said, "Repping BK to the fullest!"

Far right: When James "True" Carter demo'd the Puerto Rican Pro League they nicknamed him "El Presidente." Here we see him at St. Thomas Aquinas College wearing Pro Stars, circa 1984.

19139 Natural Trim Ox, 3-15, 16, 17

19136 Red Trim Hi, 3-15, 16, 17

19140 Red Trim Ox, 3-15, 16, 17

19137 Navy Trim Hi, 3-15, 16, 17

19141 Navy Trim Ox, 3-15, 16, 17

19138 Lt. Blue Trim Hi, 3-15, 16, 17

YOUR FEET HAVE WINGS

Clyde's got a new pair of wings

SPALDING

eet that feel good fly

JORDACHE®

JORDACHE

JORDAC

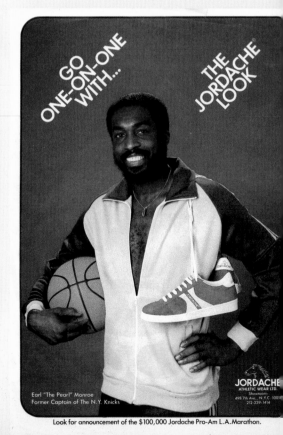

GO ONE-ON-ONE WITH... THE JORDACHE LOOK

Earl "The Pearl" Monroe
Former Captain of The N.Y. Knicks

JORDACHE
ATHLETIC WEAR LTD.
Showroom:
498 7th Ave., N.Y.C. 10018
212-239-1414

Look for announcement of the $100,000 Jordache Pro-Am L.A. Marathon.

Middle left and bottom right:
Once Knick teammates, both
Walt Frazier and Earl Monroe
endorsed their final sneakers at
the twilight of their NBA careers
(the Spalding Clyde and Jordache,
respectively).

■ Spalding Clyde, **suede low top in white on black, white on red, white on blue; leather low top in black on white; leather high top in *light blue on white**

Clyde was at the end of his career when he signed on with Spalding in '79-'80, but truthfully they didn't need his endorsement to sell these. The three wing logo looked hot and the "Wings for your Feet" tagline worked. This was my first step away from canvas sneakers. I had a healthy imagination from reading Marvel comic books, and the wings reminded me of super hero Prince Namor's winged ankles. I also had pride in my Clydes because they shot the poster ad right in the Goddard Riverside court on 92nd St. where I played all the time. They had biddie courts there with eight-foot high rims. We'd play 21 with no rules for goaltending, so the only way you could score was by yamming that sucker through!

■ Jordache, **leather low top in black on white, white on white; suede low top in *white on red**

At the height of the designer jeans era Jordache came out with their own model of basketball sneaker in '79-'80. I'm embarrassed to admit this, because they were borderline skippies, but I owned a pair that I copped down on Delancey St. They lasted a lot longer than I thought they would!

■ Nike Legend, **leather high top and low top in white on white, navy blue on white, *red on white, *purple on white, *white on green**

The '82 Legend was a mean shoe. The leather was so brick that I washed them once with too much Clorox bleach and they cracked at the crease on the high top! I had to slice the high top off to try and salvage them as 3/4 mids. Exclusive, son! In the summer of '83 at a RYA game behind the Rangel Houses, I saw a kid with a low top pair in purple with a college name on the back. Ugh! I couldn't concentrate and went on mega donut. It was a long ass court with double rims so I had an alibi.

Top left: A young Pete Nice shows how high he can jump (on a seven foot rim!) with his Converse canvas Pro Models.

Top right: That's me at the Central Baptist Kings basketball camp in 1981.

Bottom middle: A.C. Green (pre-Jheri Curls) at Oregon State, wearing orange Nike Legends.

■ **Nike Sky Force, leather high top and 3/4 in white on white, navy blue on white, *red on white, *white on white patent**

The '83-'84 Sky Force were integral for Nike. They were the first sneaker Nike put out that was listed as 3/4. The Blazers were technically 3/4 mids in height, but everyone just called them high tops cuz we didn't know any better. The Sky Force was also the first Nike sneaker to feature patent leather, and it was their only patent leather release through the '80s and early '90s until the '95-'96 Air Jordan XI.

Andre Kyles: Kenny Anderson (a.k.a. "Chibbs") wore Sky Force in navy blue on baby blue patent leather in a game for Archbishop Molloy H.S. I didn't even want to watch the game. A tear came to my eyes looking at them. For him to have those in high school was magnificent.

■ **Nike Blazer, leather high top in white on white, red on white, blue on white**

The '82 Blazer was a very modest shoe and caught the least amount of attention of any of the Blazer family, but was actually the most functional as a ball shoe. The loop on the achilles for double lacing the ankle was a nice little morsel.

■ **Converse All Star Canvas Pro Model, canvas high top and low top in navy blue on white, red on white, *white on blue; Converse All Star ABA-USA, canvas high top and low top in navy on white, red on white, *white on navy**

The '75-'82 canvas All Star was the first Converse basketball shoe to feature the star and chevron logo on the upper. They were the poor man's Dr. J signatures if you couldn't fund up for the leather jammies. The '83 ABA-USA make-ups were still out seven years after that league packed its bags.

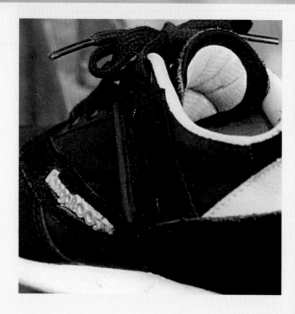

Top left: Classic headspin, classic nylon Cortez.

Top right: Young head playing skellsies, rocking cut-offs and Oceanias on a hot summer day, just waiting for someone to open a fire hydrant.

Bottom right: Frosty Freeze doing the Russian at Lincoln Center while wearing Kangaroos, circa 1981.

■ **Pro-Ked Super Plus a.k.a. "suede 69'ers," suede high top and low top in black, red, blue, *green**

The '81 suede 69'ers were semi-suspect, but are in this book on the strength of my man Mr. Freeze of Rock Steady, who somehow finessed them into looking fresh.

Emz: Pro-Keds were getting a little played by this point, but I wish I had a put a pair on ice.

Basic Classics—Other

■ **Nike Cortez, nylon/suede low cut running shoe in navy blue on white, white on navy blue, *burgundy on gray**

Nike can go on and on about how they are an authentic athletic apparel company, but I'm sure no one in their sales team was upset by the acceptance of their running category as good, functional shoes to break in by the b-boy community. The '79-'84 Cortez was the grand daddy of this phenomena, and as b-boying grew into a global movement, so did these sneakers. I have such vivid memories of seeing Ken Swift and Doze in front of Rock Steady Park with white on blue Cortez, with dukey fat white laces, standing side by side in their best exaggerated b-boy poses.

Crazy Legs: One of the best shoes to b-boy in because they were so light.

Doze Green TC5: I couldn't b-boy that well in the Cortez. They were light but the outsole was jagged and raised. They were good for sporting.

Scotch: I would rock the burgundy on gray ones with burgundy Lees that had gray pinstripes, a gray Le Tigre, and a burgundy Le Tigre hoody that folded up into a pocket pouch.

Anthony Alonso a.k.a. "Nymflow 9": Cortez were the official sneakers for Puerto Rican troublemakers! It had to be! Cortez, DAs, BVDs, and Newport cigarettes.

■ **Nike Oceania, nylon/suede low cut running shoe in white on blue, *white on burgundy, *white on gray, *red on white with blue accent, *burgundy on gray;**

■ **Lady Oceania in blue on white, blue on light blue, pink on gray, purple on light lavender**

The '80-'83 Oceania wasn't as supreme looking as the Cortez, but Nike still sold a ton of these. And rest assured, Shell toes and Clydes may be the current enduring image of breakers prior to '83, but the Oceanias deserve a historical spot not too far behind. You have to remember that unlike the current trend of kids spending exorbitant money on sneakers they can't afford, back in the days a low price point and a decent design were enough to move quantity in a particular style.

■ **Kangaroos Roos, nylon/suede running shoe**

The '81-'85 Roos may not place high on my personal list, but neither I nor any connoisseur can deny that they saw a lot of these. Okay, okay, I had a pair too. What can I say, the pouch gimmick worked, especially for latch-key kids like myself, although that pocket broke pretty quickly and then you were fucked:locked out of your crib with torn sneakers. Not fresh.

Bottom: Rammellzee rocking the mic in his Wimbledons. What was he thinking wearing an Adidas track top with Nikes on his feet?

Ahmad: I had wanted a pair of British Walkers, and my mom brought me home a pair of blue suede Kangaroos instead. She was amped. She said, "Look, baby, they got pockets." I threw them shits against the wall, man! But I couldn't hurt my mom's feelings so I wore them to school. And cats were on my jock! I couldn't believe it.

Frosty Freeze: I had a pair of Nike Cortez but I couldn't break in them, so I bought the Roos just before our performance outdoors at Lincoln Center. They gave me good grip on the slippery stage. I kept a stash of weed in the pouch pocket!

Fabel: You could pull like eight joints out of that little pouch!

■ **Adidas Rod Laver Super, nylon mesh/suede low cut tennis shoe in white with green or blue out sole**

Tennis legend Rod Laver helped design his signature shoe in '70. The polyurethane green and blue out sole first appeared circa '80. In '83-'84 Adidas got fly on us and put his grill piece on the tongue. A definitive cool out classic.

Haydee, community activist: Summers wouldn't be the same without Rod Lavers.

Ahmad: I was killing them in white/blue Rod Lavers. They were sick.

■ **Nike Cortez, leather low cut running shoe in red on white with blue wedge**

The '73 Cortez is one of the few sneakers to have been a constant in Nike's catalog from day one to today, but don't

think for a second that Forrest Gump was the only one who put these on the map.

■ **Nike Challenge Court, leather/nylon mesh 3/4 tennis shoe in burgundy on white, blue on white with red accent, *white on white with gray accent**

John McEnroe used to flam on line officials in '83 Challenge Courts. Even though they were tennis shoes, a couple of ballplayers wore them on the court. You could never go wrong with nylon mesh, nor the burgundy, ya' heard.

■ **Nike Wimbledon a.k.a. "McEnroes," leather low cut tennis shoe in light blue on white**

It wasn't until UNC's huge merchandising success in the mid '90s that sneaker companies figured out that light blue was a hot color. The '76-'81 McEnroes simple design resembled b-ball sneakers, which made them choice sirloin steak.

■ **Nike Glacier, nylon/suede low cut running shoe in white on white**

The '80 Glacier was similar to the Oceania except a little thicker on the midsole, and a little thicker style-wise. They shined like ice, and no jewels were necessary to accessorize these. A clean, white outfit to match and you were strills-naight.

adidas ®

ABDUL-JABBAR

Abdul Jabbar

Top right: New Yorkers may have loathed the Celtics (and many still do), but we loved "Tiny" when he wore these suede Dr. Js.

Bottom right: Bronx native Ricky Sobers of the Bullets doing the dipsy-doo in his rare blue on natural suede Dr. Js.

Rare Gems—Basketball

■ **Pro-Ked Court Wizard, leather/suede high top and low top in white on white, red on white, royal on white**

The '81 Court Wizard was so magically delicious that it did a disappearing act before it even appeared, right before our eyes. Big Shucks!

■ **Converse All Star Pro Model Suede a.k.a. "Dr. Js," high top in *natural on natural, *white on green, *white on navy blue, *white on black; 3/4 in *blue on white, *red on white, *white with no logo; low top in *natural on natural, *natural on rust**

While Converse was killing it with their leather Docs in playgrounds and b-boy circles, their '80-'83 suede counterparts constituted one of the most impossible to find joints this side of the GW. Tiny Archibald's game may have been slowing down, but that was a good thing, because we could get a longer look at his black suede Dr. Js running up and down the court from our $3 discount seats at the Garden.

Prof. Will Strickland: My uncle had a pair of white on burnt orange suede Dr. Js in '79. Burnt orange! I don't know where he got them and I'd never seen them before.

■ **New Balance Pride 480 a.k.a. "M.L. Carrs," nubuck high top in natural on natural, *white on dark green, *blue on white**

William Riley founded the New Balance Arch Company in Massachusetts in 1906. In the early '60s they gained a solid rep in the runner's market by making customized widths for different runners. In '82-'83 they put forth their first offering in the basketball category. Hardly anyone was up on 480s or even up on New Balance as a brand in '82. These were strictly ballplayers dominion. M.L. Carr of the Boston Celtics wore them in white on green. We all watched in amazement.

Sake: I balled in "M.L. Carrs" exclusively for two years. The bottoms had shock absorption and bounce, so I felt like I had extra hops. Every time I wore those I got sucked because nobody had them.

■ **Adidas Jabbar Blue, suede high top and low top in *white on navy blue**

The white on blue suede '80 Jabbar low tops were ultra magnetic, and were the first sneakers I'd ever seen with a colored outsole to match the uppers. It had no functional purpose, but man did it look correct.

Steve Brock: I treasured my suede Jabbars so much. I never went out and played kickball in them. I didn't care if I was 50 blocks from home, I'd run home and change out of them before I would play.

This page: What was M.L. Carr doing dragging his foot and scuffing up his gorgeous NB 480s? I'm sure if he knew how scarce they would become in the years that followed he would've taken better care of them.

Opposite: Believe it or not, Schott Free still has the original tongue tag from his NB 480s, and voíla—here it is!

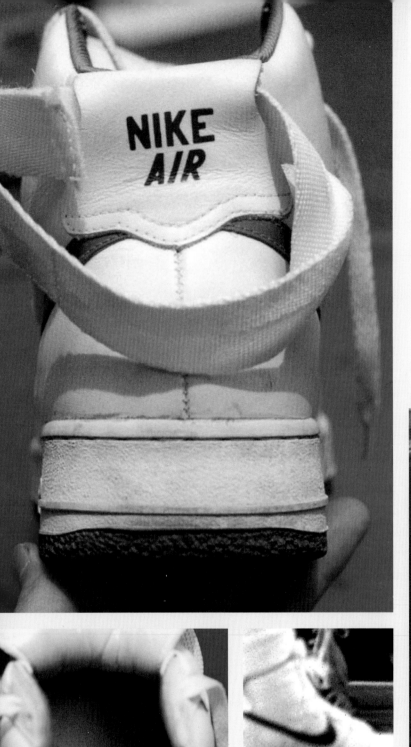

SIZE 12½ #Z0810TN7

Bottom right: Mark Jackson takes it to the baja at St. John's in Air Force Zeros. You didn't know he used to jump that high did you?

■ **Nike Air Force 1 a.k.a. "Air Force Zeros," leather/nylon mesh high top in *gray on white, *purple on white, *black on white, *red on white**

Although Nike designed them in '82, the Zeros didn't come out in stores until '83. I first saw them at the Athlete's Foot in the Galleria Mall in Philly. I honestly thought they were hiking shoes upon first glance. I had never seen a bottom so thick for a basketball shoe. It was like a dream come true for someone like myself, who played outdoors so much. They were 90 balls, which was way out my price range, but luckily a month later we got the hook up through Lower Merion H.S. The heel was unsurpassed for comfort, the leather was thick as shit but still supple so I had mobility, and the padding on the ankle was bushy. The original Air Force 1 featured a pretty roomy toe box that was longer than usual because the laces started a little higher on the foot. The nylon mesh on the uppers was a nice feature to allow my foot to breathe since the leather was so thick. These were strictly ball kicks, you didn't rock them to sport and people who didn't play ball knew nothing about them. Air technology in the sole was a revolution that changed people's approach towards grips forever, but it was initially a quiet storm. It wouldn't be until three years later that the Air Force would really catch on outside of ballplayers and become a staple of the Nike catalog and hip hop circles.

Sake: The only thing I had on my feet to play ball in from '83-'88 were Air Force 1s. My signature was the Air Force Zeros, the simple no holes in the front with the little gray check. That was my shit!

Ahmad: I wore my first pair of Air Force 1s until the sole came completely off! I was stutter stepping on this cat, and he stepped on my sole, which was talking a little. As I left the ground the whole bottom of my shit came off! You could see the air bubble! To wear a pair of Air Force 1s out like that was real, because they are still, to this day, the perfect shoes.

Serch: I wore them on the train one day, years after they were out of circulation. I had my back to this dude, and I heard a rustle by my foot. I turned around and it was a derelict bent down over my sneakers, and he kissed them! He got up and told me that they were the first pair of sneakers he played in at Lincoln H.S., and that it was the greatest year of his life. That was the nuttiest shit.

■ **Pony All American, leather high top and low top in white on white, silver on white, red on white, blue on white, *green on white**

The '83-'84 All Americans were strictly for balling. Not to boast, but I'm the only person I've ever seen in N.Y. with a pair.

Rare Gems—Other

■ **Patrick, suede/nylon low cut court shoe in gray on burgundy**

Patrick was a French company that was imported by Carlsen Import, and they were the only store I ever saw carry them. My brother Ray sported them, but rest assured that these were rare, slept on, and hot sex on a platter with seedless grapes.

Slept On Butters-Basketball

■ Nike Franchise, leather high top and low top, red on white, white on white, *blue on white, *gold on white, *purple on white, *black on white, *burgundy brown on white, *light blue on white, *green on white, *light blue on black

The '81-'82 Franchise is my favorite sneaker of all time, period, end of story! Nike originally released them in '79 to Pro and college players with rare leather toe caps, and some even rarer ones with no toe cap. By the time they fully reached stores in New York in '81 they had suede toe caps. There were also extremely rare ones with gum bottoms. The Franchise was only available until '82 and had so many different looks. That's what was so ill about it. You could have three people with the same model on, and yet all three could've had slight differences from each other. Only another connoisseur might've noticed the difference, but that was the point. Another great thing about the Franchise was that if you saw someone wearing them in red or white (the colors available in stores), you could rest assured they were serious about playing ball. If you saw someone wearing them in any other colors like green, burgundy, etc. then you knew they were crazy nice too. The special team colors weren't available in stores. You had to earn them. The wildest special make-up of the Franchise was the

customized Columbia U. Lions in light blue on black! Everyone flipped over the Air Jordan 1 when they came out in all black in '85, but for those who were up on the Lions' Franchise the Air Jordan 1 was old hat. To bring the Franchise up a notch in value Nike customized the box above the heel and put "Lions" there in light blue where they usually printed "Nike". Whether these customizations were intended to help market Nike or not, they basically drove us insane. Nike's stock with connoisseurs who played ball rose about 80,000 points with the Franchise.

Ted Nitro: My coach "Pudgy Mike" had a connection to get the Columbia U. customized Nike Franchise with an all leather toe cap. It was like seeing a UFO! It was unidentified bananas! I couldn't get those. Those are *the* hottest sneakers I've ever seen.

Jazzy Art: When I saw the Columbia Lion's Nike Franchise I screamed! I didn't know who Nike was, and I didn't know nothing about Phil Knight. It was one of the few times when I said, "These people are on the same exact wavelength as I am. I don't know who thought this up, but they did their homework."

Sake: I was at West 4th and saw my man with the Columbia U. Franchises and was like, "Woo-hah!" Those shoes split my head open. I don't know how Columbia got them made to this day. Why would Nike make special issue sneakers for an Ivy League school with no TV exposure, no nothing? Those sneakers were *the reason* I went to Columbia. Of course by the time I arrived they didn't have them anymore. My man had a pair in my size. I was trying to trade with him, and was throwing everything but the kitchen sink at him but he wasn't letting them go. I had Franchises in red on white with a gum bottom and no toe cap. I never saw anyone else with Franchises without a toe cap. I wore them at my West 4th games because that was a high visibility tournament. When John got the Nike Franchise with Spartans customized on the back they were definitely the hottest Franchises out.

Top middle: An example of the rare and elusive gum bottomed Franchises.

Bobbito: To this day, I still rate John's game a little higher than it actually was because when he put the Spartans on he was transformed.

Sake: There were people who had nice sneakers but didn't wear them properly. They disgraced the shoe in the way that they laced it, or their foot was too narrow, or they'd only wear one pair of socks. John wore his Franchises correctly.

Ted Nitro: John's Spartans with the blue stripe were like seeing an extraterrestrial. The only way I could recover from that was by buying the low top Franchise in red on white *and* white on white. Low top Franchises were hot.

■ **Converse All Star Fastbreak, nylon mesh/synthetic leather high top and low top in white on white, navy blue on white, red on white, *gold on white, *navy on gray, *navy on khaki**

I loved my '83 Fastbreaks. They were so pretty. Nobody had them. I copped them in gold on white from Gerry Cosby's. I wore them my senior season at Lower Merion H.S. even though the team had been issued Nike Air Force Zeros. The Air Force Zeros were the greatest sneakers ever made, but even they couldn't hold me back from rocking my Fastbreaks. They were great for herky jerky moves cuz you could really stop on a dime in them.

Ahmad: I went on a hunt for Fastbreaks. Isiah Thomas wore them, and it was all praises due to #11. He was the lord, dribbling between his legs mad fast, dipping it on big men. They were so light. I could be wearing cut off sweats and a dogged t-shirt, but as long as I had on my Fastbreaks motherfuckers were moved.

■ **Nike Dynasty, suede/nylon mesh/leather high top and low top in white on white, navy blue on white, *purple on white, *green on white**

The '81-'82 Dynasty was just as fly as the Franchise. The stripe on the white on white pair was suede. It became one of my earliest canvases for customizing.

■ **Pony #1 a.k.a. "Three Ring Ponys," leather high top and low top in blue on white, red on white, black on white, white on white, *burgundy on white, *green on white, *silver on blue, *silver on red; nylon mesh/leather in white on white, *silver on light blue, *burgundy on gray, *gray on burgundy, *white on forest green, *white on blue, *white on red**

I twisted my ankle pretty bad a couple of times in my '82 #1s so I had to stop wearing them to play competitively, but they looked so dynamic I still rocked

Previous spread, left: The most sought after Nikes ever were the customized Columbia Lion Franchises, seen here on Vernon Outlaw. If only this photo was in color!

Top right: If I had twenty more inches of ups, I would've hanked it on this kid. Instead, I got called for an offensive foul, but it didn't matter--I had on gold Fastbreaks.

Bottom right: Tony "Red" Bruin with the flush at Syracuse, wearing Dynasties.

Bottom left: "Gimme that rebound!": Brooklyn's Roosevelt Chapman playing for the University of Dayton, circa 1983.

LIGHTWEIGHT FOR THE HEAVYWEIGHT.

The Converse Fastbreak.™ It's easy to see why top pros
siah Thomas wear it.
It's designed with a super lightweight nylon/leather
r that has the kind of support you'll find in full leather
rs. But it weighs a lot less.
Plus, we designed the Converse Fastbreak the way we
n all our athletic shoes. By working with top athletes and
ng up with improved biomechanical designs to satisfy
needs. Which is the reason
e as light as the
rse Fastbreak carries
ch weight with the pros.

nverse Inc.

Reach for the stars. Reach for Converse.
The Official Athletic Shoe of the 1984 Olympic Games.

CONVERSE

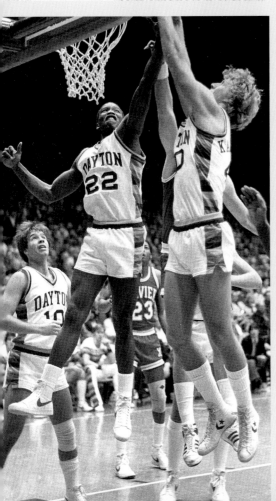

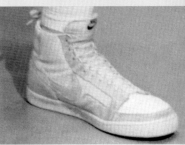

PONY
BASKETBALL

Competitor Lo
2 col. × 85 line

Top right: DeJuan Wagner's father Milt had the perfect form at Louisville, and the sweet nylon Competitors to boot.

Bottom left: All-time New York high school and playground legend "Pearl" Washington was the premiere guard in the country while playing for Syracuse.

them when I practiced jump shot drills at night. They were the flyest Ponys ever made.

Mike Drake: My prize sneakers were Pony #1s in burgundy on gray. I'd never seen that color combo before or since, and it made me think I can wear burgundy and gray without being a fool! Nobody had them until a year and a half later. I was pretty proud of that. I bought them at the Athlete's Foot outlet store. They'd get sneakers that were factory defects with crooked eyelets. You wouldn't realize they were crooked till you got home. You'd put your laces in and it would look like Gumby's head!

Emz: Burgundy on gray #1s were fresh!

■ **Pro-Ked Competitor a.k.a. "Milt Wagners," "Lancaster Gordons," leather high top and low top in red on white, royal on white, natural on white, *green on white, *white on green; Competitor Mesh, nylon mesh/leather high top in royal on white, red on white, natural on white**

The Competitor hung around from '82-'84, and it was the last Pro-Ked model to receive attention in New York. However popular Pro-Keds became in hip hop circles, it was fitting that their last hurrah was a high performance basketball shoe, which is what they had entered the NYC market with a decade and a half before.

Ted Nitro: John gave me a pair of the Competitors in green. They were too big

but I wore extra socks with them because they were so hot. I called them the "Lancaster Gordons" because he wore them at Louisville.

Tony "Red" Bruin: "Pearl" Washington was so into sneakers that his freshman year at Syracuse he wanted to wear his Pro-Keds instead of the team sponsored Nikes! He was the first player Coach Jim Boheim allowed to wear whatever he wanted.

"Pearl" Washington: I wore the nylon mesh Competitor. There was a Pro-Keds rep that approached me about wearing their sneakers when I was in high school, with the understanding that when I left college to go pro they would be interested in signing me to an endorsement contract. It was only a verbal agreement, and then he left Pro-Keds so the contract never materialized.

■ **Avia Basketball, leather high top in white on white; low top in *white on red**

Jerry Stubblefield founded Avia in '79 in Portland, Oregon. Their first basketball sneaker in '83 was incredibly designed. It featured a raised heel outsole with suction cup-like grippers and a nifty removable neoprene insole that was curved at the edges for a better fit and comfort. The high top cushioning and reinforcement was a bite of the Adidas Top Ten, but to counter that the logo stripe was totally original. This was an extremely well made, functional basketball shoe that went over a lot of people's heads.

Scotch: They looked like strange boots. I loved the neoprene insole because I could fold up a ten dollar bill, weed, and a razor blade, and stick them underneath. I was ready at any time to get knocked and go through Central Booking. They'd never find that on the pat down. They'd take your shoe, bang it, shake it, and look in it, but the insole

This page: While Magic, Larry, and Kareem argue over who'll win the series, Gerald Henderson (#43) smiles at how fresh his customized Competitors are.

Opposite: Yet another classic sneaker match-up: James Worthy of the Lakers wearing NB 640s and Cedric Maxwell sporting green nylon Pony #1s.

stayed attached. Nobody knew that it came out. If I got knocked on a Friday, I was gonna be in there all weekend so I had a little legal tender to work with. It just made the bid a lot more comfortable. I rocked those whenever I went on a boosting mission.

■ **New Balance Pride 640, leather 3/4 in white on white with gray accent**

James Worthy had signed with New Balance as a rookie in '82-'83, and during his second season in '83-'84 a lot of ballplayers started taking notice of what he had on and started searching these out. The 3/4 cut was the first New Balance sneaker to catch the eye of hip hop heads, although it was only a handful.

■ **New Balance Pride 780, leather high top in white on white with gray accent, *purple on white; leather/nylon mesh high top in blue on white**

As with most companies in the early '80s, every year New Balance improved their design, function, and comfort. The '83-'84 Pride 780 featured an extremely well-padded tongue and improved ankle support which was attractive for ballplayers but a little bulky for chilling.

Ahmad: The mesh on the uppers was murder. I wore them to my first tournament game ever when I played with the Upward Fund up at Dyckman. The Worthys were their first ball kick with "umph". He'd come down the baseline with a tomahawk slam like "hah!" so I had to get a pair, word up!

■ **Pro-Ked Final Four Mesh a.k.a. "Top Tens," nylon mesh/leather high top in white on white, red on white, royal on white, *green on white; leather high top in red on white, royal on white**

The '81-'82 Final Four Mesh was my first serious basketball high top. I dug them so much I drew a picture of them underneath my bed for my freehand drawing class at Brooklyn Tech. Pro-Ked switched up their logo in '81 again and included a bit of an arrow on the thicker stripe. It made them look sleeker.

■ **Pony Slam Dunk, canvas high top and low top in white on white, royal blue on white, black on white, red on white**

The '81-'82 Slam Dunk low top was a can't-miss with its white on white upper and gum bottom. Unfortunately it was also a can't-find.

Slept On Butters-Other

■ **Nike Daybreak, nylon/suede low cut running shoe in orange on tan with waffle bottom**

Tan and orange are earth tones you couldn't go wrong with, and they were also a ballsy color combo for '80. The waffle bottoms were kind of noisy to walk on indoors but extremely comfy-womfy.

■ **Nike Escape, suede/nylon low cut trail running shoe in rust orange on tan**

The '80 Daybreak broke ground, and then the '83 Escape broke the earth's crust. Don't front and tell your girlfriend, "I remember those!" because you don't. These were the last hand me downs I got from my brother Ray. After '83 my sniffing ability far surpassed his, but he put me on to these.

■ **Nike Lava Dome, suede/nylon low cut hiking shoe in orange on tan**

The winter of '80-'81 was the earliest sightings of Timberland tan work boots in N.Y. Cats were getting tired of wearing canvas Pro-Keds in the snow and finally getting up on functional outerwear. If boots were forward thinking, you can imagine that hiking shoes were way out the fashion frame. Had these come out in '87 they would've hit. Their offshoot, the Son of Lava Dome, would resurrect them in '89.

■ **Pro-Ked Royal Serve, velair leather tennis shoe in royal on white**

Ah, yes, I would've been doing exactly that, royally serving them well in '79-'80 if I had seen these. But I didn't, and neither did you.

■ **Adidas Achille, nylon mesh/suede running shoe in white on blue**

The Achille was Adidas' first pure running shoe designed to protect against injuries to the achilles tendon. To quote from the Adidas catalog, "This shoe not only protects against sport injuries, but is also beneficial in rapid healing." How you figure? Originating in '72, the '80-'82 design hit it on the head with a white tongue and a gold Adidas logo on it to offset the white on blue uppers. Flavorious!

■ **Nike Waffle, nylon mesh/suede low cut running shoe in yellow on blue**

You couldn't have offered me a year's supply of homemade waffles with Vermont maple syrup and fresh blueberries in exchange for the '81 Waffle. Wearing these was the best way to start your day. I would've slept in these if I had a pair.

■ **Nike Equator, nylon mesh/suede low cut running shoe in blue on tan**

Color, color, color. Comfort, comfort, comfort. The '80 Equator turned my world upside down!

■ **Etonic Trans Am, nylon/suede low cut running shoe in burgundy on flesh**

Charles Eaton started manufacturing shoes in 1883 in Brockton, Ma. In 1976 the company changed its name to Etonic. I had a pair of the '83-'86 Trans Ams in high school and learned quickly that you can't play ball in running shoes. I would attempt to just sport them but I couldn't resist picking up a rock if I was near a court, so I tortured these suckers through lateral movements they were never made for. The end result was that they got dogged and couldn't be worn for anything but chancletas to go to sleep in! Sweet dreams were made of these.■

A Holcombe Rucker game at the Dyckman site circa 1982. Witness the plethora of sneaker brands, from left to right: Converse Dr. J, Pony #1, Nike Challenge Court, Pony #1, Nike Legend, Converse Pro Mesh, and Adidas Superstar. That's our boy Mike Drake with the goggles on.

This photo of members of the Lolifes taken in 1987 illustrates how Asics, Avia and other brands became relevant on the streets of New York.

'84-'87 The Emergence of High Tech and Subtle Flamboyance

'84-'87 was the period when New York sneaker style went global, as rap and breaking gained mainstream exposure. Everywhere in the world, from suburbs to foreign countries, kids wore their basketball sneakers with fat laces untied, and picked up on the models that were popular in New York from '79-'83. The sneaker connoisseurs in New York then pushed the envelope and expanded the style beyond basketball and track sneakers to include tennis, hiking, and cross training shoes. It was a time when anything went. Blake sums it up best:

Scotch: When Union Square and Latin Quarters were both bubbling in '86-'87, people got *really* experimental with sneakers. Cats were wearing sneaker brands like Prince, Diadora, K-Swiss, Saucony, Spot-bilt, Avia, Lottos, Kangaroos, and Bally, plus Gucci Moccasins and Polo deck shoes. It was no longer just the big three—Adidas, Puma, Nike. People tried to get as flavorful as possible. One week everybody was rocking high top Chuck Taylors, but they'd wear one red one and one yellow one with a long Mickey Mouse red & yellow shirt. Everyone was trying to top each other. Then Osh Kosh blue/white striped engineer suits with an engineer hat and a Guess rugby with Spot-bilts became fly. Around my way they'd call me "Choo Choo Charlie". As soon as everybody caught on to it, you would have to flip something else.

Instead of everyone having a mono-chromatic uniform of burgundy Pumas with burgundy Lees, burgundy Izod, etc., which had been the steez for a long time, everything just exploded. Kids started rocking yellow/orange outfits with money green sneakers. Lottos came out and you could change the flavor of the emblem. The flyest shit was the leather Gucci boat shoe skippies with the red and green stripes down the back or the Polo skippies. It was about staying one step ahead of cats.

Basic Classics—Basketball

■ Nike Air Jordan II, leather low top and high top in red on white

The Air Jordan 1 sold a lot of shoes in New York no doubt, but it was the Air Jordan II that really set that model apart and gained ferocious acceptance with hip hop heads and ballplayers in New York. It was the first Nike basketball shoe that didn't have the long swoosh on the upper. Even connoisseurs who rejected the shoe because of its popularity had to applaud its design. The low top ones looked particularly aerodynamic.

Kari Agueros, sneaker consultant: People went berserko over the Jordan II. He was *the* player, but Jordan mania was as much about his sneaker as it was about his hard play.

■ Adidas Ewing Rivalry, leather high top in white on white, *gold on white, *black on white, *red on white, *red/white on white, *royal blue on white, *purple on white, *orange on white, *green on white, *light blue on white, *burgundy on white, *white on black; Ewing Rivalry, leather low top in blue/orange on white, white on white, *red/white on white

Run DMC's "My Adidas" was pumping out of soundsystems galore in '86, and while they were rhyming about Shells, loyal Adidas heads in New York who wanted something more current rolled out with the '86-'87 Ewings. Sneaker companies finally got wise and made team colors more available, and the Ewings definitely capitalized on this trend.

Come Chantrell: I have a horror story. There was a big outdoor concert, and I was hanging backstage with Bambaataa. It was muddy, and this girl said, "Your shoes are too clean." She purposely put her muddy foot on my brand new Ewings to get them dirty. I thought I was going to kill her. And she was pretty, too!

■ Adidas Ewing Conductor, leather high top in blue/orange on white, white on white, blue on white with red accent

The '86-'87 Conductor was the more souped-up version of the Rivalry.

Ahmad: Them bullshit Patrick Ewing El Dorado and Cadillac shits I never wore! Understand I'm a big Knick fan and Patrick was my man, but nah. I couldn't do that to myself.

■ Spot-bilt X-Press, leather high top in green on white, white on white, red on white, blue on white, red on black, *purple on white, *white on black

Spot-bilt is made by Hyde, which also makes Saucony. Hyde jumped off in Massachusetts in 1912, founded by A. R. Hyde and Sons. The '85-'86 X-Press in green were Xavier "the X-Man" McDaniel's shoe when he played with the Seattle Supersonics. "The X-Man" was infamous in the NBA as a hardrock, but he definitely had game. When he was a senior at Wichita State in '85 he was the first D-1 player ever to lead the nation in scoring and rebounding in the same season. As hip hop searched for new boundaries outside the main sneaker brand choices, Spot-bilt scored big.

Ahmad: Xavier McDaniels' Spot-bilts were "Oh my God!" unreal, dun. Then they had the nerve to bring those out in colors! That was ridiculous! I *had* to have the purple on white ones to match our uni's at Hunter College.

Right: Adidas released the Rivalries in an unprecedented number of flavors.

Far right: The Conductors were the high-tech version of the Rivalries.

JERRY
McCULLOUGH
1987

Left: A young Jerry McCullough
poses for this Gauchos photo
with his X-Press.

Scotch: We got into Spot-bilts real hard. Other companies were flipping their stripes. Spot-bilt flipped the whole shoe.

Dante: BK took those to heart, especially the black and green joints.

Sake: I thought the Spot-bilts were hot and then Celtic center Rick Robey wore them. He was just over. Then this kid on my team wore them with tight shorts and put the x-factor on them. I was like, "Oh man, I gotta burn my Spot-bilts right now!"

■ **Nike Air Force a.k.a. "Barkleys," leather high top and low top in white on white, black on white, red on white, blue on white, *gold on white, *green on white, *blue on white/blue with yellow accent, *blue on white/blue with red accent, *white on red**

Nowadays people generally refer to the '86-'87 Air Force as Air Force 2s. The illest version of these was the white/blue/red model. These were the flavors of Charles Barkley's Illadelph crew, and were the first sneakers that Nike produced in those colors. The '86 Air Force hit the pavement hard and caught rek immediately for sporting and for playing.

Kari Agueros: Barkley was magical, and his sneakers were even more magical. Those were some serious joints.

■ **Reebok 5600, leather high top in white on black, blue on white, red on white, *green on white**

Joseph William Foster started Reebok in 1900 in Bolton, England. Until the '86-'87 5600 came out, Reebok as a brand was strictly, to me, for women, but these changed all that. Not even Danny Ainge of the Celtics, the most hated ballplayer in the world at that time, could ruin these by wearing them. They were slick and Reebok wouldn't make another relevant basketball shoe until the first Iversons a decade later. More importantly, after the 5600 proved that Reebok could be cool on the court, their aerobic shoes followed suit and became the move for hip hop heads.

Come Chantrell: I had these and stopped in a café with my father. Some kids were coming out of school, and they were glued to the window and started to yell about my sneakers. And in my head I was like, "Yes!" My father couldn't believe it.

Sake: Dennis "DJ" Johnson and Ainge of the Celtics wore them and they were hot. I searched high and low for them.

Kari Agueros: You motherfucking right I had a pair of those! Those were serious.

Dante: The worst was seeing dudes in the hood wearing those Dennis Johnson Reeboks with the tongue crazy big in the front. That's how heavy metal cats from New Jersey wore them. That was a bad moment in sneakers for me.

Top left: Harlem's Kevin Williams of the Sonics rocking green '86 Air Force.

Top right: Private school star Mike "Butters" Parker at McBurney, rubbing his nuts on one of his opponent's heads.

Bottom right: Danny Ainge of the Celtics, wearing Reebok 5600s.

Reebok 🇬🇧
Because life is not a spectator sport.®

Adidas Forum, leather high top in blue on white, white on white, *red on white, *white on black, *white on green, *white on red, *white on blue; leather low top in blue on white, white on white, *white on black

The '84-'89 Forums didn't hit New York until '86. The Forum had the best system for ankle support ever with its crisscross velcro strap that went across both sides of the ankle. I copped the white on black low tops in New Orleans and caught fame when I was pictured with them in The Source in '91.

Andre Kyles: Bobbito's Forums were special joints. I looked down and was like, "Wow! How does he do these things?" He humbly told me where he got them. He didn't have to do that. He could have just let the beano remain hard.

Emz: Funny story but true. I picked up a Marky Mark book around '92 and he was lifting weights wearing Forums in white on blue suede! I have never seen suede Forums to this day.

Adidas Superstar a.k.a. "Shell toes," "Shells," "A.D.s," leather low top in black on white, red on white, blue on white, white on white, * "money" green on white, *white on forest green

Still popular in '84-'85, by '86 the Shells were seeing their final hours. By '87, store stock had dwindled and they became very hard to find by the end of the decade.

Puma Clyde, suede low top, red on black

The Clyde ran pretty much the same course as the Superstar during this period.

Jack Steinweis, former Puma worldwide President: In early '84 I saw a lot of kids wearing lumberjack jackets in red and black on 125th St. Soon after we responded and put out the Clyde in red on black. It was a monster color for us and was one of our best sellers ever. This was even before Nike's Air Jordan.

Adidas Campus, velour low top in white on light blue, white on burgundy, white on gray, white on navy blue, silver on black, white on green

Originally called the Tournament, it was renamed the Campus around '81 and hung around until '87. The Tournament was a serious pair of ball kicks, but the Campus didn't follow suit. No ballplayers wore them to play in. They were strictly a hip hop phenomenon. Similar to what happened with Run-D.M.C. and Shell Toes, once the Beastie Boys became pop stars in '86 and were seen wearing them, the Campus' were quickly deemed played out in New York.

Emz: When the light blue suede Campus first came out in '84 I begged my grandpops to get them for me. The first day I wore them was in gym class, and after school I was so tired that I left them on the bus. I lost them and could've cried!

Scotch: When the Beasties hit, I had to leave Adidas alone. I was a die-hard Adidas head until them dudes just

FALO U.

killed it. Cats started calling me, "Yo Beastie Boy!" up in Latin Quarters since I was basically the only white cat who rhymed there. It annoyed the shit out of me because I remembered those guys from St. Anne's, when they had mohawks. The insinuation that I was imitating the Beastie Boys really got under my skin.

■ **Pony MVP, leather high top in blue on white, red on white, black on white, *green on white**

Pony's popularity was waning by this point because the comp was making leaps and bounds in the tech and design fields. Pony couldn't keep up, but the '84-'85 MVP was their last hurrah. Louis Orr of the Knicks wore them that season, as well as a host of high school players throughout the Bronx and Manhattan.

■ **Converse Weapon, leather high top in white on black, purple on white/gold, navy blue on white, white on white, *white on orange, *white on purple, *white on forest green, *white on royal blue, *white on light blue, *white on brown, *white on gold, *white on maroon, *white on red, *white on navy blue, *orange on white/orange, *forest green on white/forest green, *light blue on white/light blue, *blue on white/blue, *brown on white/brown, *gold on white/gold, *black on white/black, *red on black/red**

I wore the '86-'87 Weapons in white on black my senior season at Wesleyan U., but I got heated when I saw mad college teams had them in colors in *Street*

and Smith's College Preview the next season. They didn't have the ill ones available at retail. Other than on the fans of Bird and Magic, I didn't really see these too much on people's feet outside of the court.

Ahmad: Magic Johnson wore them. He was a big 6'10" motherfucker coming down the court looking like Lurch from the Addam's Family, hooking people with no-look passes. He had them in purple and yellow, but I'm not a Laker fan so I couldn't wear them. In contrast you had the white on green Weapons that Larry Bird wore. He was your basic hit-you-on-the-head-with-a-three-to-win-the-game type cat. I couldn't wear them either cuz I wasn't a Boston fan. They didn't have my blue and orange Knick colors, so I bought the white on white pair and customized them.

Prof. Will Strickland: When I wore Weapons in high school I'd try to shoot my free throws and my jumper just like Larry, and I didn't even like him!

■ **Adidas Pro Shell, leather 3/4 in white on white, blue on white**

Obviously inspired by the Superstar and Pro Model, the '84 Pro Shell was proof that the street had strength. Everyone called the Superstars "Shells;" someone at Adidas must've heard them. It was one of the first model names ever that reflected popular street lingo.

Top left: Louie Orr of the Knicks taps in the offensive wearing Pony MVPs.

StarTech™ Colors

18915 Navy/White 18916 Green/White 18917 Red/White 18985 Lt. Blue/White

StarTech Hi's in body colors provide a great new look. It's the same performance basketball shoe with the biomechanically designed uni-saddle that has established itself as a proven winner. Men's sizes 5-12, 13.

StarTech™ Mid

19175 White/Natural 19176 White/Navy 19178 White/Red 19196 White/Maroon

A performance basketball shoe designed to meet the needs of most players featuring the biomechanically designed uni-saddle* which provides superior support in critical foot and heel areas. Also features variable lacing for width adjustment, and a two-color natural rubber outsole with pivot point, flex grids and heel wear area for superior performance. Men's sizes 3-15, 16, 17.

*patent pending

*Available in Team Bank Only.	19174 Black Hi 19194 Black Mid	19193 Lt. Blue Mid 19192 Lt. Blue Hi	19197 Orange Hi 19198 Orange Mid
	19199 Gold Hi 19200 Gold Mid	19201 Green Hi 19202 Green Mid	19212 Purple Hi 19213 Purple Mid

StarTech™ Hi

19172 White/Natural 19173 White/Navy 19170 White/Red 19195 White/Maroon

A performance basketball shoe designed to meet the needs of most players featuring the biomechanically designed uni-saddle* which provides superior support in critical foot and heel areas. Also features variable lacing for width adjustment, and a two-color natural rubber outsole with pivot point, flex grids and heel wear area for superior performance. Men's sizes 3-15, 16, 17.

19197 Orange Trim Hi, 5-15, 16, 17   19213 Purple Trim Mid,

19198 Orange Trim Mid, 5-15, 16, 17   19201 Green Trim Hi, 5-1

19199 Gold Trim Hi, 5-15, 16, 17   19202 Green Trim Mid, 5-1

Top right: That's me at Wesleyan wearing my Star Techs. I'm about to rip the kid with the ball for wearing four-year-old, dirty-ass Ponys.

■ **Nike Delta Force, leather *3/4, high top and low top in black on white, white on white, red on white, *white on blue, *white on red**

The '87 Delta Force, similar to the '83 Sky Force, simply came out at a tough time when there were other choices on the Nike roster that were just so much stronger, like the Air Force 1, the Barkleys, etc. They got overshadowed, but weren't a bad shoe at all.

Dante: I wore Delta Forces and got snapped on, so I never liked them. They were saying, "You can't afford Air Forces? Spend the extra twenty bucks!" L.L. wore Delta Forces on one of his album covers, and I thought, "Why does he got the budget joints on?"

■ **Converse Star Tech, leather high top and 3/4 in navy blue on white, red on white, white on white, *black on white, *maroon on white, *gold on white, *purple on white, *green on white, *orange on white, *light blue on white, *white on red/white, *white on navy/white, *white on green/white, *white on light blue/white, *white on green**

In '84 I played J.V. as a freshman at Division 3 Wesleyan U. (CT). We got hit off with '84-'86 Star Techs in maroon on white, but I strictly rode pine that season. The Star Techs will forever live in infamy.

Prof. Will Strickland: When Converse switched up their chevron/star so that it was under the leather instead of on top of it, we'd take pictures and place them in the star. I'd cut the outline of the

star with an Exacto blade on a flick of my baby brother and paste it in!

■ **Adidas Decade, leather high top in white on white, red on white, night blue on white, *orange on white; low top in navy blue on white, white on white**

In '85-'86, Adidas really went for the flush and expanded their basketball line like never before with a variety of models. The '85-'86 Decade was an economical take down of the Forum, minus the ankle strap.

Mike Drake: Decades in orange—No one had them. No one! I'd rock orange Decades with orange flower print shorts in the summer.

■ **Etonic Hakeem Olajuwan, leather high top in white on white, red on white**

The '85-'86 Hakeem was Etonic's first basketball shoe after they signed a young Olajuwan to a contract when he was rocking with the Houston Rockets. Big shout out to Arnold "A-Train" Bernard of the Gauchos and James "True" Carter of St. Thomas Aquinas College for wearing these that year. They were two of the most exciting guards in the city at the time. "Train" went on to take the high school state championship at Our Savior Lutheran, and "True" went off to Puerto Rico and became a legend in the pro league there. Hakeem, incidentally, didn't have too bad of a career himself. Good things happened to people who wore these.

Prime Minister Pete Nice: All of the sneaker companies would try to cut

Top left: Cash Money, money!

Top right: Thirstin Howl III, on the left, rocking Hangtimes, about to get paid in full.

Bottom: James "True" Carter wearing Hakeems.

deals with high school teams, especially with new models. Etonic had the Hakeems, and they hooked up with my father who was the coach at Bishop Ford H.S. Ted had a pair of light blue Airs that I wanted, so I proposed a trade.

Ted Nitro: I had a few pairs so it wasn't a big deal for me to trade. I gave them to him, but he shafted me. He tried throwing some bullshit Hakeem Olajuwan Etonics my way and I said, "Everybody has a pair of these corny joints!" My trading days were over after that because he botched the deal. Pete owes me around ten pairs of sneakers to this day.

Prime Minister Pete Nice: From that day on I've been known as Pete Sell Out! And someday Ted is going to get a package from me.

Ted Nitro: Maybe one day he might catch me on the low, like, "Ted, I didn't forget you after twenty years. Bam."

■ **Spot-bilt Hangtime, leather high top in white on black**

If you couldn't afford the X-Press and you dug the Spot-bilt logo, you rocked with the '86-'87 Hangtime.

■ **Puma Stepper, suede 3/4 in white on turquoise, white on red, white on blue**

The '84 Stepper was like the cousin of the Adidas Pro Shell, basically a 3/4 update of a classic low top.

Basic Classics—Other

■ **Nike Air Trainer 1 a.k.a. "Bo's," "McEnroes," leather cross trainer shoe in black on white/gray with green accent, *black on white/gray with purple accent**

Cross training shoes? Incredible concept on Nike's part. '87 Air Trainer 1 crushin 'em Uptown? I would've never forecasted it. I never thought these were all that, but their popularity and comfort couldn't be denied. DJ Cash Money wore these on the cover of his "Ugly People Be Quiet!" 12". How's that for cross training!

■ **Fila T1, leather low cut tennis shoe in blue/red on tan, tan on tan**

Dr. Enrico Frachey founded Fila in 1926 in Italy. Better known for their gear than for their kicks in the '80s, the '85 T1 was one of their first joints to catch attention, along with their Fitness shoe. Fila flipped them in tan to match their cream and french vanilla tennis suits. Fila has always been most popular with Brooklyn heads.

The Lolife member on the left sports the NB 576. They look menacing, don't they?

Serch: It was a time when sneakers were really territorial. An Air Force 1 was an uptown sneaker. Queens was Adidas central. Fila was really a Brooklyn sneaker, and you had to go to Albee Square Mall to get them. Biz Mark, Big Daddy Kane, Clark Kent, Stetsasonic, that was their shit. You had to pay your homage. You couldn't go into the East, into Clark's basement, without a pair of Filas on.

■ Adidas Stan Smith, leather low cut tennis shoe

In '71 Adidas named their trademark tennis shoes after tennis great Stan Smith. It is one of the best selling shoes of all time. I never liked them because I thought they looked too narrow, especially when you laced them and could barely avoid choking them since the space between the uppers on the tongue was minimal. However, when hip hop style became more relaxed, colorful, and quasi-preppy around '86, like you was on a yacht or some shit, the Stan Smiths excelled.

Brother Bill: I never liked Adidas Stan Smiths. I was a ballplayer, why would I even bother making a cultural statement like that—wearing tennis shoes was blasphemy!

Scotch: I loved them because you could rock them with anything casual. Cats had to look at them twice. At first they'd think they were blank, but then they'd say, "Oh, OK, they're Adidas. They're official."

■ Reebok Ex-O-Fit, leather low cut work out shoe in black, white

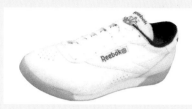

The '86 Ex-O-Fits weren't an immediate hit Uptown, but by the late '80s a classic Harlem silhouette was a pair of Gap jeans, a Champion hoody, an olive green Army jacket, and a pair of black Ex-O-Fits with the laces untied and the top half of the tongue sticking straight up, perpendicular to the foot.

■ New Balance 576, low cut running shoe in red, blue, purple, black, green, burgundy, white, gray

Have you figured out the repeating trend yet? A sneaker company with no props on the street puts out a dope basketball sneaker, earns its stripes, and then other joints of theirs start popping off. With the underground success of the 480s and then the celebrated Worthys, New Balance's name garnered lots of interest by the late '80s. The '87 576 was so butter it was worn as if it were a casual shoe.

Kari Agueros: My mom's boyfriend told me New Balance was the butter running joints, so I copped them in '85 when no one was up on them yet. When New Balance came out with the 576 in all the different flavors in '89, that's when they really caught fire.

Middle left: We all felt like we had a little Italian in us when we donned the Diadoras with the flag on the heel.

Ahmad: I used to sell sneakers near Delancey St. in the late '80s. All these cats from the projects on Ave. D would come into the store, and all they'd want were Jordans and NB 576s. Shit'd come out to a buck-fifty, and they'd hand me a brown paper bag with 150 singles in it! I'd ask them, "If I take a whiff of this bag am I gonna get high or faint?"

■ **Diadora Maverick, low cut tennis shoe in black on white, sky blue on white, white on white, red on white, silver on black**

Diadora jumped off in Italy during World War 2, founded by Marcello Danielli. The green/white/red Italian flag flavors on the uppers was a nice feature on the '86-'87 Maverick. With supple leather and really comfortable insole cushioning, these were my dance-to-the-break-of-dawn-club shoes in '87 when I was going to Nell's.

Ahmad: I had the sky blue joints with the Diadora sweatsuit that looked like them Sergio Tacchini bullshits. They were smooth, and hard to find.

Prof. Will Strickland: I almost cried when I saw the light blue ones!

■ **New Balance 996, low cut running shoe in gray**

When the 996 came out in '81, it was one of the first sneakers ever to cost a $100.

Ahmad: The 996s became popular for cats with a lot of dough cuz they cost $100. They weren't buying them cuz they looked dope, they just wanted to show that they could afford them. It was a status shoe.

■ **Adidas Country, leather running shoe in green on white, black on black with gum bottom, white on blue**

Initially popular with cross country runners and non-ghetto dwellers, the '71-present Country got reinvented in late '87 by savvy hip hop heads in Harlem and the Bronx. It was a turning point at which connoisseurs recognized that they were ripe enough to be classic, because they weren't associated with corny preppy kids anymore. Adidas helped that process along by offering them with black and blue uppers so they could be finessed with jeans.

■ **Adidas Nastase Super a.k.a. "Ille McNastys," nylon/suede low cut tennis shoe in blue on white**

Ille Nastase may have had the illest sports name in history. When Julius "Dr. J" Erving signed with Converse in the mid '70s he received around $25,000 for his endorsement. In contrast, in the early '70s Ille allegedly received around a swift million. Anyone around the way wearing the '80-'85 Nastase Super had no clue if Ille was nice with his or not, but it didn't matter. Any Adidas signature shoe that had the athlete's face on the tongue was on some extra strength shit, similar to the Jabbars.

■ **Adidas Lendl Competition, nylon/leather low cut tennis shoe in lendl blue on white, blue/red on white**

I know heads that swear by the '84 Lendls, like they might do jumping jacks if they ever saw a fresh out the box pair again.

■ **K-Swiss Classic, low cut tennis shoe in white on white, white on blue, white on black patent**

Artie and Ernie Brunner founded K-Swiss in the early '60s in Southern California. The '66-present Classic was their first tennis shoe. I remember seeing K Swiss

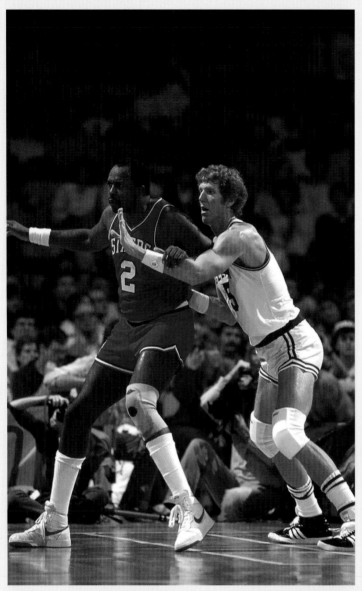

Top left: Moses Malone of the
Sixers wears Airtrains. He's about
to give the business to Bill Walton!

Top right: "Na-na-na-na-na!"
Michael Jordan sticks his tongue
out at his defenders for not having customized Airships like he
does.

Bottom right: University of
Oregon player with forest green
Airships.

in my father's tennis magazines back in
the '70s and thinking to myself, "They
outdid all the Adidas bites with four
stripes—They put five!" I was really
surprised when K-Swiss earned its
stripes in New York, but I must say they
looked hot on the right people's feet.
Heads would rock loose, heavy, colored
socks with them that matched their
tops.

■ **Tretorn, low cut tennis shoe in white**

You just got to love hip hop. Tretorn,
once the strict domain of tennis players
and prep school kids who would wear
them all dogged up, was redefined in
'86-'87 when heads started rocking the
leather and canvas model to sport on
the block. They never really took off but
they did have their New York five eye-
blinks of fame.

Rare Gems—Basketball

■ **Converse Fastbreak, leather/nylon 3/4
in navy blue on white, red on white**

The '84 3/4 Fastbreaks were even rarer
than the high top Fastbreaks, and the
only time I saw them was on Jordan in
the '84 Olympics.

■ **Nike Airtrain, leather/nylon mesh high
top in *navy blue on white, *purple on
white, *red on white**

I only saw the '84 Airtrains once in my
entire life. I was in the gym at Villanova
and one of their players had them on
silky new. I looked for them on TV when
the 'Cats would play but could never
find any of the players wearing them.

■ **Nike Airship a.k.a. "Air Force 2s,"
leather high top in white on white,
*navy blue on white, *green on white,
*red on white, *purple on white, *red
on black/red**

People generally refer to Charles
Barkley's first shoe as the Air Force 2,
but I believe the '84 Airships were actually the second Nike basketball shoe
with Air technology. Around the way we
referred to them as the Air Force 2s cuz
they resembled the Air Force 1s minus
the strap. A little-known secret: before
Michael Jordan wore his first Air
Jordans, early in his rookie season with
the Bulls he was wearing customized
Airships in red on black. SHHHH!

■ Nike Air Force 1, leather high top and low top in silver gray on white, *red on white, *black on white, *blue on white, *orange on white, *green on white; '86-'88 Nike Air Force 1 (reissues) a.k.a. "Uptowns," "Airs," leather high top in *navy blue on white, *burgundy on white, *silver on white, *gold on white, black on white, *cream on chocolate, *white on olive green, *white on patent red ('86); low top in *white on green, *white on light blue nubuck, *white on black, *gold on white

The second version of Air Force 1s became available in '84, and featured a sleeker swoosh and perforations on the toe box to make up for the missing nylon mesh of the Air Force Zeros. Nike also reduced the roominess of the toe box, which gave a sportier overall look. This shoe was the alpha and omega of sneakers. It eclipsed the Adidas Top Ten as the most func-tional basketball shoe ever, but then Nike stopped releasing them to the public by late '84. It was the first basketball sneaker that Nike ever took out of production and then brought back. Once it got reissued in '86 it became the hottest shoe in all of New York for ballplayers and non-ballplayers alike. What made them so hot in '86 was that only one store—Jew Man's in the Bronx—in all of New York carried them. In fact, only two stores, (the other was in Baltimore) in all the world carried them until about '88. The supply was truly so limited that it raised the demand to a fever pitch. Ted Nitro put me on, and I had him UPS a pair to me up at school in Connecticut in '87. I wore them to my tryout in Puerto Rico and one of my eventual teammates came up to me and said, "You're from New York, right?" I was like, "How'd you know?" He responded, "Your sneakers."

Chris Avignone, a.k.a. "Air Jesus": We got hit off with Air Force 1s for the '84 Wheelchair Classic H.S. All-Star Game. I was a 6'1" scrawny little private school kid playing with the best players in New York. I put these on and wound up winning the Dunk contest! There was no way I would have ever thought they'd be popular a decade later.

Sean Couch, Dyckman coach: The first time I put on Air Force 1s I literally felt like a superhero, like the Six Million Dollar Man!

Kurious: Once Nike said Air, that was it. Mentally you felt the springs. Compared to Dr. Js, where you felt like you were walking on the floor, Airs felt like you were in space.

Prime Minister Pete Nice: I had been searching for Air Force 1s for a year until I found them at Jew Man in '87. I bought five pairs, stocking up for the next year because I didn't know if they'd be available ever again. I bought the white on green, the cream on chocolate, and the orange on white. Earlier I had gotten a pair in brown on white through my pop's connection with St. Bonaventure. Those never came out at retail.

Rakim: I rocked Air Force 1s in blue on white on my album cover for "Don't Sweat the Technique." That's the illest sneaker Nike ever made. Jew Man's had all the flavors. Heads would ask me where I got them and I would give them all kinds of wrong directions, especially when I was wearing the beige on chocolates with beige laces. I bought two pairs.

Dante: I had on my chocolate Airs when I took Eric B. and Rakim to get signed to MCA. I was their road manager. Ra was bugging on my joints! He called them the Terminators, then he started calling me the Terminator for wearing them. Nothing will ever look better than those. Ra was one of the first cats to notice my sneaker jones. Another was Jam Master Jay (RIP). When I wore the silver Airs, Jay said, "I got to give it to you. Those shits are crazy!" This was right before the Run-D.M.C. Adidas came out and he was Adidas-ed down.

Kurious: I caught the all sky-blue Airs at Jew Man in '88. They didn't have them anywhere else. They were my favorite pair of all time.

Sake: Thou shalt not wear any sneaker post Air Force 1s. Nike peaked with them in '83-'84. There hasn't been a relevant sneaker in the last twenty years since.

Mike Drake: My man copped the Airs in white on green up in Boston. Then I saw them in burgundy in Philly. I didn't see them in New York for another nine months. They were releasing different colors in different markets. In North Carolina they had powder blue.

Sake: We got lucky once down in Virginia in '85, right by UVA. We went into this sporting goods store and my man Dan Kealey came out with orange on white Air Force 1s. That was one of the hottest sneakers anybody ever had.

Top right: Yale University, of all schools, was fortunate enough to have their name customized on the AF1 ankle strap.

Middle right: I cherished my AF1s and wore them the season I played pro in Puerto Rico.

Bottom right: Danny Ainge of the Celtics has no idea how much props he got in New York for having white on green AF1s.

Left: Brooklyn's Roosevelt Chapman claps boards at U. of Dayton.

New York City playground iron-man Tony Hargraves at Iona College with customized red on white Double Teams.

■ **Nike Double Team, leather super high top in navy blue on white, white on white, *red on white**

The '84 Double Teams may go down as the highest mega-high tops ever. They featured a built-in ankle brace on the inside of the collar that practically reached the bottom of your calf muscle. The leather and flexibility were almost identical to the Sky Force. I doubt there was ever a case in the world of someone spraining their ankles in these.

Jazzy Art: The Double Teams took five minutes to remove with all the straps and extra laces! You'd lose your wood trying to get some ass with them on, because by the time you undressed out of them, the chick would be turned off!

Sake: Chris "White Jesus" Avignone was the first person I ever saw wearing Double Teams, and I couldn't figure out whether he was wearing a blue sock or an ankle brace. When I found out they were part of the shoe I knew they were excellent. I combed all five boroughs of New York City for them. Then I saw Ralph Dalton from Georgetown wearing them up to his knees, which killed it. But those are definitely in my top five sneakers of all time.

■ **New Balance Pride 991 a.k.a. "James Worthys," leather/nylon mesh high top in black on white with gray accent**

By '85 Worthy's name and New Balance were synonymous, so basically all New Balance ball kicks were nicknamed "Worthys" whether they officially were or not. The 991 and the 999 should've and could've been equivalent to what Air Force 1s meant for Nike. The 991 was a well designed performance shoe that looked so butter, but they were barely available, and what few pairs were out there went over people's heads. New Balance—if you are reading this right now, do one sample in a size 10 1/2 and just hit me off! Hot cocoa butter!

■ **New Balance Pride 999, leather high top in blue on white**

The '85 999 was simply the illest basketball sneaker Nubies ever made. Top of the line, and top of the morning to ya'.

■ **Adidas Concord, leather high top and 3/4 in silver on white, *white on red patent, *white on blue patent with red accent, *white on black patent with red accent, *blue/white on metallic green patent**

The '83-'86 Concords were basically the same shoe as the Top Ten with a velcro strap. They really didn't pop up in stores until '84. These were the first patent leathers to really gain the favor of connoisseurs.

Turk: I never liked playing in brand new sneakers, but I was playing in a tournament and had just gotten a pair of Concords in white on red glossy patent leather. I picked them up at Carnesseca-Sarachek's. They were very rare. I hobbled out of the gym with a twisted ankle. I knew I shouldn't have worn them. I threw them out onto the train tracks and went home in my socks! Brand new joints left there on the tracks, what a shame!

Ted Nitro: One time Bobbito was in Philly, and he copped me the black patent Concords with the white suede tip. They were so hot I didn't even wanna wear them in the street and scuff them up. But finally I broke down.

Sake: Billy Goodwin played at St. John's and had black patent Concords. They were ridiculous. I was fiending, so I went to Carnesecca-Sarachek's. That was the spot where you could get fly ass St. John's basketball gear on the down low. I went there and asked, "Yo, who got the patent leather joints?" Red Sarachek was a 75 year old Jewish man, and he

looked at me like I was out of my mind! Those Concords fucked my head up completely.

Steve Brock: It was a street sneaker. A patent leather shoe was not meant for middle aged men to play ball in, it was targeted towards urban consumers.

■ **Nike Terminator a.k.a. "Hoyas," leather high top in blue on gray/blue**

The '86 Terminators were the Georgetown Hoyas' butters. Modeled after the '82-'83 Legends customized exclusively for their squad, the Terminators available at retail had the Big Nike logo on the heel. I wasn't particularly a fan of the Hoyas or their style of play, but I couldn't front on their joints. I couldn't avoid seeing them either. Georgetown games, during Pat Ewing's era from '82-'85, had to be some of the most consistently televised of any college in the country. As visible as the Terminators were on television, you rarely saw them on people's feet.

Schott Free: My favorite kicks, still to this day, are the Hoya Terminators. You could rock either the blue or the gray shoestrings that came with them. I wore them with a blue leather front and a blue furry Kangol. Kid, I'd pay $500 for a pair right now. Straight up. I was the first cat on the Island with the Terminators. Every two blocks heads were all in my feet when I walked in Park Hill with them.

Bottom: Georgetown player David Wingate takes Chris Mullin with his customized Nike Legends, which were later released commercially as the Terminators.

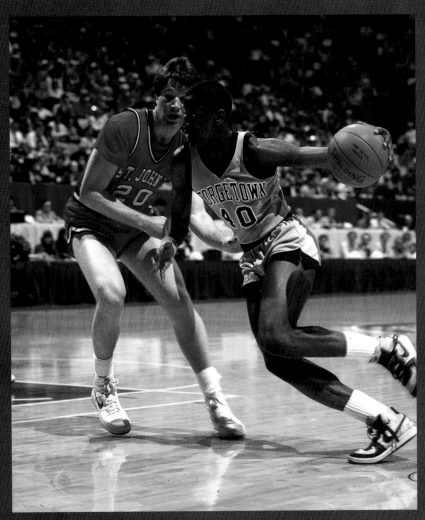

adicolor markers

Special marker for adidas sport shoes. Quick drying, waterproof, lightfast, weatherproof.

Art. No:	
gold	88000
silver	88010
yellow	88020
pink	88030
red	88040
burgundy	88050
light blue	88060
dove grey	88070
dark blue	88080
green	88090

Top: The Adicolor page from the 1984 Adidas catalog.

■ **Converse All Star Quantum, suede mid and low top in *tan on maroon, *silver on quantum, *gray on navy**

The Dr. Js weren't doing it for anybody anymore in New York by '84, so when the Quantums came out they didn't get much play, since they were pretty much the same shoe just a little jazzed up. Even if they weren't so hard to find they still would've been slept on.

■ **Adicolor, leather high top in white on white with color markers**

We had been customizing our sneakers for years by the time the Adicolor came out in '84. I never saw these anywhere and I'm glad because I would've been vexed. Customizing was for the intuitive connoisseur to figure out how to do, not for sneaker companies to mass produce and promote.

■ **'84-'85 New Balance Pride 590, leather high top in blue on white**

The Pride 590 came out circa '84-'85.

■ **New Balance Pride 650, leather low top in white on white**

I never knew the '84-'85 Pride 650 even existed until I found them in a dusty old basement of a sporting goods store in New Jersey in 2002. If only they were my size!

■ **New Balance Worthy 785, leather high top in black on white, *red on white**

Other New Balance basketball sneakers were called Worthys, but the '84-'85 785 was the officialness, with his name on the tongue and the whole nine.

■ **Nike Big Nike, leather 3/4 in white on white, blue on white**

The Nike lettering was not subtle which was a minus, but as many Nike schools wore the high tops, the 3/4 were hard to find.

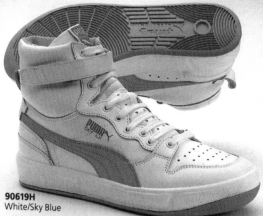

90619H
White/Sky Blue

SKY LX™ Engineered for top performance. Rubber outsole features pivot circles and flex grooves for super traction/pivoting and durability. Lightweight PU wedge system absorbs shock and padded tongue and collar offer cushioning. Dual heel counters and ¹/₂ Texon® innerboard give rear-foot stability. Velcro® strap plus staggered lacing system for superb fit. **Sizes: 5-13, 14, 15, 16**

90619U
White/Red

SKY LX™ See description left. **Sizes: 5-13, 14, 15, 16**

90619S
White/Black

SKY LX™ See description above. **Sizes: 5-13, 14, 15, 16**

90619K
White/Green

SKY LX™ See description above. **Sizes: 5-13, 14, 15, 16**

90619R
White/Burgundy

SKY LX™ See description above. **Sizes: 5-13, 14, 15, 16**

Alex En
er N

9E
ite/Purple
Y LX™ See description preceding page.
Sizes: **5-13, 14, 15, 16**

90619J
White/Navy
SKY LX™ See description preceding page.
Sizes: **5-13, 14, 15, 16**

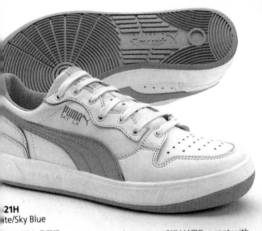

21H
ite/Sky Blue
Y LX LO™ All the same features as SKY LX™ except with
padded ankle collar. Sizes: **5-13, 14, 15, 16.** Also available in
ite/Navy **(90621J)**, White/Green **(90621K)**, White/Burgundy
621R), White/Purple **(90621E)**, White/Black **(90621S)**.

90621U
White/Red
SKY LX LO™ See description left. **Sizes: 5-13, 14, 15, 16**

Terry Cummings
Milwaukee Bucks

Ralph S

Slept On Butters—Basketball

■ **Puma Sky LX**, leather high top in blue on white, red on white, black on white, natural on white, *green on white, *orange on white, *burgundy on white, *purple on white, *sky blue on white; low top in *sky blue on white, *red on white

The '86 Sky LX was hands down the best, most functional basketball sneaker Puma ever made. My man Clay Dunbar wore a pair in burgundy on white in the inaugural season of the Ray Diaz Roundball Classic in '89. Not only was he skating on every defender in the tournament, but he caught the eye of every single connoisseur in Douglass Projects, cuz at that point they were three years past due. Paul Pressey rocked a pair in green on white while he was repping for the Milwaukee Bucks, in coach Don Nelson's point forward position.

Brian Nash, Seton Hall Assistant Coach:
The Sky LX are without doubt my favorite sneakers ever. I saw Kenny Anderson wearing a pair his freshman year at Archbishop Molloy, so I went out and bought a pair in red on white to match my uni at Bishop Ford H.S. They had the softest polyurethane bottoms and were so comfortable.

Ted Nitro: I had the Puma Sky LX in green. Bobbito got me those at a store on 42nd and 5th near Grand Central. It closed right afterwards. They were one of my all time favorites. A lot of kids were really sucking me off for them. I'd tell them, "Sorry, these were the only pair left in the store," so I could get them off my trail a little bit.

■ **Adidas Centennial**, leather high top in red on white, navy on white, white on white, *black on white/blue, *green on white; *suede high top in *white on navy blue, *natural on natural, *white on burgundy

The '85-'86 Centennial was all about Johnny Dawkins at Duke. I saw the suede version once in '87. I went up to the kid and asked him where he'd copped them. He told me Detroit. That might have been the only city in all of the U.S. besides Boston that sold them. I luckily picked up two pairs of Centennials in '91, thanks to fellow sneaker hunter Andre Kyles who found them in Queens. Queens was always Adidas domain in the '80s.

■ **Nike Dunk**, leather high top and low top in red on white/red, royal blue on white/blue, navy blue on white/navy blue, *orange on white/orange, *burgundy on white/burgundy, *blue on yellow/blue, *red on gray/red, *yellow on black/yellow

Aside from the team customized Columbia U. Franchises in light blue on black and the Georgetown U. Legends in blue on gray, I had never seen Nike come out their face with three colors until the '85-'86 Dunks. The two-tones were just as illymatic, since they were the first Nike basketball sneakers to have flavor outside of the stripe area. The low top Dunk ruled

Bottom: Left to right, Mark Jackson wears Air Jordans with a red stripe and Rod Strickland pumps the Puma Sky LX.

Marris
Chuku

159

Marris
Chuku

139

"WE BUILD WINNING INTO EVERY SHOE."

Mike Jarvis

Coach Mike Ja
Spot-bilt Advisory S

The all-new Hi-post and Lo-post basketball shoes with innovative lacing system, bio-mechanical upper and cushion insole design. Spot-bilt. The finest in athletic footwear since the 1890's. At better athletic footwear and sporting goods stores.

Spot-bilt

432 Columbia Street
Cambridge, MA 02141

Right: 1984 Spot-bilt ad for the Hi Post, the sneaker that changed the company's profile on the courts.

for chilling out, but very few heads outside of ballplayers had the eye for Dunks in '85-'86. Don't front. If you were around in the '80s you didn't have them, and you probably slept on them when they were first reissued in '99 too. If you were born after '73 you're excused. Everyone else get a late pass!

■ Ellesse Cheeks, leather high top and low top in blue on white

Leonardo Servadio founded Ellesse in '59 in Italy. I saw the '85 Cheeks signature shoe once and only once, but it made a sharp impression on my dome piece. Maurice "Mo" Cheeks ran point for the Sixers in '83 when they took the NBA chip with the devastating and vicious crew of Dr. J, Andrew Toney, Bobby Jones, and Moses Malone.

Ahmad: Ellesse were some smooth, hard to get joints.

Serch: You know the saying, "Youth is wasted on the young." I wish I knew back then what I know now. The Cheeks would've been boxed! Never worn! It haunts me to this day that I don't have them anymore. Mo Cheeks looked very fruity in the ad lying on the floor with his legs crossed.

■ Spot-bilt Hi Post and Low Post, leather high top and low top in navy blue on white, white on white, *white on green

Paul Mokeski was doo doo when he played for the Milwaukee Bucks in the NBA, but he forever gets credit for being one of the first players I ever saw rock Spot-

bilts in '84. A year later they caught their rek with the release of the X-press high tops, but the '84 Hi Post were strictly for ballplayers, and not that many were even up on them.

■ Spot-bilt Official, leather low top referee shoes in black on black

The '84 Officials were hype! I slept on them too. '84 was still a little too early to rock all black grips, but had these came out in '89 they would have done damage.

■ Adidas Strider, leather mid in white on white, navy on white, red on white, gray on white

The '85-'86 Strider was the mid cut son of the Centennial and very fly but completely overlooked.

■ Nike Vandal Supreme, nylon high top in red on silver, gold on black, *gold on white, *silver on navy, *silver on red; Nike Vandal, canvas high top in *gold on green, white on white, navy on gray, silver on black, *red on white, *gold on red, *gold on burgundy, *gold on navy

The '85 Vandal and Vandal Supreme looked exactly like the Air Force 1 at a time when the Air Force 1 was impossible to find. Considering this fact they should've blown up, but the Air Force 1 design was still a little ahead of its time, even in its Vandal form. The nylon ones were borderline corn, like on some Michael Jackson "Thriller" video shit, but the canvas ones were on the money, as witnessed by their acceptance within the graffiti and b-boy world.

Previous spread: Maurice Cheeks maxes and relaxes, stacks NBA chips, and seems happy as shit to have his own signature shoe.

VANDAL SUPREME CONT.

9479

9480

VANDAL

Upper:	Canvas
Midsole:	—
Outsole:	Rubber Cupsole
Use:	—
Sizes:	(6-12, 13)

9441

9442

9445

9446

VANDAL CONT.

9447

9450

9451

9453

Scotch: The black mesh of the Vandal absorbed any kind of ink stain. They seemed *made* for bombing. Nike called them the Vandal, and us writers were blown away. That was the official bombing shoe in '85. I wasn't a Nike fan until those came out.

Slept On Butters—Other

■ **Tiger Asics Epirus, low cut running shoe in blue on white with old gold accent**

While working for Def Jam Records in '89 I'd run all types of errands for Russell "Rush" Simmons. My favorite one was the time he gave me his platinum American Express card and told me to go buy him a pair of Reebok Ex-O-Fits. He told me, "And buy a pair of whatever you want for yourself!" Ah, now that's a cool boss. Only thing was I had to do it within fifteen minutes cuz I had other errands to run for the day too (like buying him a pack of Newports and carrot juice). So I went to the nearest store, and the flyest joints they had on the wall were Asics Gel running shoes. Never mind that I could've spent X amount of dough on some higher priced jammies. The '85-'89 Epirus were so fresh and so clean, clean.

Ahmad: Definite top ten of all time. They couldn't have weighed more than twelve ounces. Similar to the New Balance 996, you could not find the Epirus Uptown. You had to go below 96th St. to a Super Runner's Shop and pay a buck-ten for them. They were off the meter ridiculous. When I'd wear the Epirus in the South Bronx I would turn heads!

Steve Brock: I rocked Asics when no one knew what they were. My only point of reference was Bruce Lee rocking them in "Game of Death." That gave them some credibility.

■ **Adidas Marathon Trainer, suede/nylon mesh running shoe in silver on royal blue**

The trefoil logo outsole is what did it for me with the '84 Marathon Trainer. They made you look an inch taller and made music for your feet when you walked in them cuz they were so loud.

■ **Adidas Lendl Pro, leather low cut tennis shoe in three shades of blue on white**

I had heard for years that sneaker companies were experimenting with shading their logos and stripes in different colors, but that you could only see them at the sneaker shows (which were only open to retailers). Alas, the '84 Lendl Pro braved the cold territory but no one seemed to notice. These joints should have been mega-bonkers, but instead heads just walked on by.

■ **Adidas ATP Futura, leather low cut tennis shoe in silver on white**

The '84 ATP Futuras were hot sizzlers—just look at them!

■ **Saucony Courageous, suede/nylon low cut running shoe in natural on gray, blue on gray/blue**

Saucony jumped off in 1898 in Pennsylvania along the Saucony River. In 1946 they started making athletic shoes, and by the '80s had become a popular brand for jogging. The '87 Courageous was a sleekly designed technical shoe, which could've hit the same heads who were gobbling up New Balance 576s.

■ **Puma California, suede/nylon low top court shoe in burgundy on white, forest green on white**

The California became a staple in the '90s, but in the '80s it was strictly slept on.

Ahmad: One time I had on the Californias in burgundy on white in the Village and I was killing them. You couldn't really find them back in the '80s. They were hard to get joints. Now they're mainstays. ■

The End of an Era

By the end of '87, too many elements of what had been a very underground sneaker cultural movement in New York became mainstream. Sneaker design went overboard and really took a bad turn. More people than ever were wearing sneakers. It became big business, and trying to navigate around it to be a part of that tiny group of connoisseurs became more difficult than ever. This was a great thing for sneaker companies, but for those of us who lived and breathed the pursuit of rare sneakers through the '70s up until '87, it would never be the same.

Johnny Snakeback Fever: All of a sudden in the late '80s, and there were sneakers everywhere. I looked at all these people buying them and thought, "Where's the fun now?" It used to be like hunting, like the rare kill you could find. Then they just mass produced things that were rare and ruined everything. They just made the whole shit corny.

Udi: In the '80s it didn't matter if a kid was poor, rich, white, whatever--if he had on the right sneaker he was the man, because he was innovative. Every company big or small had a shot at being a relevant brand if they had the right style. Today the sneaker industry is controlled by the retailers' conglomerate of buyers that don't allow innovation and independence. There's too much marketing and billions of dollars at stake. Kids see twenty TV commercials and get brainwashed to like a brand. There are smaller companies that could give consumers options, but some of them don't even make it past the trade shows because the buyers won't order them. The big national chains like Foot Locker are in bed with all the big sneaker companies, so what happens is survival of the richest. The sneaker industry is being affected by the stock market too much. That's why they put out reissues, so they can get numbers. The fact that the industry depends on old models and designs doesn't say much for what's happening now. What is the next generation going to ask to reissue? Our reissues?

I don't know how my editor convinced me to include this photo of me looking foolio at the Goat in 1981. But it was a time of innocence that we'd all do well to remember.

In New York City, if you say ball it is understood that you're talking about basketball. There are ballplayers on our playgrounds who may not have ever played anywhere scholastically or professionally, may not ever even aspired to, whose lives revolve completely around playing ball. That mentality sustains a lifestyle unto itself. It manifests itself on and off the court by dresscodes, language, disposition, posture, stride, life perspective, priorities, everything. Native New Yorker and former Knick guard Dean Meminger said in the early '70s, "If you don't play ball, you can't hang." If a sneaker brand owns the courts, it owns the streets. This has been a constant for the last 40 years.

The only footwear beside ball kicks that mattered on the street in the '70s were shoes. British Walkers, Gators, Clarks, Ballys, Marshmallows, Chinese slippers, and Playboys were popular shoe choices and no one can deny their importance in hip hop history. But every sneaker that gained popularity amongst the hip hop community of the mid '70s earned its stripes under metal playground backboards first. Eventually, by the late '70s and early '80s, basketball culture and hip hop culture began to influence each other. Kool Herc got his nickname from playing ball, not from DJ'ing. DJ Red Alert played at powerhouse Clinton H.S. years before he started spinning on WHBI and KISS-FM. Conversely, there were kids who grew up with hip hop and then took those sensibilities to the court. If there was one common denominator among all these converging energies, it was style. Whether you were skating, scratching, hitting, or scrambling, everyone wanted some fly ass kicks to rock with their outfit. It was the quest to stay freshly dipped, and that ideal was prevalent on and off the court.

Fresh Dipped

Previous spread: Old School
Randee dips it up in Fila from his
domepiece to his toes.

Right: Keith "Silver Streak" Fryson
puts his defender in a freeze as
he mesmerizes him with his colorful Hawaiian print shorts.

It's Not Just A Game Anymore, It's Life

Ted Nitro: Being dipped on the court was about matching your tournament shirt, shorts, socks, laces, and sneakers. It gave you a psychological advantage over your opponent. I know it worked on me. If you played like shit but your gear matched, at least you looked good. If I had to choose I'd rather look hot and play wack than look busted and play dope.

Tourney Shirts

Bobbito: All of my gear revolved around ball from head to toe. By '82, I had collected 40 tournament shirts, and I wore a different one to school every day. I had shirts from the Dome, Rucker, Citywide, Boy's Harbor, R.Y.A., Goddard Riverside, Big Apple Games, and P.A.L tournaments, plus the Central Baptist Kings Camp and the Upward Fund Camp. I had my brother's Rucker and Goat tournament shirts. I had my dad's Loiza jersey from '58. I had my third cousin's club team jersey from Puerto Rico. I would hand wash them in cold water with Woolite as if they were dress shirts and then hang dry them. I wanted them to last.

You couldn't buy basketball t-shirts back then, with all sorts of college and pro logos or designs, like you can today. You might find replica jerseys at Gerry Cosby, but merchandising wasn't big business like it is now. That was a good thing though. It ensured that the only way you could look like an authentic ballplayer was by actually playing. You wouldn't see three burgers on the court all wearing the same Knicks jersey, all looking foolish.

The tournament shirts transcended all of that. If I went to play at Roberto Clemente State Park in the Bronx, where nobody knew me and the gym was packed with seven people having next, there was no way I had a chance of being picked to run. I wasn't 6'5" or diesel. The only chance I had of earning respect before getting on the court was to wear a shirt from a name tournament like Rucker or Citywide. It carried weight, but it also carried a responsibility. You couldn't have a dope tournament shirt on and then play doo doo. You had respect for the name and what it meant. You carried shame if you desecrated the name; that was our code of ethics.

Joe Cruz: In the early '60s one project would play a game against another project and that was like our NCAA. We'd wear white t-shirts and write our numbers in with a magic marker. The fly shit was to get the ironed on numbers from the stores on 149th. Then you were on!

Jazzy Art: Moe's was a spot in L.E.S. that printed shirts for tournaments. In Brooklyn, Foster Park was *the* tournament and Fly

Williams was *the* playground legend. One day Moe's had up a Foster Park shirt, and I flipped! I asked, "How much for that shirt, mine is messed up?" And he said, "Two dollars." Right away I saw dollar signs in my head! I knew there was a market for *that* shit. So I played stupid and said, "Do you have other looseys like this one?" And he replied, "I think so. Why don't you go downstairs and see." The motherfucker let me in the basement! After that if you looked at my t-shirts you'd think I was the best player in New York! I would trade my boys a Foster Park and a West 4th St. shirt for sneakers. They'd be fiending.

Turk: My homeboy went to b-ball camp once and had no gear to rock. I gave him fifteen top-notch tourney shirts so he could represent. He didn't understand their value and ended up trading them to some rednecks for family reunion shirts. The dick!

Bobbito: My basketball gear was my validation. To me just participating in New York playground culture was equivalent to being first team all state in half the U.S. All I rocked through high school was my Central Baptist Kings winter jacket and my Lower Merion H.S. Central League champs windbreaker. I got cut from Riverside Church tryouts twice in '81, but I swore if I ever made the team and got that fucking illmatic blue jacket with the yellow flap on the neck with the Hawk emblem stitched in I would've worn it at my wedding ceremony. That shit was melodramatic.

Sake: It was the Holy Jacket.

Bobbito: It was the flyest piece of clothing I've ever seen cuz it meant so much. They'd win every chip in every tournament, and in the process, were producing future college All Americans and NBA players by the dozens. Not only did they give out the ill jackets and bags, they also were the only youth team that I can remember that was giving out shorts too. They were gold cotton with the Riverside Hawks logo on the right leg.

Shorts

Ted Nitro: If I had on a pair of shorts that no one had seen before that was almost as powerful as having a hot pair of sneakers.

Bobbito: I don't think there was one game I ever played in high school or college where I didn't seriously consider vamping my game shorts. It was so hard to have a dope pair of shorts. Some sporting goods stores would carry the plain polyester jammies, but we were always searching for the double knits with some level of striped ribbing. I didn't want to wear shorts that any kid in gym class could buy. Tight shorts up on the waist, or the huggies as we used to call them, went out with the '70s . . .

Left: Rucker players with their game faces on saunter off the court in their inside-out shorts.

Right: This 1974 New York-Philadelphia Rucker shirt is one of the illest classic tournament tees I've ever seen.

Left: Our own Mark Pearson had on five pairs of socks when shooting this jumper. It was so excessive it seemed like he was wearing a cast!

Right: Greg "Elevator Man #2" Brown (#20) had a smooth handle, but he's outstyled by the kid guarding him with floppy socks on.

Ted Nitro: I'd tell kids wearing short shorts, "This is not the ABA anymore!"

Bobbito: Oversized and sagging came in with the '80s. You couldn't buy baggy long cut shorts. There was no such thing. Even if you wore a pair with a waist size twice as big as yours, the bottom of the pant leg still wouldn't reach your knee. They just weren't cut that long. You had to wear them low on your waist so that the only thing holding them up was your butt cheek, your dick, and that bone at the top of your thigh that connects it to the hip. The mentality to recreate the look of a ballplayer had settled in.

Ted Nitro: Towards the late '80s I started seeing guys who could really play wearing shorts which we called the Olaf's specials. Olaf's was a sporting goods store on Madison Ave. and 112th St. They made shorts in multiple colors. You knew that when a guy played in Olaf's (or Hawaiian shorts) he had a flashy game. The more bugged your shorts looked, the more bugged your game was. You'd be subtly saying, "You think my shorts are funny, laugh at this." I appreciated that.

Bobbito: The next step was to wear shorts and tournament shirts deliberately inside out. That was very popular from about '81 to '86. I look back and it makes sense now that my coaches in school thought I was trying to be disruptive to team unity, but I wasn't at all. I just didn't know how to look like everyone else. I wasn't socialized to do that. I wanted to wear our uniform but I didn't want to do it uniformly.

Socks

"Pee Wee" Kirkland: In the '60s, nobody ever thought the sneaker had anything to do with you becoming a better basketball player. Socks were considered more important than sneakers. The preferred sock style was thick socks as opposed to the thin ones cuz it was all about that cushion. Guys wore three pairs of socks to compensate for sneakers' thin soles.

Johnny Snakeback Fever: In the late '70s there always was a debate between wearing two or three stripes.

Bobbito: From '81 on I tried to wear strictly white socks. If I had colored tube socks, I would fold the stripes down and under to hide them. That was a good technique to add cushion to the high top, plus it added width to the shoe.

Fabel: In the '70s I wore tube socks in different colors in layers all the way up to my knee. I got that from this gang named The Outlaws who would flip socks in their gang colors.

Bobbito: Before they came out with ankle socks I had my homemade ones. I made them by rolling down my socks so that they'd form a ring like Saturn around my ankles.

Fabel: The Saturn Rings! As crazy as that was that's exactly how I rocked them, bro. They looked like a condom on your foot!

Bobbito: We would fold our socks below the heel too so that it would appear that we weren't wearing socks at all. It was a good way to catch some sun on my pale ass ankles in the summer. A tan line above the ankle was a sure-fire way to tell who was a basketball fiend down by law and who wasn't.

Ted Nitro: I always wore my socks just above the shoe, I thought people who wore their socks right below the meniscus were bone.

Bobbito: Dr. J defined that look for the '70s. He had the huge afro and his socks up to his knees. Every kid wanted to have long tube socks. I would try to stretch my socks as high as they could go in an attempt to force them to reach my knee. It was a great way of ripping open the heel by accident.

Johnny Snakeback Fever: Until I was fourteen, I always tried getting floppy socks, because it was "Pistol" Pete Maravich's style. I wore two stripe socks under them because I saw Maravich do that too. I once wore *eight* pairs of socks playing in a game.

Bobbito: The most I ever wore was five pairs. I compensated for all the holes in them by wearing a bunch at the same time!

Johnny Snakeback Fever: I wore eight because Calvin Murphy did. I would get sneakers that were too big. I had no flexibility.

Turk: The worst shit was when you rocked five pairs of socks with a fly pair of Chucks, and your fucking laces wouldn't even go up half way on the sneaker. Your grips looked like a loaf of bread ready to explode out of the cooking pan!

Sake: When I wore four or more socks I'd always rotate them. Like the sock touching my feet would become the outermost layer of sock the next day. You couldn't wear four fresh socks everyday and not reuse them before washing them, that'd be too much laundry!

Bobbito: In the '70s, we all tried emulating pro players' styles in the playgrounds as far as gear went. In the '80s though, that changed drastically. Isiah, Bird and "Magic" were gifted players, but aesthetically they looked horrible. Their shorts were huggies and their socks were up to their knees. You had to respect them cuz

SHOE LACES
BASKETBALL SHOE LACES IN 5 COLORS (54 inch)

150 White — **151** Royal Blue — **152** Scarlet — **153** Kelly
Green — **154** Light Gold. Pair, 20¢

Top right: I love the way Mount Vernon's Gus Williams laced his sneakers.

Bottom right: Crazy Legs illustrates the stepladder style of lacing your 69'ers, but why is he wearing blue and yellow socks with red laces?

they were champions, but I could only take watching them but so much. I can't name one player I ever saw in New York in the '80s whose game even remotely resembled Magic's, Bird's, or Isiah's, much less their gear. When heads on the playgrounds started folding their socks down and under, wearing their shorts sagging and their shirts inside out, it was unprecedented. You didn't see that on televised games or in magazines. It was only on the street and it was the beginning. The courts weren't that far removed from what was going on in the b-boy circles and the park jams. The movement of iron horse writers and MCs was coming from the same place that the ballplayers were making a statement from. It was time for something new.

The Dope Fiend Jelly Roll

Fabel: The Washington Boys knew how to make Pumas extra fat. They would cut the stitching where the first lace-holes are in the front so they could widen the shoe. Then they would lace them, and put jelly roll socks on to widen it even more. We called it jelly roll socks cuz the sock when wrapped around the middle of your foot resembled those jelly roll cakes you could buy at a bodega. We would wrap it around our arch then safety pin it. We would mummify our foot!

Bobbito: The first person I saw rock the jelly roll was my teammate from Douglass Projects Community Center in '81. I couldn't believe it. He had a sock that was folded three times and then tucked underneath his tongue, then he tied his laces loosely on top of it. It raised the tongue so high off the top of his foot you could see the sock peeking out of the side. I thought it was genius! It made me think of a dope fiend. I'd always see homeless dudes all strung out with their hands and feet looking mad puffy with marks from heroin. When they'd throw on sneakers they didn't need a jelly roll cuz their feets were already making their kicks look wide and fat. So I always called it the dope fiend jelly roll.

Ted Nitro: I thought it was corny. Guys would play on the court with their sneakers like that. When they sprained their ankle, it was like, "Uh, get me to the emergency room because my ankle is broken."

Laces

"Pee Wee" Kirkland: We wore different color laces to match our team color in the '60s. I used to like black laces with black Cons, so you could only see the white trimmed rubber sole.

Joe Cruz: We used to wear red and blue laces doubled up on each shoe to go out at night.

Brother Ray: The whole look on the court in the '70s was to leave your sneakers loose before you played. The Chuck Taylor laces were fat compared to the leather Adidas because the Adidas' eyelets were cut into the leather instead of metal. So you'd get fat laces to replace the skinnier ones because they'd break anyway from tying them up too tight. You'd have the fat laces and the tongue sticking up loose and then when you went to the battle you'd tie them up tight. If you showed up on the court with your sneakers already tied tight you looked like a nerd.

Fab Five Freddy: In the '70s Latin cats were doing the most extreme shit like lace weaving and overlapping.

Doze Green TC5: We met these Puertorocks from the Bronx in the late '70s who had their shit immaculately pressed from head to toe, laces, pants, shirts, even their hats.

Fabel: In the late '70s there were no fat laces. You had to make them. You'd stretch the hell out of regular laces, then iron them to death so they would keep their form. Sometimes we'd take the plastic bound end of the lace and push it inward into the lace to invert it, like an "innie" nipple!

I would claim that I introduced the fat elastic laces, but it actually started with Norman a.k.a. Door, one of the members of the Electric Company. We went to Art & Design H.S. together. One day he had put thick ribbons in his Converse. We all freaked out on it! The only drawback was that ribbons are floppy without good form. My mom used to sew, and she had all these elastic bands for making the waist on dresses or trousers. I said, "Mami! Hook me up with that!" I got one of my shoestrings, and I measured how long the elastic should be. I cut it and wrapped the end with electrical tape. I stuffed it through the eyelets of my high top Converse. I put on three pairs of socks, and then the jelly roll sock. It was like looking at a graffiti character or a drag-racing car. See, to us, everything was about exaggerating. It was about being larger than life.

In '82 I walked into Bruckner Roller Skating Rink and the Cold Crush Brothers saw me and literally fell on the floor laughing from excitement. "Look at homeboy's shit!" I had to pick them up off the floor. The elastic was my trademark, my main impact. Then it spread like wildfire.

Doze Green TC5: We also rocked underwear elastics we bought from Woolworth's for laces.

Johnny Snakeback Fever: I just remember me and Mark, two little white kids in Brooklyn in '78-'79, ironing shoelaces, playing Space Invaders, putting socks under the tongues of Adidas Pro Models. It was ridiculous. Someone should have beaten us down.

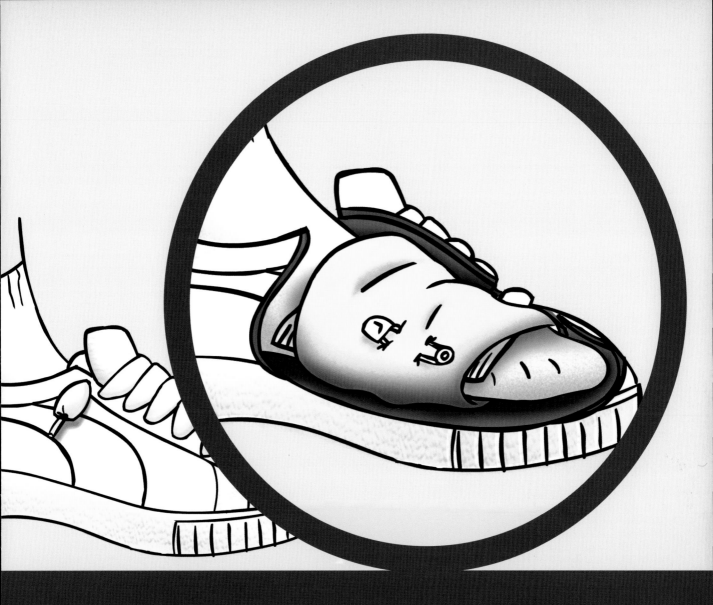

Diagrams of the two most popular
variations of the jelly roll.

Scotch: Sake put me up on hockey laces. They were the thickest laces available, but they were six feet long! I had to tuck mad extra lace inside my shoe. Walking on balled up lace plus the heavy-duty metal end would hurt by the end of the day.

Serch: In '85 I was rocking burgundy Izod shorts and shirts with Shell toes with burgundy fat laces. I'd have on white socks with a burgundy pom-pom in the back, and then another set of burgundy laces wrapped around my legs over my calf tied in the back! On bare skin! When you're an addict, nothing can be considered sacred.

Lincoln Parker: My laces were always sparkling white. I would soak them in a cup of bleach in the sink, then iron them so they'd get flat and thick. I did that on a weekly basis.

Ted Nitro: In the era of the suede Pumas, fat laces were the thing. Dancers used to break with their sneakers untied, and they'd be doing their *thing*. That looked really cool. They started lacing the laces over the eyelet instead of under towards the late '70s. Ever since then I think everyone, myself included, laces like that.

Bobbito: In the early '70s I started to see players lace the first eyelet right by the toes over the eyelet and then the rest of the eyelets would be laced under. To me that was the ultimate way a playground ballplayer could tie his shits. Then the hip hop style became pervasive on the court and in the '80s ballplayers started lacing over the eyelet too. It was such an easy way to identify whether someone was a hip hop head or not on the court. The advantage to lacing over the eyelet, besides it purely having the more vicious style, was that it kept your laces tied at a fixed tension longer than under the eyelet. It was purely functional. It had style and purpose.

I saw a lot of hip hop heads play ball with their fat laces on untied. The Goat Park was also known to the hip hop world as Rock Steady Park. There was one crew member named Woody who would call next from the sideline with his white gloves still on from popping practice. One time he was dribbling down the baseline and both his joints flew right off! He was a true b-boy. He never tied his shits up, ever. We were rolling, I had never seen no shit like that before. That was hip hop to me.

I heard a story about Sam Worthen that was similar. Sam played for the Chicago Bulls one year and spent the rest of his playing days being a street legend, particularly at West 4th St. He had mad boogie and herky jerk chicken moves on his plate. One game he was wearing low top Clydes loosely tied. The defender picked him up full court, and Sam started doing multiple spin dribbles on him while advancing up the court. Around half court

though Sam's left Puma came off, but Sam didn't stop dribbling and left his defender behind him and laid the ball in. Legend has it that after Sam scored his Puma was still spinning around in a 360 by itself at halfcourt!

Gus Williams from the Seattle Supersonics wore the craziest style of lacing. He repped Mount Vernon well in the NBA with a ring in the '77 chip. He had Nike Blazers with a green stripe and his laces were so long he'd wrap them around his ankle and then tie them in the back. To this day I've never seen anyone do that before or after him. It looked fly on him.

Off Court Lampin' With Flav

Jazzy Art: Sneakers were what we wore off the court, not shoes. If you wore the correct sneakers that matched your Lee pants and Le Tigre shirt, you was *dipped*.

Fabel: The best thing was to buy Lee's or DCs with an in-seam length that wasn't too long so my sneakers could be clearly exhibited. There was a strategic way to rock your pants so that you didn't cover the beauty of your sneakers.

Bobbito: I'd always try to rest the pant leg on top of the tongue or if it was a low top right above the knot of the lace.

Kurious: Being fresh dipped was having brand new kicks in odd colors to match with any shirt you had. It showed that you were perfectly together. I'd have some crazy light purple shirt on with Nikes in the same exact shade. It showed I had specific kicks for specific outfits. My favorite outfit was my all sky blue Airs with my Carolina tank top. I'd get a fresh cut from Jerry's Den, and I'd be killing 'em!

Emz: I'm still matching, and I'm 30 now. I'm stuck, unfortunately.

Schott Free: I not only matched my colors, I matched my brands too. If I was rocking Reeboks, I had on their socks, shorts, etc. I didn't give a fuck if no one knew but me. It just made me feel complete. What good was it if you had Adidas on with a Nike headband? It was important to play it all correctly head to toe.

Scotch: It's how you styled it. I thought Kangaroos were real garbage when they came out, but kids were making them work. NOC 167 of The Death Squad was the most out-there, futuristic space b-boy you'd ever want to meet (with the possible exception of Rammelzee). NOC was known to rock *two* pairs of sneakers at the same time. One was in a larger size *over* the ones that fit him. He had socks, sneakers, and then sneakers! It was in coordinating colors, too, and he could pull it all off. Everything was just taken to another level.

"Pee Wee" Kirkland: Believe it or not, I seen guys back in the '60s wear two different colored sneakers at the same time, black on one foot, white on the other.

Fabel: It was about shock treatment without going overboard and someone saying, "That looks stupid." We were brave. One day I was trying to figure out which pair to wear with my navy blue and white gear. So I put on one white Cortez on one foot, and one blue Cortez on the other. I stood in front of the mirror to see which one looked better with what I was wearing. And I realized they *both* looked fly! The only thing was that they both had white laces. So I bought blue laces and threw them on the white ones so it was really opposite. People freaked out on that! You definitely couldn't get away with that shit with a 69'er Pro-Ked and a Converse on each foot. People would laugh at you. It had to be the same brand model except a different color. It was just a fun thing you didn't expect.

Serch: I could literally sense my friends emotional levels based on the reactions they'd give me for my grips. If I came out with the extra shit and none of my boys were hugging my nuts for them, I'd immediately think I'd done something wrong. I'd talk to them the next day to squash whatever problem, and they'd be like, "By the way, your kicks were crazy last night!"

If the Shoe Fits

Johnny Snakeback Fever: When you're 6' 2", 140 pounds and fifteen years old with a size fourteen foot, your shit will look like El Gigante. If I walked in to a store I could tell what would look okay on my foot. A couple of times I misjudged and rolled onto the train with the El Gigante. Kids laughed at me. They broke down screaming on my legs that fucking look like threads, and shoes that fucking look like size 46! ∎

A young World B. Free at Guilford College wilds out and wears a low top Chuck on his right foot and a high top Chuck on his left!

Arts and Crafts

Johnny Snakeback Fever and
Sake hard at work customizing
Nike Legends in 1982. Note the
taped-off stripe on the sneaker
on the right.

Throughout the late '60s and early '70s, sneakers were altered minimally. But the art of sneaker customization took off in the late '70s, when the desire to have unique joints was at a fever pitch. First came little scribbles in the '60s, then painting stripes, and eventually, in the '80s, painting the whole sneaker. Some sneaker customization owes itself entirely to graffiti inspiration, but there were important reasons, beyond aesthetics, to customize. At times customization could maintain and extend the life of a shoe, but the ultimate goal was to hear the words, "I didn't know those existed!" Before '87 there were only a handful of connoisseurs who cared enough to take the time to customize (and therefore guys like me would get asked to do it for other kids on my block). It was a strictly private affair until Dapper Dan started customizing Air Force 1s with Louis Vutton stripes out of his store on 125th St. in around '87.

Brother Ray: I'd dream about designing sneakers. I'd take the glued star off my Chuck Taylors. Then I'd draw stripes and graphic shapes on sneakers with a pen or marker. I didn't want to wear anything else but sneakers all the time so I could have an excuse to have a basketball in my hand all the time. Mom and Dad told me I looked like a bum, so I started dyeing my leather ones and cutting the stripes off to make them look like something other than sneakers in the hope my parents wouldn't complain as much.

Bobbito: In the summer of '81 I played in the Rucker. Our tournament shirts were plum, so I painted my Pony stripe with a purple permanent marker. My first customization attempt failed miserably. The purple on the inside stripes rubbed off on the leather of the opposite shoe. I tried salvaging the attempt by applying Griffin shoe polish with the sponge applicator, but then they really looked like shit. That hurt.

Johnny Snakeback Fever: By '79-'80 we were completely addicted to customizing. I began to look at new sneakers as canvases. Other kids would go into the store and simply say, "I want that sneaker." I'd look at it and be like, "I'm gonna paint that leather green, and that stripe yellow." I was thirteen years old and saying to Mark Pearson, "We could open up our own business customizing sneakers." We were fully painting every shoe we got a hold of because there were so few color stripe choices available at stores.

Sake: Customization was where the whole graffiti, sneaker, and personalization flavor combined. I was already down with different kinds of alcohol markers. I had a palette. It was all about pulling it off and making that shit look factory-manufactured. They had to look as if you had an in with some team. If

you fucked up when you were customizing a sneaker and got a drip, you could blow on it ...

Bobbito: . . . or wipe it quickfast with a paper towel . . .

Sake: . . . but basically you had to live with it. That's the same as in graffiti where you would do a piece and you didn't want drips, you wanted your outline to be mad crisp.

Bobbito: I would feel like I was in an operating room asking for a scalpel during heart surgery. I would be so careful that it'd take four hours to complete a pair. First I started with permanent markers, then I graduated to Esquire Shoe Dye which was applied with a brush, then I started fucking with acrylic paint because it wouldn't crack as easily, plus I could mix the paint tubes to create hard to find colors. The ultimate was Esquire Leather Spray. That gave the truest factory manufactured look. Sometimes I would customize my sneakers in an attempt to resurrect them when they were dogged. I realized that the leather underneath the stripe would be brand new crispy white because it never saw the break of dawn. That opened up a whole new world of exclusivity because then I was able to freak the three tone customization. I once painted

chocolate on white Airs all pumpkin like the Texas Longhorns flavor. Then I razored off the original chocolate stripe to have it white on pumpkin. The outsole was still chocolate, and when I wore those people would get stomach pains! I was putting a hurting on' em!

I had a pair of Puma Sky LXs in '89. I painted them banana yellow and razor bladed off the stripes. I wore my white on yellows to this party called Paydays. De La Soul saw my joints and went up to Serch and said, "Yo, who's your man?" I will never forget that shit because De La Soul was huge at that point, and they were hawking me for my sneakers.

Ahmad: Once I saw Bob do it I was hooked. I started taking his acrylics and painting my Dr. Js. I'd paint the chevron green and the star yellow and the bottoms purple! You had

Top left: Brother Ray's customized Air Force Zeros in 1984.

Middle left: Billy Ray Bates of
the Portland Trailblazers had
these ultra-exclusive, utterly
bananas customized Nike
Franchises.

Bottom left: Pete Nice's 1978
customized Americanas, made
from white on white Jabbars.

Right: Playground legend Jack
Ryan wears customized 1979
Jabbars with a painted toe cap.

to keep pace. We'd see "Tiny" Archibald in
Pumas in white on green, and be like, "Oh
my God! We need to change our shit up."

Mike Drake: I'd try dyeing my suede sneakers
and they wouldn't come out properly. I'd
wind up with colored socks. I'd try taking
them to Solomon on 145th St. He was a professional shoe repairman and he'd tell me,
"You're wasting your time. Unless it's a light
colored leather, forget it."

Doze Green TC5: We used to paint our Puma
stripes different colors every month! Between
coloring and brushing them, they'd wind up
lasting two years (That wasn't my only pair
though, don't make me look like a bum
Bobbito!). If we couldn't find sneakers to match
our track suits we'd just color the stripes so
they would. I once took a pair of white on purple Pumas and colored the stripe lavender.

Johnny Snakeback Fever: I went to Pete
Maravich's Basketball Camp. Pony had just
come out, and I had a pair with a natural
suede stripe. I got Esquire dye and made the
stripe purple. I showed up to camp and everyone was like, "Holy shit!" across the board. I
walked on to the gym floor and saw kids'
heads explode, as if "Pistol" Pete had fed
them sticks of dynamite for camp breakfast.
It was '77. No one had ever seen a purple
stripe before, much less even imagined one.

Jazzy Art: I had the Pro-Ked Royal Flash in
black suede with the hot add on bottom. I
painted the stripe light blue. I was good for
some funky pimp colors! My teammates were
saying, "We don't know what the fuck you
thinking about, but you know what you
doing, man. You on the right shit."

Sake: I have to tip my hat to my man Blitz.
He customized a pair of Nike Blazers purple
on white, and he was so methodical about
the box on the back. He painted the Nike
lettering perfect, which was the hardest part.
The color of the check matched the lettering
in the back. He hit it off lovely.

Bobbito: It took enough hours just to get four
stripes perfect, but to paint over the thin lettering in the back box was mission impossible. This kid I went to Lower Merion H.S.
with customized his '82 Blazers to have a
green swoosh, but he even went beyond Blitz.
This kid somehow found a solution to remove
the Nike lettering, and then he freaked it and
painted his name ("Falcone") in script with
green Esquire shoe dye. He was sitting at a
table across from me in the lunchroom with
his back to me. When he sat down his pants
raised up just enough for me to peep it. His
shit was so subtle that you might not even
notice the customization, or could only appre-
ciate it in flashes.

Recreating the Suede Blazers

Johnny Snakeback Fever: We painted Mark's
Blazers in blue on white to yellow on blue.

Sake: I was still obsessed with the blue
suede Blazers after they stopped making
them, but our attempt at recreating them
was horrible. Those shits came out like
Frankenstein's shoes; they were *so* ugly.

Johnny Snakeback Fever: They were too painted! At that point people were only customizing stripes, but we took it to the next level and
tried painting the whole shoe. I told Mark that
if he wore them in the rain he'd be standing
in a puddle of paint dripping off his shoes!

 You had to customize with a new sneaker if
you wanted it to look good. The fear was that
you'd fuck up a brand new pair. They might
end up looking nice from far away, but looking
like a painting all cracking real close up.

Ted Nitro: It was hit or miss because you did-
n't know exactly how they were gonna look
until you wore them. You might even have to
throw them out because you damaged them
too much.

Recreating the Americanas

Ted Nitro: I had seen the Adidas Americanas
in Sports Illustrated, but no way was I going
to find a pair. I thought, "if I can't get that
color, I'm gonna make it." I took a pair of
Shells with red stripes and redid the middle
stripe blue so they could look like them. I
thought that was so fresh.

Jazzy Art: I took Pro Models in maroon on
white and dyed the middle stripe blue to
make them Americanas. I guess I'm a frus-
trated artist, but I got my Esquire shoe dye
which came in every color in the world. I
guess we can thank women for that, cuz
they're always dyeing their shoes.

 On the Double-R train we used to kick in
the conductor's door in the last car, get on
the intercom and rock the mic! We was
freestyling, "One two three, four five six;
check out my beat, and it goes like this."
We'd walk through the car and everybody
knew it was us, so of course they'd size us up
and down. And the minute they looked down
at my customized Americanas, I'd see heads
just punch each other over them. So you'd
spend three hours for fifteen minutes of fame
but it was worth it to see people in awe.

Sake: I painted Pro Models to make them
look like the Americanas. That was the cliché
of customizing. I give credit where credit is
due, and I definitely bit that shit off Jack

Top: Darnell Hillman of the Nets wore these customized Dr. Js in 1978.

Middle left: I customized these Franchises in 1983.

Bottom left: Emz's customized Adidas Sneekers, which he had done at a shoe repair shop.

Bottom right: DJ E-Z Rock wore these customized Louis Vuitton Air Force 1s in 1987. They were made by Dapper Dan.

Ryan. He was the first person I saw with Americanas on. I don't know if he had an actual pair or if he'd customized them. I was thirteen and he was sixteen, and down at East 5ᵗʰ he was *the man*. I wouldn't wear them to the park where he'd be, but I would wear them in my own little circle. The first time I played for the Church Uptown I bit Jack's Americanas, and kids was like, "Oh shit!"

Jack Ryan, playground legend: Americanas were impossible to find in Brooklyn, but I had to have them. I painted my Superstars to recreate them but no one knew.

Recreating the Air Jordan 1

Prime Minister Pete Nice: Before Jordans became available in stores in '85 they were totally custom made for Jordan and no one else had them. I took my 3/4 Nike Sky Force and customized them with a black/red coat. The first time I wore them was at a game at Bishop Laughlin H.S. It was a zoo. When I walked on the court people were blurring out, not realizing I had made them myself. People were going nuts. I wore them the rest of the season and opponents would ask me where I'd gotten them on the court *during the game*.

The Gladiator Batas

Johnny Snakeback Fever: Our friend Josh Laetner had an *old* pair of John Wooden Batas. It was a sin to wear sneakers so fucked up with holes, but he kept wearing them to play ball. Me and Mark were at his house and he went down to eat dinner with his parents while we were up in his room. We took a pair of scissors, and I just cut the whole upper off the sole on both shoes. Then we took the laces and tied them around the sole and then back around the tops so they would hold on.

Sake: Like some Greco-Roman gladiator shoes.

Johnny Snakeback Fever: When Josh came back upstairs, I was rocking them. He said, "What's so funny?" We were on the floor holding our stomachs. We were like, "Check it out man, we customized your Batas! We hooked them up and made them the Bata Gladiator shoe." He went bananas and was so upset.

The Silverwears

Scotch: Mark had a whole workshop of spray paints, leather dyes, tape, and Exacto knives. I copped black on white Shell toes and said, "Let's really get flamboyant now." He broke out aluminum Rustoleum, taped off the black stripes, and he sprayed the entire shoe metallic silver. Then I put fat black laces in them. You know how cars have scripted chrome letters with the model name? I tried recreating that. I caught a car that said Custom in script and pried off the two logos on each side. I mounted them in the rubber sole on the outer side of each sneaker. It was an adventure coming home on the D train. I got on the front car and walked all the way through to the back car as if it were a parade. I sat in the last car and kicked my shoes all the way out. Cats were just ogling, "What? Where'd you get those?" I said, "Custom, money. Custom!"

Sake: Lord Scotch was the only motherfucker with the balls to wear them. We knew they were ugly, but he loved attention and would do anything for it.

The True Motivation

Fabel: I had white on burgundy Pumas, and I painted the stripe gray with suede spray, then threw some gray laces on to complement it. Later I saw somebody with white on baby blue Pumas, and they painted the stripe turquoise then put turquoise laces. I was loving it because they looked like candy. I was ready to eat that shit, B, on the real! I wanted to one-up them so I removed the stripe altogether. I was wondering what a complete burgundy shoe would look like. It was very competitive. Who's gonna blow who up and be the flyest? Going to school at Art & Design H.S. was like a fashion show every day. I would want to look fly plus I was trying to impress the ladies. The ladies were feeling brothers bopping up in there with some flavorful stuff. ∎

Left: These 1982 customized Pony #1s were the first sneakers I experimented on with acrylic paint.

Middle: Ricky Sobers cut off his Converse stripes. Why? Who knows?

Right: B-boy Woody (on the left) rocks customized Nike Blazers with colored toe caps.

Before owning multiple pairs of sneakers became culturally relevant (or economically feasible) in the '80s, keeping your only pair looking fresh out the box for more than two weeks in New York was damn near impossible. Elements like gum or dog doo on the sidewalk, rooftop tar, and pigeon droppings were unavoidable, as was keeping your feet mittens from getting stepped on in a packed train during rush hour. If you were lucky enough to escape those pitfalls, then Murphy's law dictated that you'd spill pizza oil, hot dog onions, or Tahitian Treat fruit punch soda on your prized possessions and ruin your day. Even before you left your crib, the dye from brand new dungarees would rub up a shade of blue on your leather that wasn't supposed to be there. Eventually people would give up on having them look brand spanking, and would then proceed to wear them out and keep wearing them, particularly during the '70s. I would wear sneakers out so bad that my sock would be peeking out the sole, and would get ripped to shreds, so I'd have a hole in my sneaker and a hole in my socks. I'd hear snaps like, "Bobby, you're so holy!" Ha, ha, shit wasn't funny. I dedicate this section, entitled Holy Wars, to the memory of all the holes I had in my sneakers as a kid. As with most wars, it was a battle in which no one triumphed.

Gerry Erasme: I would run sneakers to the ground. I would play ball with my toe busting out on the side. I remember putting cardboard on the bottom of my insole so I could keep playing.

Brother Ray: The insole of my sneaker would wear out and then I'd stick Dr. Scholl's inserts in so they could last longer. I remember seeing guys with three inserts for cushioning.

Ted Nitro: My foot would drag on lay ups, so the leather toe part of my sneakers would split from the sole, like it'd start talking to me. I'd be vexed. I'd put Krazy Glue on it to try to keep it together. It was like fixing the Six Million Dollar Man. I'd think, "We can rebuild you. We have the technology."

Joe Ski: Some ballplayers would wear imitations called Trax. They would only last two weeks. They'd split on the side and guys would use duct tape and wrap it around the sneaker to hold it together. It would only hold for another two weeks, but they'd be out there playing.

Brother Ray: At one point people liked their sneakers so much that they would go to a shoemaker or shoe repair and ask them to glue on another pair of rubber soles.

Mike Drake: I used Shoe Goo to fill up the holes on the soles. It came out in '83, and was like rubber cement glue that you had to buy at the hardware store. It worked, too!

Jazzy Art: I walked on the side of my feet so they always wore out quickly. If you put metal tabs on the bottom of your joints though, then they wouldn't wear out. That was a trend for a minute. It'd be funny to see cats walk down the hallways of the school going "click click." You tapped up the back, and if you fucked up the front you would tap that too.

My main problem was when I wore sneakers to bomb. You could tell who wrote graffiti just by looking at their sneakers. They always had paint and ink on them. That's also how we got busted a lot by our moms.

Scotch: We were using supermarket price stamping inks, Flowmasters, and running through tracks full of grease. That stuff wasn't coming out no matter what.

Sake: Ink was *the* nemesis. Once I'd get a drop of ink on my sneaks it was over. Them shits were dead.

Jazzy Art: Mark would destroy his sneakers. He'd come out of the lay up and we'd call him "Pig Pen"!

Turk: I'd wear a sock over a fresh pair of sneakers in the lay up to protect them.

Scotch: We'd put sandwich bags on our shoes too.

Sake: TD4 a.k.a. The Deadly Four bombed Fort Hamilton. I had to give them props cuz they would change in the spot out of new Pumas and pea coats into some bummy ass sneakers and jumpsuits. They would bomb, and then leave like they were going to work. Talk about thinking ahead of time.

Fabel: Whatever you had, you had to preserve. We didn't break on cardboard all the time. We would hit the pavement too. It affected how we danced. If you did slides (or what we called floats), you would master it so it would look like you were hovering. That was partially because you didn't want to scrape any part of your kicks. Ken Swift would keep his footwork extra crispy for the simple reason that he didn't want to screw up his shoes. So the fear of dogging your joints actually improved your dancing! There was a science to it. ∎

© Martha Cooper

The Toothbrush

By the late '70s-early '80s, style on and off the court was changing. There was a higher demand to keep sneakers looking fresh out the box for longer than two weeks. Whereas in the '70s sneakers were getting restored when they were beyond repair or washed when they became totally dogged, the new mentality was to maintain your sneakers over a long period of time. I started taking care of my kicks as best possible. I knew the heel was gonna wear first, so I used to walk over metal grating on the sidewalk all the time instead of on the rubber-eroding concrete. That may have been a bit overboard, but most people did start cleaning their stompers on the daily. It was urban survival.

Doze Green TC5: We were poor so we made our shit last and looking fresh. Colgate toothpaste was the best shit to clean your joints with.

Lincoln: We religiously cleaned the rubber parts around the side of the shoe with Comet. It was a badge if you had nice, clean sneakers.

Mike Drake: I carried a suede brush for my suedes. Then I learned about saddle soap for leathers, and in a dire emergency at school I'd use chalk from the chalkboard. I learned that trick from a guy in Brooklyn. He'd take some ground up chalk and rub it on the leather then take the eraser and cover the scratches. It worked on some Puma Baskets I had that got scuffed. The eraser/chalk trick at least saved your sneakers until you got home and got your toothbrush. I saw plenty of guys in the bathroom at Tech scrubbing down. They carried their own toothbrush *and* soap.

Fabel: Everyone had a few toothbrushes. I had a whole bag of them! If you had a tooth-brush for dark colored suede Pumas you never used that toothbrush to brush a light pair because you were gonna brush some of the ink right onto the lighter sneakers. I learned that the hard way.

Serch: I had a lot of success on the gum sole with a toothbrush and baking soda or Dove dishwashing liquid.

Sake: We used Fantastik and Formula 409 on leathers.

Come Chantrell: Fantastik is . . .fantastic! I couldn't live without it!

Fabel: Oh, forget it! We were like mad scientists in the laboratory, bro! Fantastik mixed with Lysol mixed with whatever. We made our own high powered chemicals to clean the rubber parts. You had to be careful because some of those concoctions were so high post that they would take the coloring off the suede.

Ted Nitro: They had a cleaner that came with Esquire shoe dye that was poison strong. I was cleaning a pair and didn't put enough water in it to break it down. I put a plastic toothbrush in it, and it melted! I even washed sneakers in the washing machine. I'd put the shoe inside a sock and then with some clothes. I couldn't do that too much because mom would say, "You're gonna break my wash machine!" Never put a sneaker in the dryer because it will shrink down about one size.

Fabel: The mistake was wearing them before they dried completely. They started to smell!

Mike Drake: I stayed away from throwing my sneakers in the washing machine because the soles would get real soggy. I did a lot of quick dunking in the tub then brushing them off with a horse hairbrush.

Andre Kyles: I used hand lotion to moisturize the leather.

Jazzy Art: They had products out that would fuck your shit up like Sneaker White, Sneaker Bright, whatever that shit was. I did-n't fuck with that.

Serch: It was White Bright by Kiwi, then they changed the name to Sneaker Bright.

Sake: Fuck Nurses All White or Griffin shoe polish, all that shit that you put on with a sponge to make your sneakers white. That was ghetto. If you had to use Nurses All White then it was over. You were better off throwing them out.

Dante: If it rained you'd have white Griffin coming off your sneakers. I'd say, "Stop fak-ing it and buy some new joints." I coated my suede joints with 3M spray so they wouldn't stain from the rain.

Emz: The way to keep the shits right was to use a dry-cleaner on the white midsole. It got everything out without staining it. The real way to keep your shits clean is to have a mil-lion pair rotation and never wear them.

Steve Brock: Even the poorest kids in high school had at least a four kick rotation. The big joke was that you had to have a good pitching staff, because a good pitching staff always had a five man rotation. ■

kelly's
cobler
PROFESSIONAL GRADE
DRY CLEANER
FABRIC AND LEATHER CLEANER
Apply sparingly to stain with clean white cloth. Rub in circular motion.
WARNING: VAPOR HARMFUL! MAY BE HARMFUL IF SWALLOWED.
CONTAINS: Trichloroethylene and Petroleum Distillate. Avoid contact with eyes and prolonged contact with skin. Use only in well ventilated area. Avoid prolonged breathing of vapor.
FIRST AID: In case of eye contact, flush thoroughly with water. If irritation persists, get medical attention. If swallowed, do not induce vomiting. Call a physician. Keep out of reach of children.
Used by Professionals Since 1899.
4 FL. OZ.
KELLY'S
120 mL
Geo. J. Kelly Co. Div. of Fiebing Co., Inc.

TAKE CARE OF YOUR LEATHER SPORTS SHOES

1 — After use, brush away mud.

2 — Allow the shoes to dry naturally. Do not place near any source of heat.

3 — Brush your suede shoes regularly.

4 — Do not use grease or oil, it may be harmfull to the adhesion of the sole.
Polish with a relable wax polish.

PATRICK cannot accept responsibility for neglect/or maltreatment of footwear.

⮞P PATRICK®

Left: Emz recommends this dry cleaner as the best solution for crispy kicks.

Once heads got really serious about preserving their sneakers by cleaning them daily to keep them looking well groomed, the next step was to figure out how to preserve them in between use. This was the distinction between the daily wearer and the developing collector. A collector had to be cunning in how he stashed his joints. Johnny Snakeback Fever explains, "A quiver was your arsenal of shoes. Like a medieval marksman kept his arrows in his quiver, an urban shoe hound kept his collection in a quiver." And as time passed, connoisseurs realized the better and longer you kept your quiver on ice, the greater chance you had at blowing people away with some shit they had never seen or had forgotten about years later.

Scotch: I never understood how people stashed, because as soon as I got a fresh pair I was even wearing them to the laundromat! Nothing felt better than fresh out the box kicks. My pockets weren't deep enough to have mad kicks to rotate. It was hand to mouth.

Johnny Snakeback Fever: When I got new sneakers I had to break them out right away. Mark was good for buying two at a time starting in the '70s. He'd have an Adidas box up on his shelf and I'd say, "You got to break those out!" He'd be like, "Nah, not till the spring." I couldn't believe he had the willpower.

Sake: If I found dope sneakers and had the dough, I would buy three or four pairs. I would wear the first two pairs, then keep the other two on ice for a while so I could slip some other shit into the rotation.

Ted Nitro: My willpower wasn't strong enough to preserve them. I would lose that battle. I could keep a sneaker on ice for three months and all of a sudden I'd look at them one day and say, "I gotta wear these." It's like being on drugs. The sneakers were calling me, "Ted. Ted. Put me on, B. I look fresh. I'm clean. I'm ready to go." If I knew back then what I know now I would have put so many joints on ice. I'd be one of the sneaker kings. Old-timers would say, "Were you born back then?"

Jazzy Art: I bought canary yellow Air Forces. I kept them under the bed. My girlfriend was like, "You bought them, wear them." She didn't understand that I had to let them marinate! The next winter I walked in my gym class with the cleanest pair of canary Nikes. Kids went cuckoo.

Udi: My family owned Broadway Sneakers and me and my brothers knew every inch of that store. In the basement I hid the first pair of shoes I ever stashed, so my father wouldn't know that I had taken them. If I was supposed to take $50 for my salary, I would hide another pair in the basement and not take the money. I stashed Dr. Js, Top Tens, Campus, Diadoras, and Etonics. I've put over 400 sneakers on stash in the last twenty years, never worn.

Mike Drake: I kept the boxes. Even before I brought them home, box tops would spread out, so I started taking duct tape and reinforcing the corners. This way they'd be flush when I'd put the top back on.

Serch: I stack them according to size so that any adverse weight shifts don't dent the boxes. I now have over 300 pairs of unique, original, and well preserved grips. People try to battle me and I take out their whole collections with one pair!

Come Chantrell: Ten years down the line the box counts as much as the shoe. Plus, if you're gonna store 150 pairs of sneakers without boxes you're finished.

Fabel: I stuffed newspapers in suede shoes every day after I took them off. It'd keep them puffy so they wouldn't cave in. Then I'd wrap them in plastic and put them in the shoebox. Then I'd put the shoebox in plastic just in case there was ever a leak in the closet. It was my version of a ghetto incubator. I bust out my old pairs now when there's a reunion of old-timers. I do it more for the reaction from them because the new kids don't know that much about it.

Kurious: The best way to have it on ice is just to have mad new ones. Then there's no ice needed. You *are* the ice! Bobbito and Kirk Rodriguez had the illest collections. Bob had the originality crown, but Kirk had sheer numbers of fresh, always clean kicks. Even the stuff he would throw out looked brand new!

Schott Free: The illest collection besides Bobbito's would have to have been Raekwon the Chef's. You never knew what that motherfucker was going to wear.

Mike Drake: When Walter Berry went to St. John's, they seemed to be feeding him sneakers like three meals a day! Every time I saw him he had on a different pair.

Ahmad: In '85 playground legend "Master Rob" had a whole wall in his living room that was lined up with nothing else but sneaks from the floor to the ceiling. He was 6'1" and the pile was higher than he was! He'd brag, "These here I only wore once."

Serch: Sneaker collections shouldn't be sneakers on a pedestal. Each sneaker should have purpose and reason. I've worn every sneaker in my collection at least once. ■

Left: Johnny Snakeback Fever's
quiver in 1982.

Middle: A third of my quiver in 1991.

GERRY
cosby

HOURS:
MON. - FRI. 9:30 - 7:30
SAT. 9:30 - 6:00
SUN. 12:00 - 5:00
OPEN AFTER ALL
 &
HOME GAMES

When sneaker companies' sales agents present their catalogs to stores, it's up to the store to take a chance on ordering that oddball shoe or bugged out color. No store wants unsold product taking up retail or storage space, so most of them order the sureshots, i.e. the sneakers they know are popular and will move. Some stores in New York were popular because they did just that, sold the basic classics. But this book is about digging beyond that, and every couple of years a handful of stores would show forward vision and take chances on new brands, odd sizes, unusual colors, etc. Whether they took chances consistently or just for one season, we sniffed them out. Sneaker missions were one of the most exhilarating things that a connoisseur could experience. There was no home shopping on your computer. It was all word of mouth. We traveled borough to borough, walked for hours and got lost, braved getting vicked in unknown territory, and followed vague directions from strangers like, "yeah, I copped these at a store Uptown near Colonel Young, but I don't remember exactly where." They knew, they just wanted to keep down low spots secret so they could have the exclusive. But we found them, and the pay off was awesome if the store had some extra incredible doobiness, in our size of course. The following are some of the best stores between '70-'87 for finding rare gems and slept on butters. Unfortunately, and undeservedly, most of them have gone out of business. These stores need to remembered as the ones responsible for the whole limited edition craze that has made the sneaker industry so much profit. These were the stores who fed the original hunger of the sneaker connoisseur of New York and started it all. Years before Prohibit, Training Camp, and Ebay, there was Carlsen Imports, Gerry Cosby, and Jew Man's.

A Hunting We Will Go

Top Rank:

■ CARLSEN IMPORTS,
Broadway and Spring (now closed)

Brother Ray: Carlsen Import was the only spot that consistently had shit that was very, very different. I found out about it through word of mouth from other ballplayers. It wasn't even a store. You'd go up a freight elevator into this dusty showroom with sneakers all lined up. I don't even remember a cash register. It was a wholesaler, but it sold retail too.

Bobbito: Carlsen was on the third floor. Ray bought his first Nike Blazers, Ponys, Pumas, Patricks, and Batas all there. They were the importer and distributor for Adidas in the real early '70s, and then Pony, Tiger, and Nike in the mid '70s. Around '79 they stopped carrying Nikes, and I know they probably regret it to this day.

Johnny Snakeback Fever: It was the closest thing to an orgasm a preteen sneaker hound could experience. I recall the Dr. J poster in the window on the third floor that you could see walking down lower Broadway. It was like Mecca. I was nine years old, and would go with an older friend, whatever. I was taking trains on my own and my parents weren't telling me shit.

Jazzy Art: Not everyone knew. Now people speak of it in hushed tones, like, "Oh, you knew about Carlsen?" They always had squash sneakers on display, and hot joints tucked away.

Sake: Fuck yeah! Carlsen Imports was a mission spot. They always had the weird funky shit like Batas.

■ PECK AND CHASE,
Orchard St. off Delancey (now closed)

Jack Steinweis, former Puma worldwide President and salesman: Delancey was such a sales hub for us, and Peck and Chase was *the* store.

Lincoln Parker: If you wanted to be a fly brother, then you went to Delancey St. It was on the money. You could bargain for a decent price. That was the original head to toe hook up. It was ill.

Seth Rosenfeld: We called Delancey "D St.", but we never actually shopped on Delancey. It was always Orchard, but the train stop was Delancey so that's why we called it that. You had to go there with your boys because the area was infamous for stick ups. It was all cash business back then.

Storeowner on Orchard St. below Delancey (requested anonymity): Peck and Chase had three locations on Orchard St. just North of Delancey. All the Black and Latino kids would go there. The night of the blackout in '77 I was in my store with a twelve guage shotgun scared shit of all the looting, but you know what? None of the kids came South of Delancey, they broke all the storefront windows on the North side. That's where all the sneakers and leathers were!

Sake: All three Peck and Chase spots were flavor. If they didn't have your size at one store, they'd call up the block for you.

■ **SNEAKER FACTORY,**
Sterling Place, Brooklyn (now closed)

Jack Steinweis: The Sneaker Factory was the first store to ever carry strictly sneakers. They were so ahead of their time. The owner sold his own brand of sneakers called Newcons.

Sake: That was *the* spot for Pro-Keds, you could find them in every color there.

■ **PARAGON, 18th and Broadway**

In the '70s Paragon had a small sneaker wall on the first floor towards the back, and was (and still is) one of the best true sporting goods stores in all of New York. They've always carried the widest array of running, court, and basketball sneakers. It is one of the few independent stores left standing (outside of runner's shops) where the sales help will actually tell you how a shoe performs for the sport it was built for.

Honorable Mentions:

❑ **Broadway Shoe Center,**
103rd and Broadway (now closed)

The Broadway Shoe Center was ground zero for Upper West Side sneaker fiends in the '70s. They caught rek by being one of the few stores in all of New York to carry the extremely rare Adidas Americana circa '76. For carrying that shoe alone, they make this list.

❑ **Tom, Dick, and Harry's,**
105th and Third (now closed)

Tom, Dick, and Harry's had a few stores in New York, and I big this Spanish Harlem location up since it was the first place I purchased Pro-Keds.

Top Rank:

■ **GERRY COSBY'S, 32nd and 7th**

Jim Root, former buyer/floor manager at Gerry Cosby: We opened in 1937 and moved to the lobby of the Garden in '79.

Bobbito: Gerry Cosby's was the most important store for connoisseurs in the '80s until Jew Man's got hot.

Sake: Cosby's would have a dozen amazingly rare sneakers on shelves on the front wall as you walked in from the revolving doors.

Johnny Snakeback Fever: Cosby's was like a museum stop to see the Adidas Half Shells.

Jim Root: We would get a team order and put extra pairs out to see how the public would respond to different colors and styles. We noticed that people started coming in to check out our "museum pieces" as they called them. NBA players started coming to shop at our store. We'd exchange t-shirts for their extra pairs of unworn sneakers. And we'd put them out for sale because our customers wanted something unique. Then we started contacting the sneaker companies to sell us the customized sneakers they were making for colleges. They had extras that they weren't doing anything with. They'd have random selections and sizes left but we knew we could sell them. We had so many random different models we couldn't fit them all on display. We'd rotate them in and out as they sold from our back storage room.

Sake: The first time I discovered the back of Cosby's was when I bought Nike Blazers. The guy brought them out with the fat belly swoosh and "Lions" on the back. They were customized for Columbia University. The swoosh was the type of blue that you couldn't customize. It was too hot! I was with John and a light bulb went off inside of our heads. The clerk had tried to bring me out the plain Nike Blazers, and instead he brought me out the extraterrestrial shits. So we knew the Holy Grail was in the back of Cosby's.

The next time we went the clerk brought us back there. It was like magic. I saw this Adidas box, and I knew this was some extra shit. It said GRSUE-the abbreviation for green suede. I pulled them shits out and it was like, "Aaaaahhhhh!" I had found the Holy Grail-green suede Half Shell Adidas. The quest was over.

Johnny Snakeback Fever: They were too overpriced, but when Mark bought them I broke down and got the Nike Franchises with the Spartans customized on the back.

Sake: His Spartans were the hottest Franchises next to the Columbia black/light blue joints.

Ted Nitro: They had Dr. Js in white on green suede also, but didn't have my size. They would've looked like boats on my feet! When I went Uptown and told people, they said, "Ah, get out of here. You can't get those." Sure enough, I went back there the next day and they were gone. I couldn't believe they sold that quickly.

Jim Root: We stopped selling shoes after the Nike Air Jordans came out. It changed the industry. The Foot Lockers and other chains would get their shoes three months ahead of us smaller stores. It was very unfair. They made it impossible for us to compete.

■ **THE BACK OF MADISON SQUARE GARDEN, 33rd and Eighth**

Jazzy Art: My boy John Merz was *notorious* for asking players for sneakers! I would never ask them, not even for autographs.

Johnny Snakeback Fever: From '81-'84, Mark, Red Finimore, myself, and this homeless dude we named Homeboy we'd see at every game, would all go behind the Garden to the player's exit to ask every player for their sneakers.

Sake: "A Humming and Bumming We Will Go!" Red put me up on it. He's coaching at Michigan State now. The players would come out wearing their kicks over their shoulder. We would just ask them straight up, "You had a good game, why don't you hook me with your sneakers?"

Johnny Snakeback Fever: Homeboy would yell and stutter, "B-B-B-Buck Williams!"

Sake: One night the Knicks played the Celtics. Homeboy was all bummy and dirty, and stuttered, "D... D... D... Danny A... A... A... Ainge... give me your chooz." That motherfucker didn't give him shit.

Johnny Snakeback Fever: I went to 30 games a year because they had $3.50 per game student discounts. We followed these motherfuckers onto the bus. We were not letting them go. We used to ask them for practice jerseys, anything. Clinton Daily from the Bulls gave me suede Converse Pro Models. Isiah Thomas promised me sneakers, but he never came through. My friend Brian got Bill Cartwright's Nike Franchise. They were size 21, so they were useless. He had them hanging on his door for years.

Sake: Reggie Carter (RIP) hit me off with some feet. I was claiming St. John's and Riverside

Church, so he hit me off with some Bernard King Converse joints. They were doo doo!

Johnny Snakeback Fever: I'll never forget Reggie Carter because he walked me over to his Volvo on 34th St., opened up his trunk and gave me a fresh pair of Dr. Js. He wore an eleven and a half. I was wearing a thirteen and a half. I wore them for two practices and hell yeah I was in utter pain. Try running suicides in a pair that are two sizes small! My toes are still hurting!

■ **CARNESECCA-SARACHEK'S CIRCLE SPORTING GOODS, Flatbush and Bedford/Foster, Brooklyn (now closed)**

Jazzy Art: If you bought sneakers in Brooklyn and were in the know, then your main spot was Circle Sporting Goods. Former St. John's U. coach Lou Carnesecca and Red Sarachek owned it. This is back when St. John's was terrible, before the Big East Conference existed. My boy Roger McCready who played at Boston College would get hooked up for free with the flavor shit, and we would be like, "Where'd you get that color?" I guess when you're 6'9" with a game, people will do that. When you're 5'7" and 150 pounds like me, they want to see the money.

■ **THE TINTED WINDOW a.k.a. "THE BULLETPROOF WINDOW," 149th off the Grand Concourse, The Bronx (now closed)**

Ted Nitro: The "Tinted Window" was an import place where you could get sneakers nobody had.

Bobbito: They didn't have chairs for you to sit down. The salesman was behind a bulletproof window like in a ghetto liquor store. That was my spot for all the team color Dr. Js you couldn't get anywhere else.

Ted Nitro: It was like a prison when they gave you your belongings. The guy would be like, "What shoe you want, the right or left?" He'd only hand one side to you, and sometimes he *might've* let you try it on real quick, but only if you stood up to do it.

■ **SPIEGEL'S, Fulton St.**

Jazzy Art: I bought my rare Wilson Batas at Spiegels in the Wall St. area. They would get a lot of defects. Understand, defects made shits hot because it made you stand out. Sake: Speigel's was a favorite because they'd have new shit and old stock that was a little left field. I copped my rare leather toe cap Franchise there.

■ **THE AQUEDUCT FLEA MARKET, Far Rockaway, Queens**

Serch: Sneaker Steve's had two stores and one was in Fleaport which was the flea market on Rockaway Blvd. that was only open on Friday, Saturday, and Sunday. He'd have so many hot grips that I'd offer to help him pack up at 8 pm in the hopes that he'd put sneakers on the side for me since I never had enough ducats.

Bobbito: I heard through the grape that they had Nike Blazers there four years after they were out of production, so in '85 I took the hour long A train ride from Manhattan on a hunt. I came up empty. Someone must have gotten there before me, or maybe it was just a myth.

Honorable Mentions:

❏ **THE ARMY AND NAVY, 124th and Lexington (now closed)**

Ted Nitro: It was one of the few spots in the city to carry money green Shell toes.

❏ **THE ARMY AND NAVY, 149th and Third, The Bronx (now closed)**

Almost as potent as the "Bulletproof Window" down the block, and together they were a serious one, two punch on a sneaker mission to the Bronx.

❏ **CLARK'S, 42ND bet. 6th and 7th (now closed)**

The best store in the city for Chuck Taylors in low top flavors. The sneaker section was down in the basement, so even though it was on the Deuce, not a lot of people knew of it as a mission spot.

❏ **CAPITOL STORES, Ave. I and Nostrand (now closed)**

Capitol was one of the first stores in the city to carry New Balance basketball sneakers in '82-'83. That was gutsy in Brooklyn, considering that New Balance wasn't a popular brand outside of the runner's market, and wasn't even known for basketball. Props.

❏ **ROYALE'S, Van Cortland and Broadway and 90th and Broadway (now closed)**

Royale's lasted a millisecond on 90th circa '80-'81, but they were the spot to pick up Nikes in flavors when they were just on the come up.

Top Rank:

■ **JEW MAN'S, Southern Blvd, the Bronx**

Mike Drake: I heard about Jew Man's in high school, and I tried to find it five times and couldn't. I was hurt!

Ahmad: Jew Man's was off the Freeman stop on the 2/5 line. There were two Jew Man's. If the first store didn't have your size they'd just call down the block and in one second the man would have your shoes for you. Back in the day you'd get your summer job paycheck, get on the #11 bus cross-town, and cop your hot joints at Jew Man. It was a little old shack, but they had everything with flavor. They'd be like, "What you want, duke? You want to try this on, hah? No, no, that's wack, money, this is the butter right here!" The workers were all young Puerto Rican and Afro American brothers. The older cats that worked there all had pot bellies and they'd sit back and say, "That's my man, hook him up."

Ted Nitro: *The* spot up in the Bronx on Simpson St. was Jew Man's. I bought low top Converse Bernard Kings' with the wide suede toe cap in white on white there which were extremely rare. Those were one of my hottest pairs ever.

Lincoln Parker: Jew Man's was a 45 or 50 minute train ride from Manhattan and then an eight block walk. It wasn't even a store. It was more like a storefront that you'd walk into and there would be boxes of shit. My man would only let a few people in at a time, and they would sell shit no tax.

Andre Kyles: Saturdays and Thursdays was when Jew Man got their new shit in. The guy always told me that the earlier I got there the more likely they'd have my size. If they didn't have my size the trip wasn't worth it. Nobody wanted to make a trip from Queens for an hour with connecting trains for nothing so we would get up there when the store opened. When I found myself waking up at 9 am, especially on a Saturday, and getting on the train just for sneakers I realized I was an addict!

Prime Minister Pete Nice: I was a kid in a candy shop there. It was the Holy Grail for Air Force 1s when they were scarce.

■ BROADWAY SNEAKERS (NOW TRAINING CAMP), Broadway off Canal (now closed)

Udi: Broadway Sneakers started out as a variety store called The Boss Is Crazy. One day my father bought a case of roach motels and we sold them like wildfire. We were in Chinatown and didn't know they had roach problems! We brought in Pro Jogs sneakers which were a knock off of New Balance, and they too sold like crazy. We started carrying more sneakers, but we still carried roach motels! In '84 we really got behind the sneaker business and named the store Broadway Sneakers.

I was fourteen years old. We were buying 600 pairs of white on white Superstars. All the sales reps thought we were wholesaling. Our retail following was that strong. Adidas wouldn't want to sell us any colors so we made them ourselves. We'd buy special markers at Pearl Paint right up the block from us. Instead of having only one style in white, we had thirteen styles. We did them in Rasta colors and it blew up with all the heads from Flatbush.

Sales reps would come in and tell us, "This is what other stores are buying, and this is what you should buy." We'd wind up arguing with them! They'd tell us, "You can't buy that, nobody did," or "that's only for Florida." Bullshit! We had a reputation for having colors and brands first or that no one else had. We were able to form a loyal cult following of hunters who wanted new shit. We were the first to carry Etonic Trans Ams outside of runners' shops. We were early on Lotto, Diadora, Le Cox Sportif, and New Balance while the rest of the business was only thinking about the major brands. I knew what I loved and what the Bobbito types around me loved. I used my peers as my judge and jury.

Mike Drake: That's the first place I saw sneakers wrapped in Saran Wrap.

Dante: I'd sell fireworks on Canal St. and then spend all my money I'd just earned at Broadway Sneakers.

Bobbito: Broadway sneakers was always good for prime burgundies and forest greens.

■ FRANKEL'S, 40th St and 3rd Ave., Brooklyn

Sake: Frankel's was the incredible super come off spot. My grandfather (R.I.P) took me there in '87 and they had the original, original Nike Air Force Zeros. I'm not lying, I bought twelve pairs of them that day. They were $15 per pair on a close out. I spent my whole Big Apples Games check. I've gone back there, but that was a once in a million opportunity. I wish I still had a pair on ice right now, I'd split everybody's head open.

■ VET'S, 125th off St. Nicholas (now closed)

Mike Drake: Italian guys with fake hair on top ran Vet's. They never changed the décor in all the years they were open. They had choice colors and you didn't have to pay tax.

■ CENTRAL'S ARMY AND NAVY, Jamaica Ave., Queens

Andre Kyles: Central's was a local undercover spot because it wasn't fully a sneaker store. I'd always find the gem, the sneaker that nobody would be looking at, on the bottom shelf. All of the kids from Hollis or South Jamaica Queens would go to Jamaica Avenue to shop at Central's or Mr. Lee's. That was the Mecca in Queens to dig in the trenches.

Honorable Mentions:

❏ BOSS, 125th and Adam Clayton Powell Blvd. (now closed)

Boss lasted a flash of a second, but was the only store in the city (maybe the world) to carry high top Air Force 1s in white on olive in '89.

❏ OLYMPIA'S, Grand Concourse off Fordham Rd., The Bronx

Olympia's was always worth the trip to the Bronx.

❏ K.P. CONS, 125th off Amsterdam and 144th and Broadway

The sales help at K.P. Cons knew their customers well, and you had to love how they could barely speak English but they knew when to say, "Word up!" and, "Those joints are butters!"

❏ Choi's, 103rd and Broadway

Once Choi's got up to speed with Air Force 1s in '88, there was no more need to travel up to Jew Man's. ■

The old Army & Navy on 124th and Lexington, which is now closed.

ALWAYS
ETTER
HEAPER
ARMY
NIKE
adidas
PUMA
Sporting
Goods
Lee Jeans
Jackets

When cats started getting bumped for their feets en masse in the early '80s, it wasn't just about stick up kids not being able to afford new sneakers themselves. It was more also a sign of the rarified status that sneakers had attained. The thing about hip hop back in the day was that it wasn't easy to stay dipped without getting tested. If you wore your hat backwards, someone was going to regulate you to see if you were a real hardrock or not. Popular sneakers were being taken right off people's feet, and the culprits were keeping them for themselves (or their cousin who wore the right size). The easiest way to avoid drama was to wear some slept on butters or a brand that was so rare it'd go right over a stick up kids head. Regardless, the season of the vick changed everyone's comfort zone about wearing their sneakers out the house. You could put all the effort into finding dope sneakers, keeping them clean, painting them, only to lose them in a gut-wrenching infinite second.

"Pee Wee" Kirkland: Stick up kids wouldn't even go after someone else's sneakers in the '50s and '60s. Sneakers didn't represent what they did when leather models started coming out in the '70s.

John Snakeback Fever: My boy Clinton was on Fulton St. and he got his Adidas stolen off his feet. He had to walk home in his socks. *In the winter*. A sneaker was like the coveted sheepskin coat. I lived in constant fear. The sucker image of going home in your socks stuck with me. All of a sudden from '79 to '81 people were getting their shoes robbed left and right.

Bobbito: Whenever I'd travel to Bed Stuy, Harlem, the Boogie Down, or L.E.S., I'd make sure not to wear fresh out the box sneakers. I didn't want to have on kicks that were too dogged up either because then you looked like a herb and they'd really fuck with you. So I had to put a lot of thought into choosing sneakers that were going to be comfortable to play in, stylish enough to look cool, and worn enough to avoid getting burped.

Jazzy Art: In Brooklyn, especially, it was common for a kid to sit next to you with his crew on the train and look at your shit. If your shit was butter, he'd then size your shit up next to his. So you either had to punch the brother in his grill or just jet. It got so bad in Brooklyn they was robbing kids for their sneakers then killing them. Kids were getting *killed* for their *sneakers*.

Scotch: I vicked a pair of Jabbars at Modell's the day they hit Fulton St., and all I wanted to do was floss them. There were these two Puerto Rican kids from Gowanus. Wyckoff Projects and Gowanus Projects were separated by one block, and I lived smack in the middle of both of them. I knew one of them real well from school. I didn't trust him though. They were talking to me and my radar went up. I notice his man is creeping around behind me and he threw the yoke on me. He was a real tall kid, so he was able to lift me up in the air. The other cat pulled the kicks off, which wasn't hard cuz we didn't tie anything, so they would just flop off your feet. They snatched them and jetted. I went back in the house and put on some raggedy Clydes that I was using like house slippers with the heel flattened. I was hurt. I rounded up about five kids and we ran over to Gowanus. Luckily, the two kids were arguing over who was gonna get to rock my sneakers. They realized their dilemma: they had two sneakers and four feet. They were no longer a unified crew by the time we got there. We quickly overpowered them and got my shits back. And of course, after three days they were dusty and scuffed so I no longer gave a shit about them, but I was willing to risk my life to walk into Gowanus Projects, which was basically enemy territory, to get them back. So if that ain't an addict, I don't know what is.

Ted Lake: You would have some grimy characters in the Bronx looking for a quick vick. This guy came up to me once and said, "Yo, what size are those in the box?" I thought to myself, "If I got his size he might try to rob me." I glanced at his feet, and gave him a size I knew wouldn't fit him. "Yeah man, these are size 13 and a half." And he said, "Oh word? Ai-ight."

Ahmad: I bought high top Air Force 1s in white on black at K.P. Cons on 125th. I had been everywhere in the Bronx, Brooklyn, and Queens and couldn't find them. I went there on a payday and paid $80 for a pair of $65 joints because I was fiending. I didn't even make it to the train station. I got burped right across the street from Grant Projects! Money walked up to me and brushed my left shoulder. I ain't no punk. I looked at him and gave him the grid like, "Back up off me." And then on the right side another kid walked up on me and stuck it in my side and said, "Yo, give me the bag." Snatched my bag and ran up into the projects. I took off after them. I got four steps into the projects and thought, what the hell is wrong with me? I can't chase these cats. I turned around and walked to the train station burped and pissed. I wanted those sneakers so bad I almost walked back to K.P. Cons and bought another pair! You know what I'm saying!

Seth Rosenfeld: I went shopping with my sister once on Delancey in '77. I had just gotten kicked in my balls, so I had to walk with my legs wide apart. I had ten bags of weed and $150 worth of Sassoon jeans and Pumas. I was a vick waiting to happen.

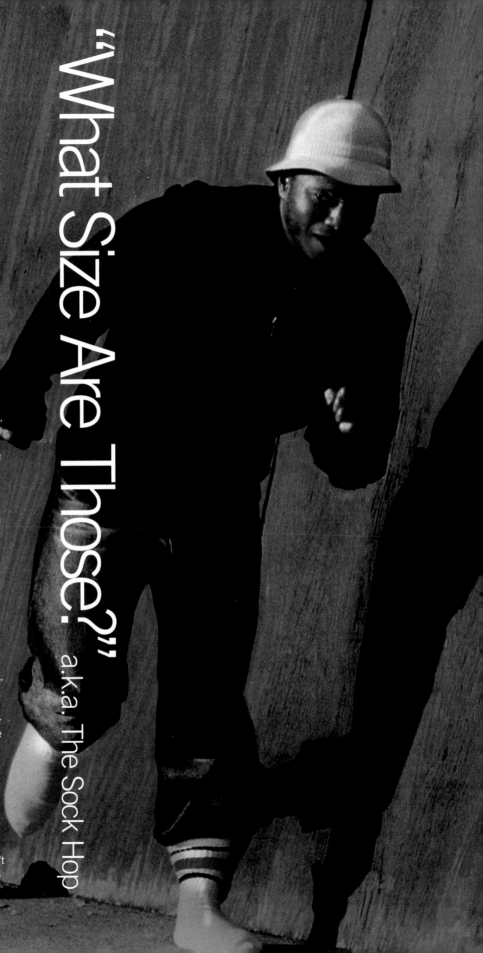

These six kids had been on the train with us since Delancey and my senses went off. I couldn't run because of my nutsack and my sister was only eleven, plus we had mad shopping bags. Basically I was done. They told us to follow them up the street when we exited on 96th. I was trying to stall and then one of the kids pulls out a meat cleaver and says, "Give us your shit!" I pleaded with them to at least let my sister go. They did and when she walked away I saw a cop car at the stoplight. When I screamed to her, "Get the cops!" the dude took a swing with the cleaver, missed, and then jetted. The cops wanted to chase them, but I still had ten bags of weed of me! I told them my sister was experiencing mental trauma and that we just needed to go home.

Dante: Cats tested me for my shits when I was thirteen. I told them, "Yo, you take my sneakers, you might bust my ass, but my moms is really gonna bust my ass." Cats started laughing, and I left. My moms taught first grade to most everyone around the way, so I got a little leeway.

Prime Minister Pete Nice: This kid tried to rob my bike and my sneakers. I knew this other kid named Wubbs who was just the man. So, I said, "Man, you try to take these and I'll get Wubbs after you." The kid was like, "Wubbs, that's my fucking brother!" So, the next thing you know, I'm giving the kid a pound and he's letting me go.

Serch: I had Puma Super Baskets that were bananas rare. Coming home from school one day, this kid was like, "Yo, money, come here. What size are those?" So I was like, "C'mon man, we go to school together." "Fuck all that. What size are those?" "Fuck it, they're your size." Thump, thump and we were scrapping. I caught a bad one but he let me keep my sneakers. It was worth it. I had them for almost two and a half years.

Schott Free: I knew these young kids around my way who had copped a little gun. They told me to run my Worthys. I thought, "Be smart and give 'em up, cuz they wildin' out." At the same time I figured, "These little motherfuckers? Fuck that!" For a split I thought, "Damn, I'm about to die over a pair of sneakers." Luckily, they said, "Psyche, we were testing you."

The Season of the Vamp: Introducing The Boosters

The desire to illegally obtain hot joints wasn't just the domain of stick ups kids, hardrocks,

"What Size Are Those?" a.k.a. The Sock Hop

or cats that were broke. The desire simply stemmed from the basic human emotion of always wanting what you don't have. My generation's fix to have ill sneakers was sometimes satisfied by boosting someone's personals, boosting from a store, or boosting from a school. And if you were a fiend and none of these were ever attempted, then admittedly they were often schemed on with no follow through. I do not in any way condone sneaker burglary, and am not attempting here to glorify it. I am only trying to show the lengths that people would go to get sneakers to illustrate how intense this time period was for sneaker afiicionados.

Stomp

Fabel: I don't want to incriminate myself! Someone is gonna be like, "You're the one who took my Pro-Keds!" Well, for any of you that I might have vicked that're reading this, I thank God that those days are over. Our motto was, "If you like it, take it." We weren't rich. We were poor kids facing a whole bunch of social ills. We would walk up, stand next to the person, and put our shoe next to theirs to see if it was the right size. A lot of times the guy wouldn't want to get stomped out, so he'd just say, "Ai-ight, you got it." The next thing you know, you see someone with socks sitting in the last seat of the train with his head down crying. That was on the regular back then. It was the climate of the time.

Soggy Socks

Crazy Legs: Most of the members of Rock Steady used to go on vicking sprees as the Yoke City Mob. We'd roll twenty deep and yoke people up for their shit, hit them over the head with nunchucks. Crazy shit! One time I stuck up this Puerto Rican kid in Central Park. I sat next to him on the park bench, sized up his Puma Baskets, then told him to run 'em. They fit me perfectly. Then I told him to walk into the lake with his socks on! We were walking away and he screamed out, *"Pero, dame mis zapatos!"* We got over the hill and saw 50 Guardian Angels walking our way so we ran!

All About the Germans

Scotch: In the early '80s I ran with a little clique of strong arm stick up kids. We used to hang out in a park that separated Myrtle Ave from Brooklyn Heights. It no longer exists. We would wait there for kids from Brooklyn Heights who would creep through there to cop their weed. We would yoke 'em up for their smoke, and sneakers were com-

ing off. If they were cleaner than mine, it was on. You'd find someone in the clique who'd fit them! The vickees weren't wearing any slouch shoes. They usually had Dassler brother German technology on their feet. I thought anything made in the U.S. was garbage, like McDonalds and Budweiser. If you can get something imported, it's just that much flyer. That winter we made a lot of cats walk home barefoot.

Catholic Guilt

Bobbito: Lincoln Parker gave me canvas Dr. Js. He had worn them out so crazy on the ball of the foot that they had a hole that looked like a bullet shot through them. I went to Macy's with them on, and went to the fifth floor where they sold sneakers. They had the Nike Equators on a table with a bunch of other sneakers that were on sale. I put them on and I put the dilapidated Dr. Js back on the table where the Equators were. This was the only time I ever vicked a pair of sneakers. My heart was pumping so fast. As I approached the exit I saw a security guard talking on his walkie-talkie and looking at me. All I could think was, "Fuck!" He walked right past me and I walked out of Macy's with brand spanking grips. I jetted across 34th St. in a sprint to the 2/3 train. I got off on 96th St. and went straight to Holy Name Church and prayed for forgiveness for stealing a pair of sneakers that I still had on. Even worse was that I left Lincoln's old shits on the table at Macy's as if they were for sale. Some kid probably picked them up and said, "Mom, I want these," without even looking at the bottoms.

"Can I See Your Receipt, Please"

"Pee Wee" Kirkland: When I'd go to Paragon's in my youth, I'd steal all the time. You paid for your sneakers right by the entrance. They didn't have detectors back then, so often I'd walk out with a pair of Converse right past the cashier. When there was a guard, one of the tricks we used was to pay for a pair, and then come back inside with the receipt. Then different people would walk back outside, fifteen different times, with the same receipt! Same size, same receipt. They had sales people but they only helped you if you didn't know your size. The sneakers were stacked in boxes where you could see the sizes, so you could just pick them up yourself and then be out.

Para-gone

Dante: My man's older brother worked at Paragon and he would put expensive sneakers for us in the irregular bin. You could buy two irregulars out the bin for $10! I got Nike Franchises and Pony McAdoos. I was only twelve and my moms questioned how I could afford them. I told her, "Don't worry about it."

The Pinball Wizard Meets the Garden Hoe (Sneakers weren't always vicked, sometimes they were schemed away)

Johnny Snakeback Fever: Blitz a.k.a. "Z" loved his Nike Franchises so much he customized the stripe to a lavender/sky blue. We were competing for gear by playing pinball at Buzzarama on Church Ave.

Sake: I thought Z's Franchises looked hot. Whatever he bought looked good on him because he had the prototype foot. I had to figure out a way to scam them so I suggested we up the stakes.

Johnny Snakeback Fever: Z and Mark went head to head and Z put up his Franchises. He lost the pinball match. We walked Z home . . .

Sake: . . . and he got them out the super duper special drawer.

Jazzy Art: You know how you got a sock drawer, an underwear drawer, the shit where you stick your porno mags underneath drawer. My man cleared out a special drawer in his bureau solely for his sneakers!

Sake: He kept them in his drawer in its original Nike box, *maybe* he kept some loot in the drawer but that's it. Z would be taking them shits out the drawer slowly and methodically, making sure everything was correct. It was a shrine to his Nikes.

Jazzy Art: I ain't gonna lie, he put a towel inside the drawer under the box! It wasn't velvet, but that was the image he was trying to get.

Johnny Snakeback Fever: When he had to give them up to Mark, Z was practically in tears. He said, "Yo, Mark, I can't believe you're taking them from me."

Sake: I told him, "You lost, give up them feets."

Johnny Snakeback Fever: Arthur was laughing. He was dying. The next day we were playing cards for gear at Mark's house. Z came over and wanted to win them back. Mark's father called from the backyard and said, "Marcus!" He walked in the room with tennis shorts on and a dress shirt, and Z's Franchise!

Sake: They looked bananas with the shape of my foot, so I gave them to my dad. He has feet that go up in the front like a motorboat. The Franchises looked like crazy magic carpet shoes on him. With my dad mowing the lawn in them, getting them all green, it was over!

Johnny Snakeback Fever: We were all stunned, as it crystallized that Mark's father was wearing them to garden. The sneaker was taken so far out of its intended sphere that it was truly an insult. They were in a universe they never expected to be in. That was a funny moment, but it was sad too. I believe Z started to cry.

Nice Rack

Jazzy Art: It was an unwritten rule, you never robbed your friends, but everything else was fair game. I was always down for the jack move. I worked at a store that we called The Rack. The owner was a cheap motherfucker. I did have some loyalty to him though, but then he gave me a $5 Christmas bonus in a card. After that I said, "It's on!" He got a deal with New Balance when they started making basketball sneakers. They were hot, and nobody had 'em. He was one of the few distributors for New Balance basketball sneakers on the East Coast.

A lot of kids got fired before me for getting caught boosting. They'd throw sneakers in the garbage, then try to get them out after work. Mark would come in and I would let him steal pants cuz he was constantly growing. He'd ask, "Yo, what's up with the sneakers?" I'd say, "Don't worry. We gonna do this shit right cuz this clown is playing me." I used to *work*, and he gave me a crab $5 Christmas bonus. I was gonna give it back to him, but then he would have known I was vexed. The minute I got the five, I said, "All right, this five times a thousand. That's how much I'm gonna get. Cuz that's how you played me."

Mark had his mother's Reliant K-car, which we called the Cop Car. I said, "Drive by the job, park on the side, and look in the alley." That morning I packed a New Balance duffel bag's worth of their sneakers in Mark's size and my own. I also packed in underwear and about every pair of Adidas socks we had in the store! That bag weighed about 40 pounds! Mark parked in the alley, so I opened the back door. There was a twelve foot high fence, and I flung the bag over it. Mark's looking at me, and I'm like, "Get the fucking bag!" So he gets it, puts it in the trunk, and he's ready to drive off. I said, "Nah, wait, we

gonna do more, it's payday." After the third bag, my arms got tired cuz those shits were heavy! I loaded up the fourth bag with Adidas Stan Smiths, and tried to throw it over the fence, but it got caught on the top! The bag was sitting there, and the owner is walking around inside the store. I was the only one that worked in the sneaker section, and I got this big New Balance duffel bag full of shit hanging on the fence.

Sake: I couldn't do shit cuz I was the worst fence climbing motherfucker there ever was. I was too tall.

Jazzy Art: So I came back all sweaty and told my co-worker the deal. He goes, "Oh, shit! You robbing out the back? Let me pack up some shit now too." I screamed, "Yo, you don't understand! I got a bag full of shit hanging on the fence! If the owner sees this, we all getting fired." He's like, "Damn, I'm on parole; I can't get fired." I said, "I'm gonna climb up the fence and unhook that shit, just watch my back." I fucking climbed up the fence and unhooked the bag. Now I'm holding a 40 pound bag in my hand, hanging on to the fence, twelve feet above the ground, and Mark's going, "Throw the bag over!" I couldn't generate enough force though. Finally I did, and he was like, "Are we doing any more?" I said, "Nah, but come back tomorrow." The owner never really caught on, cuz I was in charge of the inventory, and according to me New Balance was selling like crazy!

Turk: Mark and Art were so bold that it was comical. Our motto was, "If it ain't nailed down its ours!"

Nice Socks You Have There

Sake: Vicking and racking goes back to the relationship between graffiti and sneakers. Me and Turk used to be able to rack anywhere. I'd lift ten cans of paint with my Riverside Church gym bag and sling it over my shoulder and be out of the store in no time. Me and Turk were two clean cut, college looking white kids so they never suspected us. As I got older I didn't want to steal from my favorite sneaker stores and burn out my spots, so we went on missions. We'd make the trip out to Marshall's in Long Island just to vick. I would walk in with socks and walk out with low top Adidas Top Tens in red on white.

Johnny Snakeback Fever: From '84 to '87 it was open season on Marshall's. Mark used to walk in with no shoes on. Dead up! He would walk to the back of the store in his stocking feet, find a nice pair of sneakers, put them on, rip their tag off, and he'd walk right out of there. He'd do this consistently. It was amazing.

Home Court Disadvantage

Jazzy Art: I would check the other lockers on away games to see what I could vick when I played for Fort Hamilton H.S. By junior year I was getting more playing time, so the coach trusted me to open up our gym during first period. The motherfucker was probably hanging out in his office drinking, so I had all these keys. He'd say, "Go open up the gym, I'll be up there in a minute." On the way to the gym was the storage room for all the team sports. They kept like $1,000 worth of M&M's for the teams to sell in there. So I took mad boxes of M&M's and I stuck 'em in my varsity locker. When our team Dr. Js came in, I vicked a couple. He called the company up. He didn't think anybody was stealing because he had the key, there was nothing ever missing up there. But I really didn't like Dr. Js much, so I just traded 'em off.

Turk: No matter where I went or played I was constantly scheming on dudes' gear, watching and observing like a hawk on a mouse as to where they'd laid down their shit and when the time was right to swoop down for the kill. The shit was like animal kingdom only the gear was the prey. I don't know what it was but stealing gear and spray paint was the ultimate high.

Stooping too low

Dante Ross: This one cat in my neighborhood used to talk a lot. Cats got sick of him and took his sneakers and *all* his shit and made him walk home in his bathing suit. I was never with that though. If my moms caught me doing that shit, I'd be dead. Maybe a marker or pen, but stealing sneakers is stooping too low. ■

Skippies and Rejects

"Skippies, they make your feet feel fine, skippies, they cost a $1.99!"

I don't care what you say—if you were born before '80 then you wore skippies as a kid! My parents' generation sewed sneakers together, wearing them into the ground, and they made sure they reminded us of that fact when we came of age in our quest to get brand name sneakers. It wasn't until the '80s that the major brands released sneakers in infant and child sizes. So essentially anyone growing up during the '60s or '70s—whether they were of means or not—wore skippies through their early childhood. That said, it's certainly not a blemish on your past record. But the blame begins to accumulate if you were ten or eleven years old and still wearing skippies, or, even worse, if you were of high school age and showed bad judgement in choosing skippies you thought were going to pass. Make no mistake: Skippies weren't just poorly made bargain price shoes. Oh no! The title "skippies" applies to any sneaker—regardless of brand—that was poorly made, or simply looked really cacahuetes. Here are some of the worst of the worst.

Johnny Snakeback Fever: When I buy a shoe it's almost like I'm drunk. Afterwards I'm walking down the street thinking, "Yeah, I'm rocking shit," but then I'd look down and say, "Oh shit, these are wack!"

Turk: It's funny how fake Ponys had an upside down arch. The funniest shits I saw were these fake Ellesse grips on some jackass in the village. He must have bought them on 14th St. from the same guy that sold VCRs in a box. Then when you got home inside is a fucking brick wrapped up in newspapers!

As this 1978 photo proves, it was OK to wear skippies around pigeon coops, just in case one of the birds had an accident on your kicks.

The worst sneakers to grace New York sneaker stores' wall space

The '70s
■ **Keds Decks**

Fabel: The nastiest sneakers I had were the stupid white Keds skippies. They looked like nurse shoes. In Spanish Harlem girls would wear Keds all the time and fuck around with click-clacks.

■ **Pro Specs, suede low top in white on green, white on blue, white on tobacco**

Frosty Freeze: They stole my pair at the 110th St. Pool. I put them down for a second cuz all the lockers were taken. Why would someone steal Pro Specs?

Ted Nitro: The Specs were definitely the worst. They were my first pair of sneakers. My mother purchased them and I told her, "Mom, I rather have Pro-Keds." She wasn't trying to buy me anything expensive. She was like, "You're a little kid, these are good enough for you."

Andre Kyles: Pro Specs were the supermarket specials.

■ **Pro Players**

Maddie Fontanez, old school Bronx hip hop head: I used to braid hair for money to buy sneakers because the only time we got kicks was back to school, Christmas, and Easter. Three times a year and that was it. Kids are spoiled now getting kicks every three weeks. I made $20 once on a braid and took that dough straight to Buster Brown to buy some Pro Players. That's all I could afford.

Fabel: Brothers would say, "You big imitation-Puma wearing!"

■ Fayva Olympians

Johnny Snakeback Fever: You could have flavor shit on but a pair of Fayva Olympians with it just negated everything. If your gear was plus ten in your favor, then the Fayva Olympians turned it around to a negative ten. You might as well walked out with nothing on! They were the kind of shoes that the Mafia put on people before throwing them in a river! They were so heavy.

■ Jox by Thom McAnn

Lincoln Parker: Jox were trying to knock off Asics. They were the utter wack. Nuts. Never.

Dante: My man wore Jox once and we giggled on him for *months*.

■ Trax and Fast Trax

Sake: Fast Trax were the ultimate fake Adidas of all time, and they didn't even have a shell toe. Skippiados.

■ John Havlicek

Dante: They were crazy bone imitation Adidas with four stripes. My man had a pair and we used to snap on him and say, "Just cut off one of the stripes and you can say you have Adidas on!"

Brother Ray: I wore them to the park for a week and totally ripped them to shreds! The worst pair of sneakers I ever had.

■ Champion

Fabel: I don't know if they were the same company as Champion hoodies, but in '70 there was a brand called Champions. My mom called them Championes and then Spanish speaking mothers, grandmothers, and aunts started calling every sneaker Championes. Old-timers are gonna know. *Championes!*

■ Stadia by Kinney

Pro Players and Fayva Olympians should have had legislation preventing their manufacture, but as bad as they were you'd still see kids wearing them. Stadia were so scud that you wouldn't even see the worst skippie-wearing mug wearing them.

■ Mach 5

Anthony Alonso a.k.a. "Nymflow 9": Those were sneakers for toys!

The '80s

■ '85 Nike Air Jordan 1

Jordan may well be the best ballplayer in history by far, but that doesn't excuse his first signature shoe from criticism. Put it in perspective: the Jordan 1 came out after the Air Force 1 and it just didn't compare. The Air Force 1 was the standard, but most people in '85-'86 outside of the connoisseur circle weren't up on them. The Dunk came out right around the same time as the Jordan 1, and the Dunk's design simplicity, sleekness and colorways were far superior. But the Dunk was slept on at first too. The worst thing about the Jordan was the wing logo on the high top. Neither fresh nor subtle. Magnify that by every herb in the world who wore these, and you have one of the worst signature shoes from the glory period of sneaker design.

Jazzy Art: The first time I saw black/red Jordans in '85 that went straight back to the Columbia Lions' '81 Franchise. I never bought Jordans. I just thought they was too out there. I said, "The guy who's designing Nike right now must be on crack!"

Johnny Snakeback Fever: I stopped sneaker collecting in '86 when Air Jordans came out. They were the ugliest sneakers I had ever seen. When he kept coming out with these ridiculous looking sneakers that looked like ballet shoes, the whole thing made me sick.

Kurious: The first Jordans got too overexposed. Everyone had them. I never got them.

■ Lotto

Lotto is an Italian company. I always looked at them as poorly made "boe boes" as they said in Philly, especially when they came out with the knock off Converse Pro Stars.

Fabel: Wiggles and I went to Europe to perform with The Magnificent Force, and Wiggles came back with a pair of Lottos. He tried talking me into buying a pair, but I wasn't really feeling them. When I saw how people were sweating him, I got a pair the next time we went. Then they hit like wildfire.

Scotch: I thought they were mad cornball but kids were somehow making them work.

Ted Nitro: The Lotto shoes were terrible, just terrible.

Johnny Snakeback Fever: Why did people like those sneakers? Weren't Lottos women's sneakers?

Ahmad: I hated them "change-your-color" shits that Lotto made. Fucking hated them!

Steve Brock: They had a little triangle that came in a bag of fifty colors that you could pop in and out. That brought everything to a different level in terms of customization. The industry got a little ridiculous with the sheer amount of foolishness they were making.

■ Patrick Ewing

After a successful short stint with a signature shoe with Adidas, Pat ventured out in '89 with his own brand. Some kids tried their best to finesse them, but they just couldn't be pulled off as being hype.

Johnny Snakeback Fever: I tried those on and they were Frankenstein shoes. When you put those on, bolts almost spontaneously popped out of your neck!

Roos

Clyde Drexler of the Portland TrailBlazers wore Roos one season. It was the equivalent of a top Indy 5000 race car driver riding a unicycle with a flat tire. What was he thinking? Clyde never won a NBA Championship. Is that a coincedence?

Prof. Will Strickland: They were the worst shoes ever.

Wilson

Somehow Wilson got Trent Tucker of the Knicks to wear their sneakers one season. You couldn't have tempted me with a date with Jane Kennedy and Pam Grier to get me to wear those. Trent should've gotten a technical foul called on him at the beginning of every game he wore them.

NBA's

Ted Nitro: In the '70s NBA's were fake canvas Cons. Terrible.

Dante: Later they made imitation Adidas with four stripes. My man bought them for $5 at a department store that was going out of business. He was on mad welfare. His moms bought all his six brothers NBA's. My man Benji could snap, and when he saw them he said NBA stood for "Nothing But Ass!" I'll never forget that snap! We called that kid and his brothers Nothing But Ass for years.

Balloons

Dante: These sneakers had balloons on them, and were fake Reeboks. I know about them because I dated a lot of Spanish girls who were broke!

Steve Brock: Sears put out Balloons. I remember seeing some dope girls rocking Balloons and I would just lose interest!

Troop

"For any rapper, who attempts to wear Troop, and step in my path, I'm willing as an A-1 General"
—*Kool Keith of the Ultramagnetic MCs "Give the Drummer Some" Next Plateau Records 1987*

Andre Kyles: The Troops were hideous.

Bobbito: They were built horribly.

Udi: Maybe for you guys, because you're connoisseurs and athletes, they were wack, but Troop mattered a lot. A small Korean guy started Troop and woke up the whole sneaker industry. They were always in denial that millions of sneakers were bought in the inner cities. They always wanted to stay sport specific, like their shoes were only for runners. Bullshit! Troop was the first brand that let these big five of the sneaker industry realize either you address this inner city business or someone else will. They were the first company to identify with hip hop culture. Stetsasonic wore them and their spokesperson at that time was a very young and exuberant L.L. Cool J. In the business sector of the footwear industry at that time, Troop was critical.

Carlsens

Carlsen Imports had a pair of imitation Adidas with four stripes. One day my former radio partner DJ Stretch Armstrong came back from Carlsens all happy thinking he had come off with some ill suede Adidas. When he showed them to me, of all people, I laughed so hard I remember feeling bad afterwards. He fell asleep and I put them in a salad bowl and hid them in his refrigerator!

Johnny Snakeback Fever: My high school team was given Carlsens. I saw the four stripes and all I could vision was putting a fifth stripe across the four to make a five like when you're counting. It was the biggest sign of shame to rock those.

Zx 1200

Anthony Alonso a.k.a. "Nymflow 9": They were the never to be forgotten classic skippies straight from the Indian discount store, with styro-foam soles!

Wildcats

Anthony Alonso a.k.a. "Nymflow 9": I'm embarrassed to admit that I know about so many skippies, but these were top five worst of all time.

Spalding

Kurious: The only shoes they ever had that mattered were the Clydes. Besides that they were some real backyard, fake rims, falling down sneakers. I'd only wear them if I was fighting!

Dante: The logo with the diamond in the circle was bananas. They should've stuck with the three wings logo.

Reebok Pumps, leather high top in black with white/red accent, white with blue accent

Sake: The '87 Pumps were an offense to mankind. They were stupid and ugly.

Ted Nitro: The Reebok Pumps were overrated. Everyone was so souped up like, "Oh the Pump." I thought they were corny.

■ Nike Air Pressure

Jazzy Art: After Reebok came out with the Pump, Nike came out with their own version in '89 called the Air Pressure. They were so wack and crazy ugly. No one really remembers them and I'm sure Nike wants to keep it like that!

Dante: I never liked them. They looked like when you pressed the shoe you were going to float away!

■ Avia 830

Ted Nitro: I should have bought Avias when they first came out and Clyde Drexler was wearing them, but I bought a couple of terrible Avias when they were on their way out. They were just disgusting. Bad move.

Sake: The Clyde Drexler Avias were hot for a minute but then I saw Clyde Drexler play in them. He did one of those right handed swooping moves, where he dribbled the whole time with his right hand and did a finger roll with his right hand. After that them shits were out. I could never think they were fly again.

Prof. Will Strickland: Avias were the biggest violations to me.

■ Bally

Kurious: Ballys were the worst of all time.

Bobbito: Brooklyn heads thought they were fresh and looked cool in them, but I could never fuck with them either. Like Dougie Fresh said to Slick Rick when Rick told him to put his Ballys on, " . . . the shoes always hurt my corns!"

■ Fila
Ahmad: Filas were always wack. I don't care if Brooklyn repped them hard, they had poor construction and were skippies to me.

■ Converse Jack Purcell
Ahmad: I swore that if I could freak Purcells, cats would get up on them. But no matter where I wore them I would get laughed at. I thought they were dope. I wore them to Philly, Boston, Virginia, and New York. Heads were like, "No!" I can look at a sneaker and say it's hot. Because I'm confident, I can rock it and cats would be on it. It didn't work with those. Not at all. Cats were calling them clown shoes, bobo toes, saying, "What's that Hoop?"

■ Timberland
Serch: Timberland started making sneakers in '86 and I don't give a fuck how hot their boots are, their sneakers were the worst. They should burn the tree on their logo for making them.

The '90s

■ Xanthus
Xavier McDaniel had the hot Spot-bilt signatures, but then he bugged out and put these out. Pat Ewing should have warned his former teammate about these types of bad moves.

Sake: Oh, Xanthas. Fucking horrible!

■ British Knights
Turk: The BKs Derrick Coleman wore were ridiculous. His sneaker contract should be placed in the Smithsonian right next to Daniel Boone's musket!

Kurious: It's not even worth mentioning them. I don't even want to give them publicity.

Prof. Will Strickland: I would never wear British Knights. They were a fucking coon shoe. They probably said, "Let's put some baubles and doo-dads and lights on this shit, and sell it to black folk." I'm serious. Fucking British Knights were garbage!

■ L.A. Gear
When I saw Karl Malone wearing L.A. Gear I knew from that point on he would never win a NBA championship.

Johnny Snakeback Fever: Clown shoes. ■

Top left: We couldn't give our coach any love for wearing Jox by Thom McAnn. Plus he had on the huggies!

Top right: My parents could afford to get me a new bike, but they fronted on getting my feet out of skippies.

...TO YOUR DEALER FEATURING:
FICIAL NBA BASKETBALL SHOES

$ 1.99
SALE
$ 1.99

LL.COOL.J

PRO EDITION

TROOP

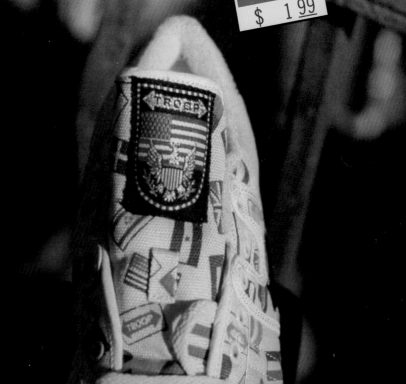

TROOP

Don't be fooled by imitations! adidas is the original 3-stripe shoe. You may see other shoes with three stripes that appear similar in construction. adidas has pioneered all important developments and advances in sports footwear. The highest quality is built into each and every adidas shoe and this cannot be imitated. Look for the 3 stripes, the distinctive heel patch and the word "adidas".

Converse makes 'em, but Sears gives 'em soul.

padded comfort all-around

thick, tough rubber soles

extra heavy weave canvas for long wear

full cushion insoles

The Winner

★ BUILT BY ★ converse JUST FOR

At most larger Sears stores and catalog.
©Sears, Roebuck and Co., 1977

Sears
AT THE SHOE PLACE

Maroon and Light Blue join the Winner team

Introducing Trax«« ...Very Basic...
Very Competitive Footwear.

Nobody ever won anything because of the labels
on his shoes. Winning takes basics…basics like
practice, sweat, effort, desire…in short, the
fundamentals. That's why Trax are your best bet when it comes to
athletic shoes. They're built solid. They offer the support,
comfort and durability you get with
expensive shoes…but Trax give you these basic features
for under fifteen dollars. Whatever your age,
whatever your game…from men's hurdles to women's doubles
…Trax are priced to beat the competition.

$7.97

$9.97

Sold exclusively at

Kmart
The Saving Place

S. S. Kresge Company ⓚ Troy, Michigan 48084

I don't care what these ads say,
skippies are skippies. And you
wouldn't want to be caught at an
ant funeral wearing any of these.

225

The Cardinal Sin of New York City sneaker culture was wearing skippies, but sometimes people of limited economic means simply didn't have a choice. However, someone wearing the most expensive sneakers could look 80,000 times worse than a brother who knew how to wear his skippies. There were circumscribed behavior patterns within our sneaker madness, and those who knew the secret codes were down by law, and those who didn't got screamed on. The following are some of the commandments of sneaker connoisseurs. Most of these still hold true today, but some are specific to the pre-'87 golden era.

Prof. Will Strickland: Outright biting someone's kicks and then rocking them the same exact way is wack.

Lincoln Parker: Never wear your new shit to a party because brothers will step on your shit. Never wear your joints in a vacant lot because of all the dog shit. Never buy white sneakers in the wintertime. Never mix and match sneaker brands.

Dante: Nike sneakers with Adidas sweats looked retarded because the sweats had three stripes on the side. Polo sweats with Nike could pass because Polo wasn't making sneakers like that. I always hated cats wearing Hoya sneakers with a Knicks jersey. That's a no-no.

Sake: Thou shalt not lace your sneakers so tight that the sides of the uppers touch together. That shit made me want to vomit.

Johnny Snakeback Fever: Back then you would go to a store and the salesman would put on your sneakers for you and tie your shits up mad tight . . .

Bobbito: . . . As if to cut off your blood circulation. My man Tone Greer (a.k.a. "Batman") would snap at someone with their joints too tight and say, "Money, who tied your sneakers, Arnold Schwarzenegger?"

Dante: My man Wolf would choke his Polo skippies up so much we'd call him the Chelsea Choker! We'd snap, "Yo, I heard you choked a pair of sandals! Don't your ankles hurt?"

Fabel: Thou shalt not wear dirty ass laces on fly sneakers. Wash them damn things, bro!

Johnny Snakeback Fever: Colored laces were out unless they were candy-striped.

Ted Nitro: Country guys would say, "What's wrong with wearing red laces with green striped sneakers?" That was a sin. You'd be like, "Can't he afford white sneaker strings?" Some guys would have two different colored

strings on their sneakers, which I thought was very down-Southish too. Some guys didn't know when to retire shoes. That was a no-no. If you had old joints, just bronze them, but keep them off the court please.

Johnny Snakeback Fever: The all white Deck shoe were skippies that looked like a boating shoe and were completely wack. Joey Bag of Donuts always liked wearing them.

Lincoln Parker: In the '80s we'd never wear black leather sneakers, strictly because of the Celtics.

Steve Brock: Thou shalt not wear any shoes that have velcro instead of laces, Adidas Sambas, Reebok aerobic shoes, Chuck Taylors in pink, lavender, or American flags, coaching shoes, or Nike Field General turf shoes off the turf.

Ted Nitro: Guys would wear two different shoes on the court. They were trying to make a fashion statement, but they'd stink the court up.

Bobbito: The ultimate worst was a guy wearing two different brands with one new and the other old. Was your house that messy that you couldn't find a match? That was nutty magillacutti.

Pete Nice: When I played for Columbia, any player there that wasn't from New York who wore Air Force 1s just made them look wack.

Bobbito: In the '80s you had to earn the right to wear the best sneakers. Your game had to match the level of your sneakers. If you attempted to wear some shit you didn't deserve you were a fucking dick. I saw this kid with green Air Force 1s in '86 at this gym. Nobody had them. He had on a matching practice jersey from some D-1 school too, so I thought, "Money must be nasty." He got on the court and his game was trash! I really wanted to chop his head off. Nowadays it's out of control. Kids will pay $140 for a pair of ball sneakers and they don't even play. It's just for show.

Dante: My rule with old school sneakers is, if you weren't around when they first came out and you weren't even cognizant of them, you can't wear the re-issues. Don't play yourself and act like you were down from day one. When too many people rock an old school re-issue, it just deads the sneaker for me. Clydes and Shells got officially deaded for me. Girls put the whammy on a lot of sneakers too when they start wearing them too much.

Serch: Thou shalt not claim you know the difference between a reissue and an original when you don't, and thou shalt not claim origi-

nal when it's a reissue. Thou shalt not claim old school sneakers when you are under twenty. It's a violation of code. Somebody should give you two to four right now.

Brother Ray: You never wanted to play ball against someone with tennis sneakers on or running shoes. If you were on the court without basketball sneakers, you may as well have had on bowling shoes! To me a basketball sneaker had to be high top. Anything else go play paddleball with!

Ahmad: There are cats that buy joints and then pull the insole out so that they fit. I don't know what their problem is. You got to go out on a hunt and find your size. You can't be walking around with a bunion jumping out, continually taking your shoe off because the shit is too damn small. Come on man! I sit around laughing at cats like that.

Bobbito: Any Miami Vice colors like fuscia, pink, light purple, teal, etc. was major no-no, especially when sneaker companies started trying to mix them together. Two wrongs don't make a right.

Dante: Black socks in sneakers looked real stupid.

Andre Kyles: You know what I could never understand? When someone spent the money on a fresh pair of sneakers but the rest of their wardrobe was wack. It just defeated the purpose.

Kurious: A cardinal sin of sneakers is to wear some felonious shit that people laugh at. If you don't have that much dough just get yourself a pair of Chuck Taylors like they do on the West Coast. It doesn't cost that much dough to look fresh. Get blisters on your feet if you play ball, but at least look fresh.

Serch: Thou shalt not come out your crib and pound one sneaker higher than 24" and claim dominance. Subtlety is crucial. Your sneakers should merit attraction on their own without you having to ask people to look. ∎

Hey, I've got as much love for Nike as the next man (and maybe even more), but I can't excuse them, or any brand, for producing sneakers as hideously ugly as these.

Future Underground classics

Okay, hopefully by this point you've learned something about the developmental age and golden age of sneaker history in New York. I might have been extreme in saying that only a handful of dope sneakers have come out since '87. It's more a matter of there having been very few sneakers released that not everyone and their mama is up on. Sneaker companies are huge businesses, and even when they tell you something is limited edition that shoe may be selling anywhere from 10,000 to 5,000,000 pairs in a year. That's not very limited at all, but they know that the consumer still wants to feel like he or she is wearing something special so they affix the "limited" tag to it anyway. It's called marketing, kiddies.

The following selections are my favorite sneakers of the last fifteen years that were either slept on by the masses or were truly limited. Some of them I picked strictly for balling, some strictly for chill-out, and some that serve both purposes. Most sneaker companies went woefully wrong trying to keep up in the design and marketing race that Nike sparked, but thankfully in the last couple of years I'm finding some sleek, comfortable, and worthy designs from a variety of companies. Part of being a connoisseur is being a non-conformist who thrives on choice and quality. That's hard to achieve when the majority of New York stores stock predominantly Nike and Timberland. Don't buy a pair of sneakers just cuz no one has them if they're made cheaply. In New York, none of the following sneakers blew up or have blown up yet—as the pop-culture neo-classics like the first Reebok Iversons, the Nike Air Max '95, the Nike Jordan XI, and others have. All the other heavy hitters in the last ten years are all reissues or updated versions of older models. No one will ask you, "Where'd you get those?," unless you have them in a color from another locale. In contrast, all of the following sneakers were hard to find during the time they were available in New York, are even rarer now, and best represent what I'll probably be writing about twenty years from now if I do a "Where'd You Get Those? Part 2." And if you don't believe me remember this: the most popular sneakers now (like Air Force 1s) were both slept on and rare when they first came out twenty years ago.

■ **Avia 880, leather/synthetic high top in silver on black, red on white, blue on white, *orange on white, *purple on white, *green on white**

The '89 880s stand as the last release by Avia that made any noise here in New York. True high tops that were above the ankle were slowly losing favor in the face of the growing popularity of 3/4 mid cuts at the end of the '80s. Nonetheless, the 880 was worn by ballplayers in the know and select hip hop heads.

Ahmad: Avia had the high powered basketball joints in '89. They were like 190 pounds and four stories high! You could play 400 full courts in them and they'd never fall apart. Mad heads had the fruit flavors, like orange and green.

■ **New Balance 730, leather high top in black on black with white accent**

By '89 sneakers in all black broke out of the circle of connoisseurs and started to become a bit more prevalent on ball courts in New York. By the '90s black would become the preferred color choice over white for all sneaker buyers. The '89 730 appeared early in that wave and was extremely rare.

■ **Tiger Asics Top Gun, leather high top in *purple on white/yellow, blue on white/red, red on white/blue, white on white**

Asics did a campaign for the '89 Top Gun that featured New York playground stars Elmer Anderson and Tony Hargraves, but unfortunately the sneakers were pretty hard to find. My man Kirk Rodriguez caught two pairs, one with red stripes and one with blue, and he'd wear red on his left foot and blue on his right just to torture us on the block!

■ **Nike Son of Lava Dome, synthetic/nylon mesh/suede low cut hiking shoes in orange on natural/black, yellow on natural/black**

The original Lava Dome went over everyone's head in New York, but the '89 Sons caught on with a miniscule number of heads who were looking for something a little different from Timbs. These were the first hiking shoes to ever make noise because they were sleek and low top which was the antithesis of the category. I had a pair in orange, and Special Ed wore a pair in yellow on the backside of his first LP "Youngest In Charge".

■ **Nike Air Alpha Force, leather low top in white on white, blue on white, red on white, *blue on white with red accent, black on white, *green on white, *gold on white, *light blue on white, *orange on white**

The '88 Alpha Force was the low top brother of the Nike Revolution high top in their design, except the Revolutions were really ugly style-wise, I don't care what anyone says. The Alpha Force, however, was a return to the wide and thick outer and midsole that Nike had all but abandoned after the Air Force 1s release in '83. The five year wait was worth it.

■ Nike Air Force III, leather high top in blue on white, *blue on white/red/blue, *gold on white, *red on white, *gray on blue/gray; Air Force III Escape, leather/suede/nylon in *dark brown on white/brown/dark brown, *blue on white/black/blue

The '88-'89 Air Force III was probably the last Nike basketball shoe that didn't have a player endorsement behind it, but they were still eaten up by serious ballplayers and non-ballplayers alike. These were hard to find in New York. I hadn't met Dante Ross yet, but I saw him with the brown pair on at PayDays, which was the illest weekly hip hop party in '89. He was talking to Funkenklein (R.I.P.) who had "Ease Back" etched into the hair on his neck. Dante is the only person I ever saw with a pair.

■ Nike Air Ballistic, leather high top in black on white, *orange on white, *purple on white, *green on white, *burgundy on white

The '93 Air Ballistics were sort of the David Robinson signatures but not really, and at any rate a great sneaker to run up and down the court in and not catch bunionitis afterwards.

■ Nike Air Force, leather high top and mid cut in black on white, white on black/red/blue, *orange on white, *purple on white, *green on white, *burgundy on white

Mad college teams and pro players wore the '93 Air Force. They featured the same strap support system as the Jordan VIII and the Air Force Max CB (a.k.a. "Barkleys") that came out that year, but were infinitely less popular. Like EPMD said, "Strictly underground funk, keep the crossover."

■ Nike Air Strong, leather high top and mid cut in red on white (*Air Canadas), blue on white, black on white, *purple on white, *light blue on white

Luckily for me I was able to finagle a pair of the '94 Air Strong from the Canadian National Team with Canada and the maple leaf embroidered on the tongue. When I played for WalkerWear in the Entertainer's Basketball Classic up on '55th, you know I had to throw these on since there couldn't have been more than 30 pairs of them in the world period, and definitely none in the U.S. I laced them up halfway to ensure that the Rucker Park crowd could see the Canada logo, but that shit backfired. Yeah I looked good on the court and felt geesed, but by the end of the game I was still on my donut. I shot a 27 foot jumper and missed, and then announcer Duke "Tango" called me Danny DeVito (rhymes with Bobbito)! Ah, man, I can still hear the crowd's laughter echoing in my dome. I can't front, I was even

laughing at myself on the court. That shit was comedy. I haven't worn my Canadian Air Strongs to play ball since.

■ Nike Air 2 Strong, leather high top and mid cut in white on black, *burgundy on white, *red on white, *blue on white, *orange on white, *green on white

While research and development departments were bumping heads trying to compete for the lightest sneaker ever made, the '95 Air 2 Strong came in to save the day (and my feet). They were sturdy and comfortable, and my choice for best kicks to play outdoors, ever.

■ Nike Air Mada, leather/nylon low cut trail shoe in *black on tan with gold accent

The Nike Lava Dome is the classic, but the first issue of the '94 Mada is simply the creamiest of all ACG category shoes in Nike's history.

■ Nike Air Resistance 1, leather/kevlar low cut tennis shoe in white on white, navy blue on white, green on white

The '94 Air Resistance 1 were my down low cool out joints for that entire summer. I hadn't picked up a tennis racquet in ten years but who cared! The Resistance featured a Kevlar toe reinforcement that was practically indestructible. Kevlar is the same material they use to make bulletproof vests, so imagine how well it can protect your little toe from people stepping on you on the train!

■ **Adidas Equipment Basketball Boot, nubuck/synthetic high top in black on black**

The early and mid '90s was a very dry period for Adidas, and the '94 Equipment was their oasis until they started re-releasing their classics. This shoe had a removable neoprene inner sock lining which came in different colors. The only color that worked was black. The red and off blue liners were straight up butt ugly. Unfortunately the lining made your feet feel like molten lava during a hot summer day on the asphalt, so that was a minus too. Nonetheless, these were a sign of good things to come from Adidas later on in the decade.

■ **Nike Air Force Lite, leather high top in white on navy blue, white on black, white on crimson red**

I could've swore the '98 Air Force Lite were gonna blow at retail since they were designed like a lighter, updated Air Force 1. They did gain the favor of every ballplayer who played in them. They'd see me in mine and come up to me and say, "I have a pair of those too. I love them."

■ **Puma Cell Origin, leather high top and low cut in navy blue on white, burgundy on white, metallic red on white, metallic blue on black, *white on purple**

Vince Carter wore the '98 Cell Origin the first year he signed with Puma. I have gotten more "Where'd you get those?" remarks for the three pairs that I own than for any other current sneaker I've worn in the last twelve years. Supposedly the pre-orders for them were low but then they blew out of every store, so their availability was short and limited. Good for me!

■ **And One Lottery, leather/nylon mid cut in *red/white, blue/white, white/white, black on black**

The red/white '99 Lotterys were Larry Hughes' sneakers during his rookie season with the Sixers. And One was just getting off the ground with their mixtape style street videos and Set Free—who was producing their videos—gave me a pair to rock. I wore them to a game in L.E.S. and everyone, even the scorekeepers, was asking me where I'd gotten them. I dropped 30 points, which was the most I had scored in a game since '93, but I don't know if the scorekeepers were padding my stats to get on my good side. They knew I had a couple of And One Mixtape volume 1s in my bag and they wanted a copy! I would've handed them over but I was too busy nursing my feet. Yeah they looked hot but they weren't comfortable at all.

■ **New Balance 750, leather high top in gray/navy blue on white**

It had been over a decade since Nubies had come out with a decent basketball shoe, so the '98 750s were a lot to get excited over. This was a sneaker that performed on the court and could be worn with no socks while DJ'ing. I would purposely get up from behind the DJ booth and walk around when I sniffed fellow connoisseurs present, and 100% of the time they'd have a comment.

■ **New Balance 800, leather high top in black on white/silver with yellow accent**

Let's just say I practically had an asthma attack when I saw the '00 800 wrapped in plastic on the wall. The store had only ordered one pair for each size from 8 1/2 to 11 plus one size 12. That's only seven pairs total. They had one pair left, and thankfully it was a 10 1/2 but I didn't have enough money on me. I peeled off home on my bike and rode four miles round-trip in less than 30 minutes (that's fast in rush hour traffic). I was pet that someone would come in and buy them before me. Luckily I copped them, and they became my good luck sneakers.

Above: Michael Cooper of the Lakers
sports the elusive Asics Top Gun in
purple/yellow.

235

■ New Balance 600, leather low top in white on white

I don't know if the '00 600 ever came out and if they did I never saw anyone with them. If I had seen someone with these on I would've offered to treat them to a free Jamai-can chicken patty to match the gum bottoms!

■ Adidas Bromium II, leather high top in royal blue on white, black on white, red on white, white on black, * maroon on white, *purple on white, *green on white, *orange on white

The '01 Bromium II could very well be the Pro Model of the new millennium in terms of function and style. I love these sneakers. It is classic, already. If you own a pair, stop wearing them right now! Put them on ice, you'll thank me in a couple of years. I wore my burgundy pair up at Orchard Beach in the Hoops In The Sun tournament in '02. Our uni's were the exact shade of burgundy, and people couldn't handle it! Our squad (featuring John "Franchise" Strickland, Shawnell Scott, and Mike Campbell) took the chip. I didn't get much burn, but what better way to ride pine than to look mega-fresh dipped.

■ Tiger Asics Gel Drive, leather high top in *silver on white, *red on white

I had to mail order the '01 Gel Drive from California and I'm glad I did. A lot of cats from my generation secretly come up to me when I wear these and ask, "I didn't know Asics was making basketball shoes again! I

used to love Asics." Younger heads have stopped me to say, "Those are hot, let me see them . . . What are they?" Recognize and realize the realness!

■ Gravis Tarmac, leather low cut lifestyle shoe in tan/brown, white/hotwire red, white/basil

Dennis Jenson founded Gravis in '99 in Burlington, VT. I don't wear linen pants, but if I did I'd wear the '00-'02 Tarmacs with them. Gravis is the up and coming footwear company to watch out for.

■ Gravis Kingpin, leather/nylon mesh low cut lifestyle shoe in red/silver, white with gum bottom, tan/brown

The '02 Kingpin almost leans towards the Prada style high-end fashion sneakers but it's not anywhere near as price offensive. Inspired by soccer shoes, you might not actually play soccer in these but you can depend on them to give the type of comfort that a soccer shoe would give. The white ones with the gum bottom are incredible!

■ Adidas Pro Model 2G, patent leather high top in white on white, white on royal, white on navy, white on green, white on red, white on orange, white on black, white on light blue

Sonny Vaccaro was up to his old tricks again! Sonny lifted Nike in the '70s and '80s by sponsoring college teams and high school phenoms with customized sneakers with their personal and team names printed on them. With the '02 Pro Model 2G he and Adidas are now embroidering the names. Brilliant! Thankfully you won't find these in New York stores.

■ Adidas Bromium III, leather high top in white on blue, white on red, white on orange, white on green, white on light blue, white on black, white on burgundy

The Bromium IIs were my favorite sneaker of the new millennium until the '02 Bromium IIIs came out. Whew! Beware of the overkill on the ankle padding. I actually took a razor blade and cut them out, and since then these have been a great sneaker to wear and attract desired attention. ■

The customized Pump-N-Run squad's Pro Model 2Gs were so hot that I was ready to ride pine last fall just to cop a pair.

PUMP-N-RUN

NYC Ball Legends

The following is a list of some of New York's greatest ball players of all time, as well as others who I personally enjoyed watching, playing against, or hearing stories about. Between '70 and '87 these were the players who were sneaker companies' best advertising. Whatever they wore other ballplayers and the hordes of crowd participants were prone to bite. (Only players who made their names in the five boroughs after '70 and before '87 are included. For example Roger Brown, Frank "Shake and Bake" Streety, and Connie "Hawk" Hawkins all earned their rep in the '60s, and obviously their legends continued on through the decades.) While doing the research for this list many names were questioned by my contributors, comments like, "He's a bum!" and "Yeah he played in the pros but he had no rep in the playground tournaments!" So this is not meant to be a definitive list, it is both opinions and facts. Players' info starts with their youth team affiliations, then scholastic career, then pro.

A typically victorious New York City squad at the Empire State Games circa 1982, featuring both Walter Berry and Dwayne "Pearl" Washington.

Super-duper Sam Worthen was one of the craftiest passers New York has ever seen. Here he is at Marquette, skating to the hole.

Catching Rek in the '70s
New York in the NBA

■ **Rolando Blackman**-Grady H.S. '77, USA Olympic Team '80, Kansas St. '81, Dallas '81-'92, N.Y. Knicks '92-'94

■ **Dave Britton**-Dyckman, Riverside Church, Kennedy H.S. '76, Potomac St. (W. Va.), Texas A & M '80, Washington Bullets '80-'81

"He once had 56 points and 29 rebounds in one game at Kennedy."
—Colin Killian, Associate SID-Texas A & M

■ **Reggie Carter** (RIP)-Riverside Church, Lutheran H.S. (Long Island) '75, Hawaii, St. John's '80, N.Y. Knicks '80-'82

He set off the program at Riverside Church and was their first big time player.

■ **Mike Dunleavy**-Nazareth H.S. '72, South Carolina '76, Philadelphia 76'ers '76-'77, Houston Rockets '78-'82, San Antonio Spurs '82-'83, Milwaukee Bucks '83-'90

■ **Franklin Edwards**-Each One Teach One, Milbank Hawks, Julia Richmond '77, Cleveland St. '81, Philadelphia 76'ers '81-'84, L.A. Clippers '84-'86, Sacramento Kings '86-'88

■ **Len Elmore**-Power Memorial H.S. '70, Maryland '74 (2nd Team All American '74), Indiana Pacers '74-'79, Kansas City Kings '79-'80, Milwaukee Bucks '80-'81, New Jersey Nets '81-'83, N.Y. Knicks '83-'84

■ **World B. Free (formerly Lloyd B. Free)**-Vanguards, Brownsville Jets, Canarsie H.S. '71, Guilford '75 (Division 2 1st Team All American '75), Philadelphia 76'ers '75-'78, San Diego Clippers '78-'80 (All NBA 2nd Team '79), Golden State Warriors '80-'82, Cleveland Cavaliers '82-'86, Philadelphia 76'ers '86-'87, Houston Rockets '87-'88

Probably the only ballplayer I've ever seen who could shoot as well on his way down as on his way up!

■ **Stew Granger**-Riverside Church, Nazareth H.S. '79, Villanova '83, Cleveland Cavaliers '83-84, Atlanta Hawks '84-'85, N.Y. Knicks '86-'87

■ **Sid Green**-Riverside Church, Thomas Jefferson H.S. '79 (McDonald's All American '79), UNLV '83 (2nd Team All American '83), Chicago Bulls '83-'86, Detroit Pistons '86-'87, N.Y. Knicks '87-'89, Orlando Magic '89-'90, San Antonio Spurs '90-'92, Charlotte Hornets '93

■ **Ernie Grunfeld**-Forest Hills H.S. '73, USA Olympic Team '76, Tennessee '77, Milwaukee Bucks '77-'79, Kansas City Kings '79-'82, N.Y. Knicks '82-'86

■ **Tom Henderson**-Nobles, Clinton H.S. '70, San Jacinto J.C. '72, USA Olympic Team '72, Hawaii '74, Atlanta Hawks '74-'76, Washington Bullets '77-'79, Houston Rockets '79-'83

■ **Armond Hill**-Broncos, Bishop Ford H.S. '72, Princeton '76, Atlanta Hawks '76-'80, Seattle Supersonics '80-'81, San Diego Clippers '82, Milwaukee Bucks '82-'83, Atlanta Hawks '83-'84

■ **Geoff Huston**-Brownsville Jets, Canarsie H.S. '75, Texas Tech '79, N.Y. Knicks '79-'80, Dallas Mavericks '80, Cleveland Cavaliers '81-'85, Golden St. Warriors '85-'86, L.A. Clippers '86-'87

■ **Greg "Jocko" Jackson**-Brownsville Jets, Tilden H.S. '70, Guilford '74, New York Knicks '74, Phoenix Suns '75

■ **George Johnson**-Riverside Church, New Utrecht H.S. '74, St. Johns '78, Milwaukee Bucks '78-79, Denver Nuggets '79-'80, Indiana Pacers '80-'84, Philadelphia 76'ers '84-'85, Washington Bullets '85-'86

■ **Lynbert "Cheese" Johnson**-Stan Brown's Cavaliers, Riverside Church, Haaren H.S. '74, Wichita St. '79, Golden State Warriors '79-'80

■ **Vinnie "The Microwave" Johnson**-F.D.R. H.S. '75, McClennan C.C. (Tx.) '77, Baylor '79, Seattle Supersonic '79-'82, Detroit Pistons '82-'91, San Antonio Spurs '91-'92

■ **Albert King**-Gauchos, Riverside Church, Fort Hamilton H.S. '77 (McDonald's All American '77), Maryland '80 (2nd Team All American '80), N.J. Nets '81-'87, Philadelphia 76'ers '87-'88, San Antonio Spurs '88-'89, Washington Bullets '91-'92

He was the most celebrated high school player out of New York in the '70s, even more than his brother Bernard.

■ **Bernard King**-Fort Hamilton H.S. '73, Tennessee '77 (2nd Team All American '76, 1st Team All American '77), New Jersey Nets '77-'79 (All Rookie 1st Team '78), Utah Jazz '79-'80, Golden State Warriors '80-'82 (All NBA 2nd Team '82), N.Y. Knicks '82-'87 (All NBA 1st Team '84, '85), Washington Bullets '87-'91, N.J. Nets '92-'93

■ **Butch Lee**-Jefferson Park, Gauchos, Riverside Church, Clinton H.S. '74, Puerto Rican Olympic Team '76, Marquette '78 (2nd Team All American '77, 1st Team All America

'78, UPI/AP/Naismith College Player of the Year '78, NCAA Championship Most Outstanding Player '77, NABC All Star Game MVP '78), Atlanta Hawks '78, Cleveland Cavaliers '79, Los Angeles Lakers '80

■ **Nancy Lieberman**-Far Rockaway H.S. '76, Old Dominion '80, USA Olympic Team '80, Dallas Diamonds (WBL) '80-'81, Dallas Diamonds (WABA) '84, Springfield Fame (USBL, was the first woman to ever play in a men's professional league) '86, Phoenix Mercury (WNBA) '97

■ **Tony Price**-Jefferson Park, Riverside Church, Taft H.S. '76, U Penn '80, San Diego Clippers '80-'81

■ **Ed "Sky Lab" Searcy**-Riverside Church, Power '70, St. John's '74, Boston Celtics '75-'76

■ **Phil "The Thrill" Sellers**-Brownsville Jets, Thomas Jefferson H.S. '72, Rutgers '76 (1st Team All American '76), Detroit Pistons '76-'77

■ **Steve "Bear" Shepard**-Clinton H.S. '73, USA Olympic Team '76, Maryland '77, Chicago Bulls '77-'78, Detroit Pistons '79

■ **Ricky Sobers**-Clinton H.S. '71, College of Southern Idaho (J.C.) '73, UNLV '75, Phoenix Suns '75-'77, Indiana Pacers '77-'79, Chicago Bulls '79-'82, Washington Bullets '82-'84, Seattle Supersonics '84-'86

■ **James "Fly" Williams**- Brownsville Jets, Madison H.S., Glen Springs Academy (N.Y.) '70, Austin Peay '74, St. Louis Spirits (ABA) '74-'75

"He played for the Westsiders in the Pro Rucker for three years. He may have been the best of them all."
—*Butch Purcell, legendary Pro Rucker coach*

■ **Kevin "Will Power" Williams**-Each One Teach One, Broncos, Milbank Hawks, Dyckman, Charles Evan Hughes H.S. '79, St. Johns '83, San Antonio Spurs '83-'84, Cleveland Cavaliers '84-'85, Seattle Supersonics '86-'88, N.J. Nets '88, L.A. Clippers '89

"Kevin Williams was one of the toughest scoring guards out of New York ever."
—*Mr. Couch, Dyckman/Uptowners coach*

■ **Brian Winters**-Archbishop Molloy H.S. '70, South Carolina '74, Los Angeles Lakers '74-'75 (NBA All Rookie 1st Team '75), Milwaukee Bucks '75-'83

■ **Sam Worthen**-Franklin K. Lane H.S. '76, McClennan C.C. (Tx.), Marquette '80 (2nd Team All American '80), Chicago Bulls '80-'81, Utah Jazz '81-'82

New York Playground, High School, and College Stars

■ **Tony "Apjack" Spear** (late '70s-early '80s)

"He was Earl "the Goat" Manigualt's favorite player. He had no fear, didn't like dunking unless there was a man in his face. He'd take off from the foul line no problem."
—*Clark Elie*

■ **Jimmy Black**-Riverside Church, Cardinal Hayes H.S. '78, UNC '82

■ **Arturo Brown** (RIP)-Gauchos, Nazareth H.S. '79

■ **"Disco" Fred Brown**-Dyckman, Kennedy H.S. '79, Virginia Commonwealth '83

He'd dribble between one leg three or four times repeatedly real fast with either hand real low to try to shake his man to the ground.

■ **Tony "Red" Bruin**-Riverside Church, Gauchos, Mater Christi H.S. '79 (McDonald's All American '79), Syracuse '83

■ **Ted "the Sled" Campbell** (RIP)-Intersession Church, Brandies H.S. '77, Saddleback J.C. (Ca.)

■ **John Candelaria**-LaSalle H.S. '72

■ **Nestor Cora**-Riverside Church, Stevenson H.S. '74, Chippola J.C. (Fl.), Morris J.C. '76, Fordham, St. Francis (Brooklyn) '79

■ **Angel "Monchito" Cruz a.k.a. "Munch"**-Clinton H.S. '76, Essex C.C. '78, Puerto Rican Olympic Team '84

■ **Eddie "Sundance Kid" Davis**-Wagner Community Center, Dyckman, Milbank Hawks, Riverside Church, Victorville J.C. '74 (Ca.), San Diego '77

"He averaged 40 up at Foster Projects."
—*Clark Elie*

■ **Drew Doward**-Gauchos, Essex C.C. '78

■ **Arnold Dugger**-Dyckman, Riverside Church, Clinton H.S. '73, Oral Roberts '77

"He was one of my idols."
—*Leroy "La Luscious Lee" Shaw*

■ **Alexander "Boobie" Eldridge a.k.a. "Magic"** (RIP)-Jefferson Park, Riverside Church, Taft H.S. '74, U Mass '78

"He was an All American his senior year in high school. Him and Butch Lee were the best guards in the city."
—*Leroy "La Luscious Lee" Shaw*

■ **Clark "The Magnificent One" Elie a.k.a. "Big Man Little Man"** Harlem USA, Riverside Church (AAU), Gauchos (AAU), Brandies H.S. '74, CCNY '79

"When Clark played for Harlem USA at West 4th St., they took that tournament nine years in a row. He became accustomed to bringing home a TV from the Wiz. That was the prize for MVP." —Gerry Erasme

■ **Cesar "Spanish Doc" Fantauci**-Each One Teach One

"People would tell me he was one of the best latin players they'd ever seen. I would tell them he was one of the best players I'd seen period." —Butch Purcell

■ **Keith Ron "Silver Streak" Fryson**-Milbank Hawks, Brandeis H.S. '73, College of Southern Idaho (J.C.) '74, Hawaii '75

■ **"Jumping" Artie Green**-Resurrection, Trio Crusaders, Taft H.S. '77, Marquette '81

"He once pinned me on the backboard with his elbow. I'll probably tell me grandchildren about that one. His elbow!" —Kurt Mahoney

■ **Carlton "Mr. Mojo" Green**-RYA, George Washington H.S. '72, Hardin Simmons (TX) '73, Kingsborough C.C. '76

■ **Gary "Pork Chop" Green**-Mitchell Gym, Morris H.S., Harlem Prep '78

■ **Billy Goodwin**-Columbus H.S. '79, San Jacinto J.C., St. John's '83

■ **Richie Gordon**-Boys and Girls H.S. '79, Columbia U. '83

■ **Joe "The Destroyer" Hammond**-Milbank Hawks

■ **Bernard "The Knob" Hardin**-Wingate H.S. '70, Elsworth J.C. (Ia.) '72, New Mexico '74

"Bernard almost got drafted to the NBA out of high school."—Sid Jones.

"He was the truth if I ever saw it. He's on the 1st team of players who should've been pro but didn't make it."—Butch Purcell

■ **Alonzo "Superkid" Jackson** (late '70s)-Chick Jewels, Dyckman

"I saw him at the Goat Tournament. He was destroying them, so his defender's girlfriend started yapping, "Lonzo you ain't shit!" The next play he threw a pass from half court that went through three guys to his man for a lay up. He turned to the woman, dropped his shorts, grabbed his dick in his jock strap and said, "Suck my dick!" He pulled up his

shorts and kept playing like nothing happened. I never saw no shit like that!" —Lincoln Parker

■ **Bruce "Cloud 9" King**-Charles Evan Hughes H.S. '70, Pan American '74

■ **Chris Logan**-Riverside Church, Bishop Ford '79, Holy Cross '83

■ **Allen Lorick** (late '70s)-Riverside Church

■ **Bob Misevicius**-Power '74, Providence '78

■ **Eric Marbury**-Riverside Church, Lincoln H.S. '78, Georgia '82

■ **Charlie "Rock" Moore**-Trio Crusaders, Stevenson H.S. '77, Delaware St. '81

■ **Hector Olivencia**-USV Kings, Riverside Church, Clinton H.S. '74, Sacred Heart '78 (Division 2 1st Team All American '78)

"He got drafted by the San Antonio Spurs but didn't make it. He went down to Puerto Rico and became one of their all time scorers." —Mike "Nappy" Napolitan

■ **"Corky" Ortiz** (mid '70s)-Milbank Hammerheads

■ **Kenny Page**-Riverside Church, McKee Vocational H.S. '77, Ohio St. '78, New Mexico '81

"He was the best player out of Staten Island ever." —Mike "Nappy" Napolitan.

■ **Tom "Gator" Pauling**-Each One Teach One, Ben Franklin H.S. '73, UTEP '77

■ **Curtis "Cornbread" Phauls**- Riverside Church, Taft H.S. '77, San Jacinto J.C. '79, U Mass '80

■ **Mike Pyatt**-Ressurection, Riverside Church, Brandies H.S., Bishop Dubois H.S. '74, U Mass '78

"He was so bad he broke Dr. J's scoring record at U Mass." —Leroy "La Luscious Lee" Shaw

■ **Bernard Rencher**-Riverside Church, Mater Christi '76, St. John's '80

■ **Billy "White Jesus" Riser**-Dyckman, Ben Franklin H.S. '80

"He had the most insane hops I've ever seen for a whiteboy." —Lincoln Parker.

■ **Ronnie Ryer**-RYA, Riverside Church, Brandeis H.S. '77, Wichita St. '79

Walter Berry is the nicest big man I have ever seen play in New York. At 6'8", he had a handle and he had hang time, making him virtually unstoppable. In 1986, while playing at St. John's, he was a consensus choice for College Player of the Year.

■ **Bill "Daddy Boogie" Sadler a.k.a. "Fat Sad"**-Broncos, Riverside Church, Norman Thomas H.S. '79, Pepperdine '83

■ **Maurice Sanford**-Dyckman, Boys and Girls H.S. '79, Niagara '81, Hofstra, N.Y. Tech

■ **Norman "Storm" Scullark**-Dyckman, Riverside Church, Brandies H.S. '75, Lon Morris J.C. (Tx.), Centenary '79

■ **Leroy "Dome Burglar" 'La Luscious Lee' 'Mr. Excitement' Shaw**-Trio Crusaders, Taft H.S. '72, Midwestern '76

"Leroy once turned his back and dribbled right in front of his defender the whole length of the floor, dribbling behind his back without even facing his basket! Shit was crazy!"
—Ted Nitro

■ **Marvin "Hammer" Stevens**-Milbank Hammerheads, Charles Evan Hughes H.S., Central H.S. (Ga.) '67, Georgia Southern '68, Western New England '70

"I was the leading scorer in the Pro Rucker in '73. I dropped 66 points in one game. I had a big rep at West 4th St. too. People would come out the train station, and if they saw I wasn't playing that day they'd get right back on the train!"—"Hammer"

■ **Georgie "Pretty Boy" Torres**-Clinton H.S., Stevenson H.S. '77, Bethany Nazarene '81

■ **Ronnie "Twinkle Toes" Wright**-Resurrection, SUNY-Plattsburgh '77

"If Butch Lee didn't get MVP, then Ronnie did."
—Vernon "VJ" Moore

Catching Rek in the '80s
New York in the NBA

■ **Kenny "Chibbs" Anderson**-Broncos, Gauchos, Riverside Church, Archbishop Molloy H.S. '89 (McDonald's All American '89), Georgia Tech '91 (1st Team All American '91), New Jersey Nets '91-'96, Charlotte Hornets '96, Portland Trailblazers '96-'98, Boston Celtics '98-'01

■ **Walter "The Truth" Berry**-Riverside Church, Ben Franklin H.S. '82, San Jacinto J.C. '84, St. John's '86 (1st Team All American '86, UPI/AP/Wooden/NABC College Player of the Year '86), Portland Trailblazers '86, San Antonio Spurs '87-'88, New Jersey Nets '88, Houston Rockets '89

I saw him at Nelson Park in '84. This kid had a breakaway lay up and was at the foul line by himself. Walter was at half court. By the time the kid released the ball Walter had caught up and he "brrr, stick'em, ha ha ha, stick'em" boarded him. Not only did he pin him, he cuffed the ball on his forearm on his way down. The crowd lost it and ran onto the court. They had to stop the game for five minutes.

■ **Steve Burtt**-Each One Teach One, Phipps PAL Sun Devils, Charles Evan Hughes H.S. '80, Iona '84, Golden State Warriors '84-'85, L.A. Clippers '87-'88, Phoenix Suns '91-'92, Washington Bullets '92-'93

■ **Duane Causwell**-Cordoza H.S. '86, Temple '90, Sacramento Kings '90-'97, Miami Heat '97-'00

■ **Lorenzo Charles**-Broncos, Riverside Church, Brooklyn Tech H.S. '81, N.C. State '85 (NABC All Star Game MVP '85), Atlanta Hawks '85-'86

■ **Derrick "Band-Aid" Chievous**-Gauchos, Holy Cross '84 (McDonald's All American '84), Missouri '88, Houston Rockets '88-'89, Cleveland Cavaliers '89-'90

■ **Lloyd "Sweet Pea" Daniels**-Gauchos, Thomas Jefferson H.S., Andrew Jackson H.S., Mount San Antonio J.C. (Ca.), San Antonio Spurs '92-'94, Philadelphia Sixers '94, Los Angeles Lakers '95, Sacramento Kings '96-'97, N.J. Nets '97, Toronto Raptors '97, Atlanta Hawks '98

He was the first high school freshman ever to make All City. Not even Kareem did that.

■ **Billy "the Kid" Donovan**-Dyckman, Riverside Church, St. Agnes H.S. '83, Providence '87, N.Y. Knicks '87-'88

■ **Mario "The Jedi" Elie**-Phipps PAL Sun Devils, Gauchos, Riverside Church, Harlem USA, Power Memorial H.S. '81, American International College '85, Philadelphia 76'ers '90, Golden State Warriors '91-'92, Portland Trailblazers '92-'93, Houston Rockets '93-'98, San Antonio Spurs '98-'00, Phoenix Suns '00-'01

■ **Vern Fleming**-St. Rita's, Gauchos, Mater Christi H.S. '80 (McDonald's All American '80), Georgia '84, USA Olympic Team '84, Indiana Pacers '84-'95, N.J. Nets '95-'96

■ **Mark "Action" Jackson**-Broncos, Riverside Church, Gauchos, Bishop Loughlin H.S. '83, St. Johns '87 (2nd Team All American '87), N.Y. Knicks '87-'92 (NBA Rookie of the Year '88), L.A. Clippers '92-'94, Indiana Pacers '94-96, Denver Nuggets '96, Indiana Pacers '97-'00, Toronto Raptors '00, N.Y. Knicks '01-'02

■ **Eric Johnson**-Broncos, FDR H.S. '85, Baylor, Nebraska '89, Utah Jazz '89-'90

■ **Anthony Mason**-Springfield H.S. '84, Tennessee St. '88, N.J. Nets '89-'90, Denver Nuggets '90-'91, N.Y. Knicks '91-'96, Charlotte Hornets '96-'00

■ **John "Salt" Morton**-Riverside Church, Walton H.S. '85, Seton Hall '89 (Final Four All Tournament '89), Cleveland Cavaliers '89-'91, Miami Heat '92

■ **Chris Mullin**-Gauchos, Riverside Church, Power Memorial H.S., Xaverian H.S. '81 (McDonald's All American '81), St. Johns '85 (2nd Team All American '84, 1st Team All American '85, UPI/Wooden College Player of the Year '85, USA Olympic Team '84 and '92, Golden State Warriors '85-'97 (All NBA 2nd Team '89, '91, All NBA 1st Team '92), Indiana Pacers '97-'00, Golden St. Warriors '00-'01

■ **"E.Z." Ed Pinckney**-Gauchos, Riverside Church, Stevenson H.S. '81 (McDonald's All American '81), Villanova '85 (NCAA Championship Most Outstanding Player '85), Phoenix Suns '85-'87, Sacramento Kings '87-'88, Boston Celtics '88-'94, Milwaukee Bucks '94-'95, Toronto Raptors '95, Philadelphia 76'ers '96, Miami Heat '96-'97

■ **Olden "O.P." Polynice**-Riverside Church, All Hallows '83, UVA "87, Seattle Supersonics '87-'90, L.A. Clippers '90-'92, Detroit Pistons '92-'93, Sacramento Kings '93-'98, Seattle Supersonics '98-'99, Utah Jazz '99-'01

■ **Jerry "Ice" Reynolds**-Brooklyn USA, Gauchos, Riverside Church, Alexander Hamilton H.S. '81, LSU '85, Milwaukee Bucks '85-'88, Seattle Supersonics '88-'89, Orlando Magic '89-'92, Milwaukee Bucks '95-'96

■ **John "Spider" Salley**-Gauchos, Canarsie H.S. '82, Georgia Tech '86, Detroit Pistons '86-'92, Miami Heat '92-'95, Toronto Raptors '95, Chicago Bulls '96, L.A. Lakers '99-'00

■ **Carey Scurry**-Riverside Church, Alexander Hamilton H.S. '81, N.E. Oklahoma A & M J.C. '82, LIU '85, Utah Jazz '85-'87, N.Y. Knicks '88

■ **Malik Sealy**-Guachos, Riverside Church, Tolentine H.S. '88 (McDonald's All American '88), St. John's '92 (2nd Team All American '92), Indiana Pacers '92-'94, L.A. Clippers '94-'97, Detroit Pistons '97-'98, Minnesota Timberwolves '98-'00

■ **Kenny "Jet" Smith**-Riverside Church, Archbishop Molloy H.S. '83 (McDonald's All American '83), UNC '87 (1st Team All American '87), Sacramento Kings '87-'89 (NBA All Rookie 1st Team '88), Atlanta Hawks '90, Houston Rockets '90-'96, Detroit Pistons '96, Orlando Magic '96, Denver Nuggets '97

■ **Rod "Bestrough" Strickland**-Gauchos, Rice H.S., Truman H.S. '84, Oak Hill Academy '85, Depaul '88, N.Y. Knicks '88-'89 (NBA All Rookie 2nd Team '89), San Antonio Spurs '90-'92, Portland Trailblazers '92-'96, Washington Bullets '96-'00 (All NBA 2nd Team '98), Portland Trailblazers '00-'01

■ **Gary Voce**-Dyckman, Riverside Church, Tolentine H.S. '84, Notre Dame '88, Cleveland Cavaliers '89-'90

■ **Dwayne "Pearl" Washington a.k.a. "Pac Man"** Brownsville Jets, Broncos, Gauchos, Riverside Church, Norman Thomas H.S., Boys High '83 (McDonald's All American Game Wooden Award Co-MVP '83), Syracuse '86 (2nd Team All American '85, N.J. Nets '86-'88, Miami Heat '88-'89

"Pearl showed up to a game at Kings Towers on a motorcycle with a fly ass girl on the back. He drove that shit right to half court, parked it, scored 55 points, then left. That's some real legend shit, I wanted to be just like him!" —Arnold "A Train" Bernard

■ **Jayson Williams**-Broncos, Christ the King H.S. '86, St. Johns '90, Philadelphia 76'ers '90-'92, N.J. Nets '92-'99

New York Playground, High School, and College Stars

■ **Richie "The Animal" Adams**-Dyckman, Gauchos (AAU), Ben Franklin H.S. '80, U.N.L.V. '85

I heard he'd show up to games high and drunk and still drop 50!

■ **Elmer "Yak Yak" Anderson a.k.a. "Cinemax"**-Gauchos, Boys and Girls High '82, St. Bonaventure '86

He and Pearl may have been the best high school backcourt ever.

■ **Chris "Air Jesus" Avignone**-Dyckman, Bank St. H.S. '84, Columbia '88

Chris used to try to catch people on the board and then dunk it through the hoop for them so that he could say, "You suck so bad I have to score for you!"

"The first time "Tiny" Archibald coached against him he came up to me and said, "You can't have that whiteboy dunking on us like that! Who is he?" —Mr. Couch

■ **Stu Barnett**-Phipps P.A.L. Sun Devils, Riverside Church, Tolentine H.S., Kennedy H.S. '88, Wyoming '91

I heard that Stu never took the train or bus and just walked everywhere and that's how he got his hops. Like one time he had a game in Brooklyn and he walked there from the Bronx!

■ **Arnold "A Train" Bernard**-Gauchos, Truman H.S., Our Savior Lutheran H.S. '87, San Jacinto J.C. '89, S.W. Missouri '91, Harlem Globetrotters

"Our Savior Lutheran took the city, state, everything, with just five players and no subs. They may have been the best high school squad ever." —Lincoln Parker

■ **Andre Blackett**-Broncos, Gauchos, Riverside Church, Tolentine H.S. '85, Brooklyn College '86

"Crazy handle." —Al Morales

■ **Chris Brooks**-Broncos, Gauchos, Gompers H.S., Oak Hill Academy '86 (McDonald's All American '86), West Virginia '91

■ **Anthony "Cosell" Brown**-Brooklyn USA, Gauchos, Alexander Hamilton H.S. '80

"The best point guard I've ever coached." —Sid Jones

■ **James "True" Carter a.k.a. "El Presidente"** Hillcrest '82, St. Thomas Aquinas '86, Puerto Rican Olympic Team '92 and '96

■ **Roosevelt Chapman**-Broncos, Gauchos, Riverside Church, Westinghouse H.S. '80, Dayton '84

■ **Sean Couch**-Dyckman, Kennedy H.S., The Hun School of Princeton '83, Columbia '87

■ **Bruce Dalrymple**-Riverside Church, St. Johnsbury Academy '83 (McDonald's All American '83), Georgia Tech '87

"One of the toughest defenders out of New York ever." —Mr. Couch

■ **Ed "Bug Eye" Davender**-Brooklyn USA, Broncos, Riverside Church, Gauchos, Alexander Hamilton H.S., Boys and Girls H.S. '84 (McDonald's All American '84), Kentucky '88

■ **Ray Diaz**-Phipps PAL Sun Devils, Norman Thomas '81, Cheyney St. '85

■ **Dave Edwards**- Riverside Church, Andrew Jackson H.S. '89, Georgetown U. '90, Texas A & M '94 (Frances Pomeroy Naismith College Player of the Year under 6' Runner Up '94)

"He had one of the highest scoring averages in New York City High School history, and is still our all time career leader in steals and assists." —Colin Killian-SID Texas A & M

■ **Andre "Sky" Ervin**-Brooklyn USA, Gauchos, Alexander Hamilton H.S. '82, LIU '86

■ **Vern Giscombe**-Riverside Church, Cardinal Hayes H.S. '80, U Conn '84

■ **Tony Hargraves**-Gauchos, Riverside Church, Our Savior Lutheran '81, Iona '85

"I'm one of the few people who can say he held Michael Jordan under double figures. He was at UNC and only scored six points." —Tony Hargraves

■ **Greg "Boo" Harvey**-Gauchos, Andrew Jackson H.S. '86, San Jacinto J.C. (Tx.) '88, St. John's '90 (Frances Pomeroy Naismith College Player of the Year under 6' '90)

■ **Moe Hicks**-Riverside Church, Rice H.S. '81, Loyola (Md.) '85

■ **Carlton "Duncan" Hines** (RIP)-Dyckman, Gauchos, Manhattan Center H.S., Maine Central Institute '86

■ **"Master Rob" Hockett**-Rena-Coa Sonics, Gauchos, Jacksonville J.C. (TX) '87 (JuCo All American '87), New Orleans '89, Harlem Globetrotters

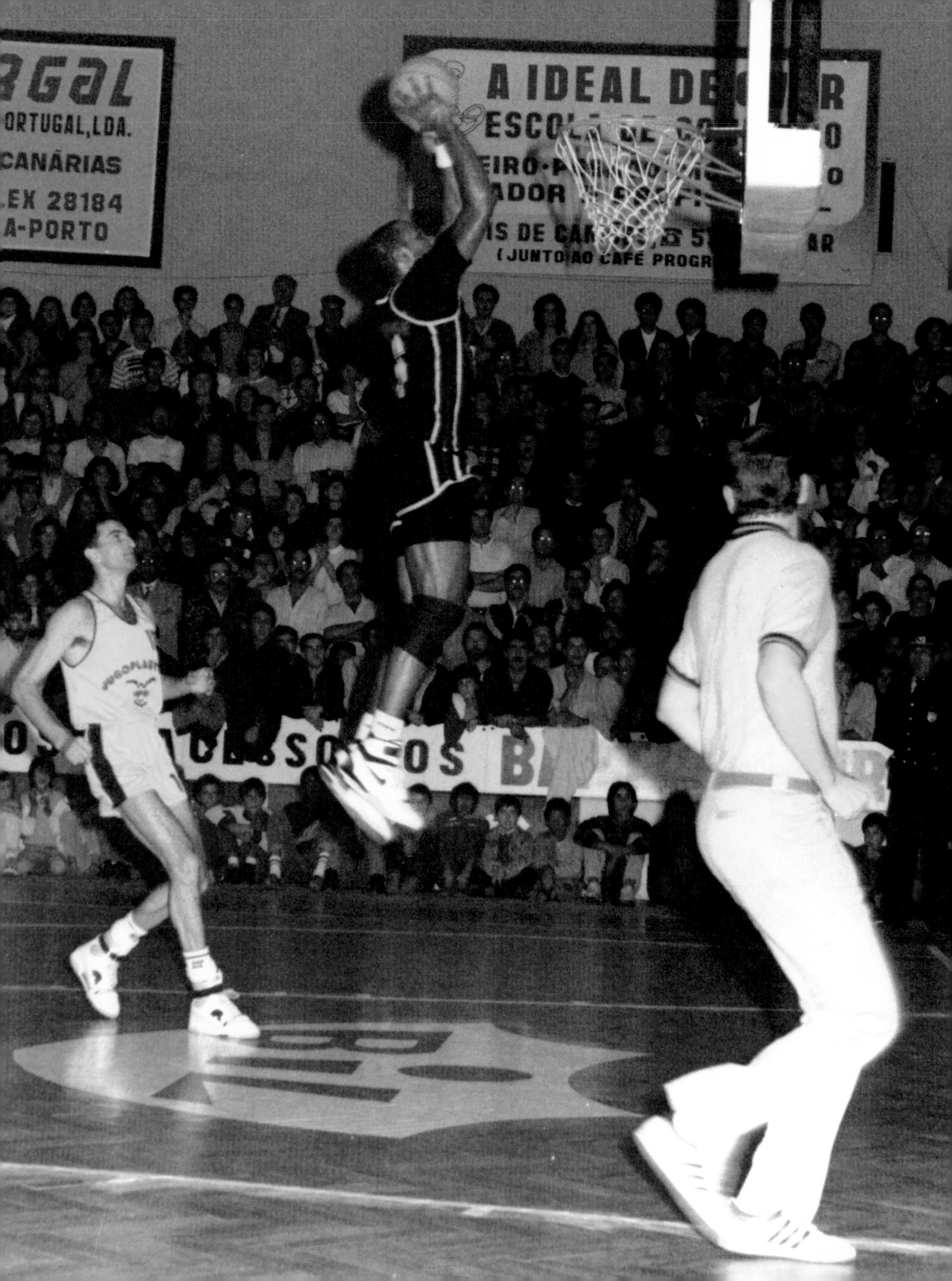
ORTUGAL, LDA.
CANÁRIAS
A-PORTO
A IDEAL DE
(JUNTO AO CAFÉ PROGR

I grew up playing against Mario "The Jedi" Elie. Here we see him playing pro in Portugal circa 1987. He played all over the world until he finally got a break as a rookie in the NBA at age 27. He went on to win three NBA rings, two with Houston and one with San Antonio.

■ **Kenny Hutchinson**-Broncos, Riverside Church, Dyckman, Ben Franklin H.S. '83, Arkansas '87

■ **Ralph James**-Riverside Church, Archbishop Molloy H.S. '87, Harvard '90

■ **Dwayne "DJ" Johnson**-Gauchos, Mater Christi H.S. '81, Marquette'84 "He owned West 4th St." Clark Elie

■ **John Johnson**-Riverside Church, Tolentine H.S. '84, UVA '88

■ **"Disco" Bobby Jones** (RIP)-Upward Fund, New Breed, Gauchos, Riverside Church, Brandies H.S. '83, LIU '87

■ **Clarence "Mugsy" Leggett, a.k.a. "Meep Meep"**-Dyckman, Kennedy H.S., Walton '81, Westchester J.C. '86, St. Augustine's (N.C.) '89

"He dropped 55 against the Gauchos in King Towers and the next game had 60 against Riverside. Gumby (the announcer) nick-named him "Meep Meep". That's the sound the Road runner makes when he bursts into high speed in the cartoon." —Sundance Kid

■ **Alvin Lott**-Riverside Church, Cardinal Hayes H.S. '82, St. Bonaventure '86

■ **Gary Massey**-Broncos, Riverside Church, St. Raymonds H.S. '85, Villanova '89

■ **Ronald "The Terminator" Matthias**-Central Baptist Kings, Gauchos, Rice H.S., Evander H.S. '84, Palm Beach J.C. '86

"Ron scored over 100 points in a game at the Upward Fund, and I heard he led in the nation in scoring when he played Junior College with 40 a game. He's the best scorer I've ever seen" —Ted "Nitro"

■ **Roger McCready**-Broncos, Riverside Church, Gauchos, Xaverian H.S. '82, Boston College '86

■ **Darryl "Mack" McDonald a.k.a. "Mr. Excitement"**-Park East H.S. '84, Westchester J.C. '86, Texas A & M '88

■ **Kenny "Mouse" McFadden**-Broncos, Cleveland St. '89

■ **Mike Moses**-Riverside Church, Tolentine '80, Florida, St. John's '85

■ **Ernie Myers**-Riverside Church, Tolentine H.S. '82 (McDonald's All American '82), N.C. State '86

■ **Molloy "The Future" Nesmith**-Broncos, Riverside Church, Monroe H.S. '83, Jacksonville J.C. (Tx.) '85, Utah St. '86

"Molloy's legend is for real. Even before he got his nickname up at '55", he once dropped 60 points in a high school game." —Mike "Butters" Parker

■ **Kenny Patterson**-Gauchos, Forest Hills H.S. '80, Depaul '85

■ **Jack "Blackjack" Ryan a.k.a. "Water"**-Ty Cobb, John Jay H.S. '80, Mt. Hood C.C. (Or.) '82-'83, Brooklyn College '83-'84

I played with Jack in the Starett City Pro-Am. He went 17 for 17 from the field all from 18' and out. The only inside shot he took was with one second on the clock to win the game. He missed the lay up and we lost! He had a try out with the Nets at age 27 and was the last man cut. Chris Mullin once described him as the best shooter he'd ever seen who hadn't played in the NBA.

■ **Gus Santos**-Broncos, Gauchos, Power Memorial H.S. '82, Wichita St. '87

■ **Carlton "Paco" Screen**-Broncos, Riverside Church, Xaverian H.S. '86, Providence '90

■ **Richie "99%" Simmonds**-Riverside Church, All Hallows H.S. '84, Iona '88

He'd hit about nine out of every ten shots he'd take at the "Goat" park. He was the leading scorer for Catholic high schools his senior year.

■ **Phil Smith**-Mater Christi H.S. '80, New Mexico '84

■ **Gary Springer**- Riverside Church, Ben Franklin H.S. '80 (McDonalds All American '80), Iona '84

■ **Byron Strickland**-New Breed, Gauchos, Riverside Church, Chelsea Vocational H.S. '81, Trinidad C.C. '83, Hardin Simmons (TX) '85

■ **Jimmy "Soul Man" Tate** (late '80s-early '90s, RIP)

■ **Gerald "Dancing Doogie (pronounced do-gee)" Thomas**-Milbank Hammerheads, Essex C.C. '83, Palm Beach J.C. '85, West Virginia Wesleyan '86

He was invited to play overseas at age 29 strictly off of street rep. He may have had the best bank shot in New York playground history next to Joe Hammond.

"Pookie" Wilson knew how to make buckets. He once scored 100 points in a PAL game in Spanish Harlem. His team's total was 102. Here he takes it to the rack while playing for John Jay College.

■ **Lamont "Tip Dog" Thorton**-Gauchos, Riverside Church, M.L. King H.S. '85, Jacksonville J.C. (Tx.) '87, New Orleans '89

Tip once stopped and bounced the ball high around his chest. He pushed his arms through the ball like he was passing but didn't touch the ball. The defender ran towards the fake to deflect it, and when "Tip" kept it the defender just kept running towards half court and then ran straight out the park! In the middle of the game! People were screaming!

■ **Mike "Boogie" Thorton**-Gauchos, M.L. King H.S. '87, Jacksonville J.C. (TX) '89, C.W. Post '90

He once threw the ball behind his back and around his defender's waist at the same time. He caught it behind the defender's back and then layed it up reverse. That was sick! I heard that he shook Rod Strickland so bad one time that Rod fell out of bounds underneath the scorer's table!

■ **Danny Tirado** (RIP)-Broncos, Gauchos, Riverside Church, Our Savior Lutheran '88, U. of Jacksonville (Fl.) '91

"He holds the New York State H.S. record with 34 assists in one game still to this day." —Broncos coach Doc Nicelli

■ **Troy Truesdale**-Gauchos, All Hallows H.S. '81, Iona '85

■ **Melvin "The Thief" Walcott** (early '80s)-Milbank Hawks, Ben Franklin H.S.

"Quickest hands in the city." —Mr. Couch

■ **Curtis Washington**-Kip's Boys Club, Riverside Church, John Bowne H.S. '80, Trinidad C.C. '83, St. Thomas Aquinas '88 (Basketball Times 1st Team All American '87, '88, NAIA 1st Team All American '88, Sport Magazine Small College Player of the Year '88)

■ **Eugene "Beetle" Washington**-Brooklyn USA, Broncos, Gauchos, Alexander Hamilton H.S. '81, New Orleans '84

■ **Maurice "Moe Blind" White**-Central Baptist, Brandies H.S., N.Y. Tech

■ **James "Pookie" Wilson a.k.a. "MVP"** (RIP)-Far Rockaway H.S. '81, John Jay College '83

I read that Pookie averaged 34.6 pts in the Pro Rucker in '85 and led the league in assists. He also scored 42 points on Kevin Williams who was playing in the NBA at the time. Definite legend.

Joe "The Destroyer" Hammond is the legend of legends. He holds the Pro Rucker single game scoring record with 70 points. Here we see him catching a woof at the Rucker in 1977 while wearing his signature low tops.

Bobbito a.k.a. Soul Food Bob
Nike Franchise in light blue on black
Nike Air Force Zero in light blue on white
Adidas Half Shell Americana
Wilson Bata John Wooden in gold on white
Puma Sky LX in burgundy on white
Converse Fastbreak in gold on white
Pro-Ked Royal Flash in white on blue
Pony '77 MVP in yellow on royal
Adidas suede Jabbar Blue low top
New Balance Pride 991

Brother Ray
Adidas Pro Model
Wilson Bata John Wooden
Pony Pro Model
Puma Clyde high top in white on white
Nike Air Force Zero
Converse Dr. J
Pony #1 in burgundy on gray
Patrick court shoes
Nike Air Trainer 1
Nike Blazer

John Snakeback Fever
Pro-Ked Royal Flash in white on blue
Adidas Half Shell in white on green
Adidas Top Ten low top in red on white
Nike suede Blazers in white on blue
Nike suede Blazer in white on red
Wilson Bata John Wooden
Tiger '75 Fable
Nike Franchise customized Spartans
Adidas patent Concord in white on black
New Balance nubuck 480
Pro-Ked Competitor in green on white

Ted Nitro
Converse Dr. Js in green on white
Nike Franchise
Adidas Americana
Nike Air Force 1 in purple on white
Adidas Pro Model Half Shell
Puma Sky LX in green on white
Adidas Top Ten in red on white
Converse Pro Star low top in white on white
Puma Sky
Pro-Ked Royal Flash

Jazzy Art
Adidas Pro Models
Adidas Top Ten
Nike Air Force 1 in orange on white
Nike Franchise
Wilson Bata John Wooden
Pony Bob McAdoo

Sake
Nike Double Team
Nike Air Force Zero
Nike '86 Air Force
Nike suede Blazer in white on blue
Nike Franchise in light blue on black
New Balance nubuck 480 "ML Carr"
Adidas Forums
Adidas Top Ten
Puma Sky LX in green on white
Reeboks 5600 in white on black

Dante Ross
Nike Air Force 1 in cream on chocolate
Nike Air Force 1 in white on olive
Nike Air Force 1 low top in white on green
Converse Dr. J
Adidas Forum in white on green
Adidas Concords
Nike Air Force 1 in white on carolina
Nike Dunk in blue on yellow/blue
Pony McAdoo
Adidas Rod Laver

Fabel
Pro-Ked 69'ers
Adidas Jabbars
Puma Clyde
Adidas Superstar
Nike nylon Cortez
Nike leather Cortez

Schott Free
Nike Terminator in blue on gray/blue
Pony # 1
New Balance 480
Pro-Ked 69'ers in red
Reebok Question 1 in red on white
Puma Clyde in light blue on dark blue
Puma Cell Origin in metallic blue on black
Adidas Top Ten low top in red on white
New Balance Worthy 785 in black on white
Polo Decks/Gucci Mocassins (tie)

Emz
Puma Clyde in rust on tan
Nike Air Force One low top in white on orange,
     white on green
Adidas Top Ten
Pony #1 in burgundy on gray
Adidas Campus in white on light blue
Nike Air Ace in aqua on white
Nike Air Max '95 in khaki/orange
Adidas Forums
Adidas Centennials
Nike nylon Cortez in red on white/blue
Nike '86 Air Force

Prime Minister Pete Nice
Tony "Red" Bruin's customized Nike suede
     Blazers in yellow on green
Player customized Converse Dr. Js
Nike Air Force One
Nike Sky Force 3/4
Nike customized Sky Force a.k.a. "Pre-Jordans"
Puma Clyde in orange on blue
Adidas Top Ten
Adidas Superstar
Nike Franchise
Super Pro-Ked

Scotch
Adidas Jabbar in natural on white
Nike Vandals
Adidas Superstar in green on white
Adidas Top Tens
Adidas Stan Smiths
Adidas Nastase Super
Adidas Rod Laver
Puma Clyde
Puma Basket
Nike Cortez in burgundy on gray

Serch
Nike Air Force 1
Adidas Top Ten in white on black
Nike '93 Air Max
Adidas Superstar in white on white
Fila T 1 in red/blue on tan
Puma Basket
Nike Air Force Zero
Nike '88 Olympic Jordan

Kurious
Nike Air Force 1 in white on sky blue
Adidas Forums in white on green
Puma Clyde in white on green
Adidas Rod Lavers
Nike nylon Cortez in white on navy
Pony Pro Model
Pro-Ked 69'ers
Converse Dr. J in green on white

Mike Drake
Adidas Stan Smiths
Nike Air Force 1 in white on green
Pony #1 in burgundy on gray
Puma Clyde in silver on black
Adidas Decade in orange on white

Udi
New Balance 1300
Pro Jogs in white on burgundy
Puma Sky in navy on white
Adidas Top Ten high top
New Balance 576
New Balance suede/nylon mesh Worthy in navy
Fila T 1 in blue/red on tan
Timberland Chuckas
Nike Air Force 1 low top in black on white
Nike Epics

Steve Brock
Puma Super Basket
Nike Air Force 1 in olive on white
Adidas Jabbar Blue
Nike nylon Cortez in burgundy on gray
Nike suede Blazer
Nike Bruin
Adidas Top Ten
K-Swiss
Etonic Trans Am
Pro-Ked 69'ers in brown

Prof. Will Strickland
Puma Clyde in blue on orange
Nike Franchise
Adidas Pro Model
Nike Air Revolution
Diadora Maverick light blue on white
Converse suede Dr. J in natural on rust
Converse Weapon
Nike Air Force 1
Adidas Top Ten

Chronological Customizations

- '81-Pony Pro Model in customized purple on white (permanent magic marker)

- '82-Nike Dynasty in customized kelly green on white (Esquire shoe dye)

- '82-Pony #1 nylon mesh in customized black on white (acrylic paint)

- '83-Nike Legends in customized light blue on white (acrylic paint)

- '83-Nike Franchise in red on customized black (leather shoe dye)

- '83-Nike Air Force Zeros in customized burgundy on white (Esquire shoe dye)

- '84-Nike Air Force Zeros in customized light blue on white (acrylic paint)

- '85-Avia in customized canary yellow/kelly green on white (acrylic paint)

- '89-Puma Sky LX in white on customized banana yellow (Esquire leather shoe spray and razor blade)

- '89-Nike Air Force One in navy blue on customized light blue (Esquire leather shoe spray)

- '90-Nike Air Force One in customized white on customized pumpkin with chocolate outsole (Esquire leather shoe spray and razor blade)

- '90-Nike Air Force One in customized white on customized navy blue with orange outsole (Esquire leather shoe spray and razor blade)

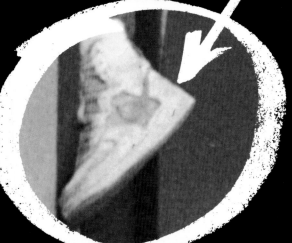

My customized Air Force Zeros in light blue may be my all time favorite work of art. Here I am with the ABC-LM crew and members of the OTB Breakers in Hershey Park, PA in '84.

Company Roster:

Adidas
www.Adidas.com
1-800-448-1796

Asics Tiger Corporation
16275 Laguna Canyon Road
Irvine, CA 92618
www.Asicstiger.com
1-800-678-9435

Avia
6077 S.W. Lakeview Blvd.
Lake Oswego, OR 97035
www.Avia.com
1-800-547-3213

Bata
www.Bata.com

Brooks Sports Inc.
19820 North Creek Parkway, Suite 200
Bothell, WA 98011-8223 USA
www.Brooksrunning.com
www.Brookssports.com
1-800-2-BROOKS

Converse
1 High St.
N. Andover, MA 01845
www.Converse.com

Diadora
www.DiadoraAmerica.com

Ellesse USA
141 W. 36th Street, 11th Floor
New York, NY 10018
www.Ellesse.com
1-800-ELLESSE

Etonic Athletic Worldwide
216 Rt. 206 South ste. 18
Hillsborough, NJ 08844
www.Etonicathletic.com
www.Etonic.com
info@etonicathletic.com
1-908-359-4887

Fila
8 West 40th Street, 3rd Floor
New York, NY 10018
www.fila.com
1-800-Pro-Fila
1-888-Fila-Net

Gravis
208 Flynn Ave, studio #2c
Burlngton, VT 05401
www.Gravisfootwear.com
1-877-247-2847

Kaepa USA
9050 Autobahn Drive, #500
Dallas, TX 75237
www.Kaepa-USA.com
www.Kaepa.com
1-800-880-9200

K-Swiss
31248 Oak Crest Dr.
Westlake Village, CA 91361
www.Kswiss.com
1-800-297-1919

Lotto
www.Lotto.it

Mizuno
www.Mizuno.com

New Balance Athletic Shoe, Inc.
Brighton Landing, 20 Guest St.
Boston, MA 02135-2088
www.NewBalance.com
1-800-253-SHOE

Nike
www.Nike.com

Patrick
www.Patrick.fr

Pony
www.Pony.com

Pro-keds
www.prokeds.com

Puma
www.Puma.com
1-800-782-PUMA

Reebok International Ltd.
PO Box 1060
Ronks, PA 17573
www.Reebok.com

Saucony, Inc.
13 Centennial Drive
Peabody, MA 01961
www.Saucony.com
www.Sauconyinc.com
www.SpotBilt.com
1-800-365-7282

Spalding
425 Meadow St.
Chicopee, MA 01021
www.Spalding.com
1-800-772-5346

Stride Rite
www.Striderite.com

Tretorn
DISTRIBUTOR-Rocky Mountain Sports
1898 South Flatiron Court
Boulder Colorado 80301
1-303-444-5340
www.Tretorn.com
1-800-525-2852

Wilson Sporting Goods Co.
8700 West Bryn Mawr Avenue
Chicago, IL 60631
1-773-714-6400
www.Wilsonsports.com

This book is spiritually dedicated to my pops Ramon Garcia (RIP) who would've been proud to tell his friends at the local bodega that his son was a published author.

Acknowledgements:

Dana Albarella for the push in '99

Ben Fasman for the research and transcriptions (additional transcribing by Ethan Flad and Adam Waytz)

Brent Rollins for bringing my baby to life with flavor

Love to my Famalam (Ramon y Ramona, Ray/Suzanne, Bill/Betty, Hiedi/Jaime, and my pineapple nephews), and to my friends who gave me the most consistent support over the last two years while I wrote this (particularly Esmé Rene, Ethan Flad, Michelle Willems, Rich Medina, Vanessa Cruz, and Sarah Zeller-Berkman)

Big thanks to everyone who took the time to be interviewed and/or allowed me to photograph their collections. The following people were also invaluable resources for sneaker info: Rickford Powell, Vaz TCK, Lord Sear, Justin Francis, Jer, DJ Spinna, Cognito, Timm "C" Hotep, Zuhairah Khaldun, Ilana Finley, Betsy Parker, Abby Guyer, Miki Bunnell, Akiko, "Hawaii" Mike Salman, Justin Leonard-Project Playground Basketball, Elly Tatum, Jimmy Smith, John Jay, Margarita Corporan, Selene Allen, Mr. Wix, K.C, Kelly Woo, Jasmine Kimera, Minya at Sportswear, Lord Finesse, Randy Weiner, DJ Kon, Manny "Agua" Maldonado, Main from Bushwick, TonX, Chino BYI, Xavier, Drew "Peets," Jamel Shabazz, Sung Choi at Clae

Big thanks to everyone who helped out with basketball resources: Gerry Erasme, Lincoln Parker, Mike "Butters" Parker, Ray Diaz, Clark Elie, Greg Brown, Sid Jones, Butch Purcell, Tone "The Batman" Greer, Sean Couch, Ray Nash, Tom Kolchowski, Dee Adams, Jorge Stork, Artie Andino, Herman Hailey, Ernesto "the Ness" Morris, Mike "Nappy" Napolitan, Doc Nicelli, Mr. Couch, Al Morales, Darren Neil, Duane Johnson-Kingston Park, Ernie Lorch, Fred Neil, Russell Shuler-Youth Education through Sports, Bill "Blast" Roberts, Vernon "VJ" Moore, Tony Hargraves, Parnes Cartwright, Arnold "A Train" Bernard, Gerald "Dancing Doogie" Thomas, Leroy Shaw, Kurt Mahoney, Harold Starks

Good looking out to my pops for introducing me to basketball in '73, to Craig Raddix a.k.a. "The Original Rocker Crazy Craig" for introducing me to hip hop in '77, to Jon Shecter for giving me my first writing gig at the Source in '90, to Tamara Schlesinger for introducing me to my first camera, and to Justine Wysong for teaching me how to use one.

Photo Credits:

All photos by Bobbito Garcia, except:

The Amsterdam News: pg. 38

Andrew Bernstein/NBAE-Getty Images: pgs. 127, 128, 129, 141, 145

Doug Bruce/NBAE-Getty Images: pg. 49

David L. Buuck/UT Photo Services: pgs. 42, 46

Martha Cooper: pgs. 54, 85, 87, 88, 91, 92, 102, 110, 112, 143, 184, 197, 198, 218

Jim Cummings/NBAE-Getty Images: pgs. 114, 116

James Drake/Sports Illustrated: pgs. 66, 234

Daniel Grogan: pgs. 94, 99

Andy Hayt/Sports Illustrated: pg. 192

John Iacono/Sports Illustrated: pgs. 78, 154

Walter Iooss, Jr./Sports Illustrated: pg. 157

Heinz Kluetmeier/Sports Illustrated: pg. 65

Ron Koch/NBAE-Getty Images: pg. 91

Neil Leifer/NBAE-Getty Images: pg. 40

Richard Mackson/Sports Illustrated: pg. 161

Manny Millan/Sports Illustrated: pg. 154

NBAE-Getty Images: pgs. 184, 197

Sean Peters: pgs. 6, 232

Dick Raphael/NBAE-Getty Images: pg. 66

Esmé Rene: pg. 120

Rayon Richards: pg. 230

Tom Richards/Syracuse U. Sports Information: pg. 97

Wen Roberts/NBAE-Getty Images: pg. 65

Jon Soohoo/NBAE-Getty Images: pg. 65

Rob "Reef" Tewlow: pg. 191

Jerry Wachter/NBAE-Getty Images: pg. 114

Matt Willigan: pgs. 2, 68, 69, 88, 90, 92, 98, 100, 103, 104, 114, 115, 120, 136, 145, 162, 256

Louisiana St. U. Athletics: pg. 241

Marquette U. Sports Information: pgs. 58, 241, 242

John Merz: pgs. 190, 206

Peter Nash: pg. 238

New Balance: pgs. 28, 233, 236

Nike: pgs. 110, 112, 154, 172, 222, 228

Oregon St. U. Sports Information: pgs. 92, 108, 154

Pony: pgs. 72, 118, 126

Pro-Ked: pgs. 40, 94

Puma: pgs. 87, 164

John Purcell: pgs. 25, 32, 36, 44, 49, 52, 82

Reebok: pgs. 140, 141

Oral Roberts U. Sports Information: pg. 240

Rutgers U. Sports Information: pg. 240

Saucony, Inc.: pg. 168

Spalding Sports Worldwide, Inc.: pgs. 30, 31, 106

St. Bonaventure College: pg. 240

St. John's U. Sports Information: pgs. 118, 240, 241, 246

Texas A&M Athletic Department: pgs. 240, 241

Texas Tech U.: pg. 240

U. of Arkansas Sports Information: pg. 240

U. of Dayton Athletic Communications: pgs. 125, 157

U. of Georgia Sports Communications: pg. 240

U. of Hawaii Sports Media Relations: pgs. 178, 240

U. of Kentucky: pg. 240

U. of Louisville Sports Information: pgs. 105, 126

U. of Maryland: pg. 240

U. of New Mexico Media Relations: pg. 240

U. of Oregon Media Services: pgs. 62, 123

U. of Texas Sports Information: pg. 96

U. of Texas El Paso: pgs. 39, 240

Dwayne Washington: pg. 126

The following photos were provided courtesy of:

Adidas: pgs. 44, 99, 102, 137, 143, 160, 162

Archbishop Molloy H.S: pg. 241

Asics Tiger: pgs. 29, 81, 231

Avia: pg. 231

B.J. Carter: pgs. 105, 148

Brooks Sports: pg. 80

Tony "Red" Bruin: pgs. 76, 125

Columbia U. Athletic Communications: pg. 122

Converse: pgs. 28, 46, 60, 145, 146

Mr. Couch: pgs. 26, 79, 180, 181, 241

Victor DeJesus: pgs. 11, 134, 148, 150

Depaul U. Athletics: pgs. 167, 241

Diadora: pg. 153

Clark Elie: pgs. 241, 250

Ellesse: pgs. 168, 170

Fila: pg. 149

The Gauchos: pgs. 50, 83, 138, 143, 240

Georgia Tech Athletic Association: pg. 241

Gravis: pg. 236

Guilford College Sports Information: pgs. 46, 189, 240

Cleo Hill: pg. 240

Iona College: pgs. 158, 241

Jacksonville U Media Relations: pg. 240

John Jay College Basketball Office: pgs. 240, 252

Kaepa USA: pg. 80

Richard Kirkland: pgs. 20, 254

Long Island U. Sports Information: pgs. 240, 241

Some sneakers in this book were photographed courtesy of generous collectors such as Chris Hall and Micheal "Emz" Greene. Other collectors include:

Milo "Mighty Mi" Berger, Michael "Serch" Berrin, Bootsy at Harput's sneaker store (San Francisco), "Big" Will Caraway, Come Chantrell, Richard "Crazy Legs" Colón, Smit-Cruyff sneaker store (Amsterdam), Alec DeRuggiero, Ethan "Chilly E" Flad, Claudia Gold a.k.a. "The Skippie Queen," Matt George at Good Foot sneaker store (Toronto), Andre Kyles, Ted "Nitro" Lake, Adam "Air Rev" Leaventon, Marlon Orr, Jorge "Fabel" Pabon, Ramon Rodriguez, Dante Ross, DJ Ted Shred, Kris Stone, Josh "DJ Language" Taylor

About the Author:

Bobbito Garcia does it all. As Contributing Editor for *Vibe* magazine, his signature "Soundcheck" column has appeared in every issue for the last nine years. As a DJ, he broke such acts as Wu-Tang, Jay-Z and Nas on his legendary "Stretch Armstrong and Bobbito" radio show on New York's WKCR.

His passion for sneakers has found many outlets over the years: He was one of the first writers to pen an article on the subject in a national magazine (*The Source*, in 1991), and he has consulted for Nike, Adidas, and Converse. He has appeared in six Nike ad campaigns from 1994 to 2002, and has displayed his prodigious basketball skills in halftime shows for the NBA.

Bobbito's writing has appeared in books such as *The Vibe History of Hip Hop* (Three Rivers Press) and *ego trip's Book of Rap Lists* (St. Martin's Press). He is also the play-by-play announcer for EA Sports' 2003 *NBA Street Volume 2* video game. A genuine hip hop legend, Garcia lives in New York, where he is currently working on "Basics to Boogie," an instructional basketball video/DVD series.